THE
BLESSING
AND THE CURSE

THE
BLESSING
AND THE CURSE

Phyllis Greenbach

The Blessing and the Curse biographical references: memoir, family saga, adoption, abortion, immigration, substance abuse, Jewish identity

email: theblessingandthecurse@gmail.com

ISBN: 0615636365
ISBN 13: 9780615636368

Library of Congress Control Number: 2012908431
Phyllis Greenbach, Palm Desert, CA

*For my family
with love*

I have set before thee life and death,
the blessing and the curse,
Therefore choose life.

Deuteronomy 30:19

AN OLD CHASIDIC TALE

Long ago in Lodz, Poland there lived a man who had a beautiful horse. People would come to say, "How lucky you are to have such a horse."

He said, "Perhaps. But what seems like a blessing may be a curse."

They laughed. They thought he was crazy. They thought he had his beautiful horse. It was easy for him to say that. But some time later that horse ran off. It was gone. The people were saddened. They came to give their sympathies.

He said, "Perhaps, but what seems like a curse may be a blessing."

Sometime later that horse returned and was followed by twenty-one wild stallions, which by the law of the land became his property. Villagers came to congratulate him. "What a wonderful thing that has happened to you," they said.

He said, "Perhaps. But what seems like a blessing may be a curse."

They laughed. They thought he was nuts. But sometime after that, when his only son was riding one of the new horses, he was thrown from the horse and broke his leg. People came to give their sympathies. They said, "What a shame it was that you ever saw those horses."

He said, "Perhaps. But what seems like a curse may be a blessing."

Shortly after that the czar came through the village and drafted every able-bodied young man for a war against the vicious tribes of the north. Every young man who went from that town was killed. The only one that survived was that man's son, who had a broken leg.

And so, to this day, in that town, they still say, *"What seems like a blessing may be a curse, and what seems like a curse may be a blessing."*

DISCLAIMER

In essence this is a true story. However, I have taken the liberty of changing the names of the people involved. In doing so, I would like to think I have provided them with at least a modicum of privacy.

CONTENTS

PROLOGUE

DANIELLE'S ADOPTIVE MOTHER, NANCY

PALM DESERT, CALIFORNIA. 1999. My body tensed the moment I heard my daughter's voice on the phone. Something was the matter. But when she greeted me and simply asked, "How was your day?" my anxiety dropped.

"You know, Our Lady of Perpetual Aggravation is always the same," I replied, hoping for a laugh. "Teaching never changes."

My attempt at humor was greeted with a stony silence. "Mom, I have something to tell you."

I always get a warm, fuzzy feeling when Danielle calls me mom. Still in a playful mood, I responded, "Sounds ominous." I was thinking her two-year old son got into more mischief. Last I heard, he slipped the remote control into the slot for the VCR and no one could find it for a week.

"What I have to say is going to blow you away." There it was again, that serious tone in Danielle's voice, the precursor to bad news. "Mom, promise you'll listen, okay?"

"Sure," I said, not knowing what was coming at me.

There was a long pause before Danielle continued. "I got a really weird phone call yesterday. A guy called and claimed to be my *half-brother*."

"Your *half-brother*? Come on, Danielle. You've got a brother and sister. You don't have a *half-brother*. Are you making this up? Is this some kind of joke?"

"No, Mom, you heard me right. It's a long story. And I don't know where to begin."

Our family had no *halves* or *steps* connected to it. Content with our lives, my husband Russell and I thought we personified the typical American family—three kids, two cars, a fluffy white Samoyed and a house in the suburbs. Everything but the white picket fence and clusters of bright yellow daffodils growing behind it. But somewhere on a deeper level, an uncomfortable knot began to swell in the pit of my stomach. Actually it felt more like sniper fire. Out of the blue and violent.

In denial, I questioned her. "What makes you think this so-called *half-brother* is on the up-and-up? Suppose he's a con artist? Some one who happened to get your phone number."

"Mom, let me explain, okay?"

Danielle's adoption happened over three decades earlier. The few facts I could dredge up were as faded and worn as an old photograph. Even in the beginning, the social worker only provided us with a few snippets of information. Danielle's *birth-father* was over six feet tall, had brown eyes and an exceptionally high I.Q.—so they said. Her *birth-mother* was barely five feet, worked as a hairdresser, and had requested her baby be placed in a Jewish home. I vaguely remembered that someone in the family was Hungarian and that the *birth-mother's* father was a doctor.

A flood of emotions surged through my body after Danielle's startling announcement about the bizarre telephone call. I bombarded her with a minuet of questions, not really listening to her answers before attacking her with the next. "I don't understand. So tell me again, who's this guy? And how did he get your name?"

To be sure, this was just as much a shock to Danielle as it was to me. But somehow she was managing to hold it together.

At that moment I feared this intrusion would ruin our cohesive family. More than anything, I yearned to backtrack, to erase everything she was telling me. I wanted to *unhear* it. Yank the rug out from under this anonymous guy. Pull the plug. Do whatever it took. Besides, the terms *half-brother* or *half-sister* have always seemed demeaning. It reminded me of the story of King Solomon and the baby he threatened to slice in two.

Everything Russell and I did to adopt Danielle was legal. We were in our early twenties and could barely afford it. But somehow we plodded through the interviews and social services, paid an attorney, went to court, and cherished the legal documents that made her ours.

Despite my shock, Danielle plowed forward.

"Mom, his name's Brandon," she explained, as if to underscore his credibility.

I didn't care. I could not bear attaching a name to this faceless stranger.

"It's kind of complicated," Danielle warned. "Brandon and I have the same *birth-father* but different *birth-mothers*. He's about my age. Married. Has a twin sister. Growing up, they lived with his mom and grandma. But he wasn't adopted."

Thus began the conversation I had always feared. It hurt me to hear what she was saying. He wasn't adopted, as if my precious daughter was a throw-away baby. "Let me see if I've got this straight," I eventually replied. "You and this person, this guy, have the same *birth-father* but different *birth-mothers*."

Parts of the conversation sounded like a needle stuck in the groove of an old-fashioned record, repeating phrases over and over. *Adopted. Half-brother. Birth-father.*

"This can't be! Your records are sealed," I protested for the umpteenth time. "How did he find you? Tell me again." Denial was the only thing working for me.

Danielle patiently picked her way through this minefield. "I don't know exactly, but somehow Brandon connected with my *birth-mother.*"

"Oh, God. Your *birth-mother.*" Just saying it aloud unnerved me.

A *half-brother* was bad enough, but her *birth-mother*, that was an indigestible piece of gristle. I felt violated, as if the outer layer of our peaceful family had just been strip-mined. Territorial rights were the only thing left for me to claim. And I claimed them greedily, ferociously. I took satisfaction in knowing Danielle's *birth-mother*— whoever she was—had not caught up to her until now.

At thirty-three, Danielle was happily married with a little boy of her own. She and her husband, Christopher, were successfully navigating their own course. Her life was rock solid, her personality fully developed, and her values set.

With more than a trace of bitterness, I regarded her *birth-mother* as a selfish intruder, an alien force stepping into my tidy, manicured reality. I imagined she wanted to pirouette into our lives now that Russell and I had paid for Danielle's braces, sent her to college, and given her a big wedding. Where was she, I wondered, when we worried about the long-term effects of her broken leg? She was nowhere to be found when we realized Danielle was in a seventy-year-old brick building in downtown Santa Cruz, the epicenter of the Loma Prieta earthquake. Or when Russell and I thought she and Christopher were lost in a blizzard while deer hunting in the Ruby Mountains.

We dedicated every moment to our three children and committed every penny—probably more than we should have—to their whims and desires. What had she contributed? A fertilized egg. That's it. I didn't want to share Danielle with some Johnny-Come-Lately. And, if I looked fear in the face, I was terrified of losing my beloved daughter.

After hanging up the telephone, I planted my elbow on my desk and propped the palm of my hand under my chin. I stared blankly at the family snapshots and cards pinned to the cork bulletin board. Like any possessive and protective parent, I wanted nothing more than to wrap my arms around my daughter and give her a big hug. But that was impossible. I lived in southern California and she in the Bay Area, over 500 miles away.

While Danielle and I had been talking, my husband Russell had been napping on the living room couch with another rerun of *Law and Order* blaring on the TV. What could I say to shield the most caring, devoted father in the world? How and when would I break this devastating news? Knowing he would be broken-hearted, I decided to postpone it until morning.

Sleep eluded me. I struggled to absorb this new reality. I tried coming to grips with the intrusion of Danielle's *half-brother* and her *birth-mother*, but I found I had more questions than answers. Just what makes a family? Is it in the DNA or is it the place where you are loved, no matter what? And who exactly were these strangers that just punched a massive hole into our well-ordered lives? Where did they come from? How did it happen that Danielle, our cherished daughter, was put up for adoption?

I was searching for pat answers—some sort of universal truths—but nothing came to mind. It was not that simple. I felt as if I were viewing the world through a sheet of wax paper.

Book One

JOSEPH AND LEAH,
DANIELLE'S
GRANDPARENTS
On Birth-Mother's Side

There is no denying it. Ancestry plays a major role in destiny. Nothing happens in a vacuum. We are molded by the experiences of those who came before us. This story would be difficult to tell without an understanding of the times and the families of those touched by this adoption.

CHAPTER 1

MAMA'S ADMONITION

CLEVELAND, OHIO. 1932. *I'm one of the lucky ones*, Joseph thought to himself as he approached Mama's apartment in the late afternoon. *With so many people out of work, the graveyard shift at the telephone company isn't half bad.*

For him money made all the difference.

Less than a month after receiving his first paycheck, Joseph rented an attic room in a rundown boarding house near Case Western University. As long as he overlooked the dust motes, the room was a vast improvement over Mama's apartment. Even though the double bed was lumpy, it still beat the itchy, threadbare couch where he slept through childhood. He could finally stretch his legs out and sleep in the first real bed he had ever known. Once more, he loved the beat-up walnut desk—even though the drawers didn't quite close all the way—and the swivel chair set between the two dormer windows. Now his time was his own. He could study at all hours of the day and night without worrying about waking Mama or Mama waking him up.

This Friday night had special meaning. *Shabbos*, the Jewish Sabbath, coincided with Mama's birthday. Even though Joseph had little time to spare, he had deliberately set aside his studies to be with her. Ever since moving out, Joseph carried around a pocketful of guilt, as if he had abandoned his widowed mother.

Just as the sun set, Mama washed her greasy hands and dried them on her flowery cotton apron. She grabbed a wooden match from the box and lit her two Sabbath candles. She covered her eyes and recited the ancient prayer:

Baruch atah Adonai, eloheinu melekh ha'olam . . .

While his mother recited the blessing, Joseph more or less repeated it from rote. All the while he stared at her, as if seeing her for the first time. He noticed her stocky, pear-shaped figure, like a Russian nesting doll, and her arthritic hands and swollen ankles. He saw the furrowed lines on her face and her salt and pepper hair. There was no doubt she was aging. For fourteen years, ever since her husband and Joseph's brother died in the flu epidemic, she had worked as a baker's helper, standing on her feet from six in the morning until two or three o'clock in the afternoon. Not knowing how to read or write, this was the best she could do and she was grateful for the work.

Green glass dishes were placed kitty-corner at the second-hand table jammed against the wall in the cluttered kitchen. A folded ironing board tilted over the light switch just behind Joseph. Even though it was Mama's birthday, Joseph sat like a prince while Mama dished up his favorite meal, chicken that fell off the bone and *luchen kugel*, a rich noodle dish laden with butter and sour cream.

Now with someone to talk to, she repeated a few tidbits of gossip about the neighbors and their children. As greenhorns most of the apartment dwellers had lived in the building for years, helping each other when they could, but never above squabbling over petty things like a real family. Since coming to America, Mama had lived a few blocks off Buckeye Road, in her cloistered world filled with Hungarian Jewish immigrants.

Although Joseph strived to separate himself from Mama's old world ways, he appreciated Mama's cooking more than ever. He listened with half an ear, more intent on eating the home-cooked supper. Ever since moving to the boarding house, he had subsisted on milk, cheese, hard rolls, and fruit. After dinner Mama sliced two pieces of the day-old honey cake she carried home from the bakery. "So . . . *nu*, Josephla. Tell me, where have you been? Always so busy."

"Mama, between med school and work I hardly have time to pee. Besides, I'm seeing someone." The instant the words slipped out, he regretted it. Joseph knew his mother well. She could be overbearing and insular and he much preferred to keep his private life private.

Mama appeared baffled. With her thick accent she asked, "Seeing someone? Oh, and does this someone have a name?"

He was stuck. How could he say he didn't know her name? "Maureen."

Mama raised her eyebrows. "So . . . what kind of name is Maureen?"

Joseph knew what she was driving at but dodged the real issue. "It's a name. What's to tell? She's a nice girl, studying to be a teacher." Already on the defensive, he braced himself for the interrogation to come.

Not known for her tact, Mama dug right to the heart of the matter. "This girl, Maureen, is she Jewish?"

"No, Mama, she's Catholic. Does it really matter? I told you, we're just friends. What does religion have to do with it anyway? Wait 'til you meet Maureen. She's a wonderful gal. You'll see. I'll bring her here for supper."

Mama continued as if she had never heard his voice. "No, Joseph, not here. No *shiksas*."

"If you don't want her here, fine. But tell me something, you think maybe this is the Taj Mahal? For God's sake, Mama, be reasonable. What do you have against non-Jews. She doesn't wash her clothes in the river or practice voodoo, if that's what you're thinking."

"You know what I mean," she said, waving her chubby finger in the air.

"No, Mama, I really don't." Joseph didn't want to fight, but his mother's narrow-minded edict rubbed him the wrong way. "Explain it to me."

"*Goyim*, non-Jews. They're different."

"How different can they be? Don't we all breathe the same air and have the same dreams? Mama, for Pete's sakes, just tell me, what's so different?"

"For hundreds of years Jews have suffered. We've been *pro*secuted."

"Wrong word, Mama. The word is *per*secuted." Normally he'd let it go, but he couldn't deal with her illogical reasoning.

Either she didn't understand or ignored his comment. She added, "But we survived. Jews survived. No thanks to the *goyim*."

"Ah, so it always gets back to that, does it? Jews suffered. Jews survived. That's it? That's your reason . . . ? Mama, times have changed. We're in America, the melting pot. Isn't that why you left Hungary?"

"*Melting pot, schmelting pot.* For this, I did not come to America. I want you should bring me home a nice Jewish girl."

"For God's sakes, Mama, this isn't about *you*. It's about *me*. Maureen's smart and funny. She makes me happy. Isn't that enough?"

Raising her finger again, she retorted, "Listen to me, Joseph. You're Jewish . . . and don't ever forget it!"

"You don't think I know that? Mama, you're unreasonable." Usually mild-mannered Joseph fought for control, knowing no amount of logic could change her mind. He pushed back the clunky spindle chair and rose from the table to clear his plate. Inadvertently he knocked over the washboard that protruded from the space below the chipped porcelain sink.

"Sorry," Mama apologized. "I meant to put that thing away."

For the moment they side-stepped the more contentious issue. Joseph tried to be amicable, but underneath his calm veneer, he continued to seethe. When an appropriate amount of time elapsed, he excused himself. "I wish I could stay longer, but I really need to study before I go back to work."

"Take the rest of the chicken, Josephla." Mama insisted, as if their argument had melted away. "You'll put it in the ice box for tomorrow's supper." She wrapped the leftovers in pink butcher paper, tied it with a thin string she saved from the bakery and stuffed it into another sack so it would not leak.

As she handed him the package, he thanked her. At the door Joseph bent down and kissed Mama's cheek. "Happy Birthday."

Joseph nabbed a seat on the half-empty trolley. For a time he fixated on his mother's uncompromising and antiquated religious views. He dismissed his mother's admonition, thinking her ways were from the old school. He was confident that Maureen was the best thing that ever happened to him. Until he met Maureen, he had been intimidated by woman, the more beautiful, the more intimidating. Maureen resembled a sophisticated Gibson Girl with her coppery hair piled on top of her head and her cute upturned nose. But there were other more elusive qualities that Joseph loved too. They had to do with her husky voice, her effervescent personality and ready laughter. Besides, she overlooked the tremor in his arm. She saw him as a regular guy.

As soon as he reached the boarding house, he called to tell her what happened. At first she didn't understand. He had to explain that *shiksa* meant a non-Jewish girl. Maureen was hurt, but pretended to shrug it off. "Forget it, sweetie. She's just old-fashioned. She'll get over it."

CHAPTER 2

SPEAKEASY

THE RIGORS of medical school and Joseph's graveyard shift at the telephone company left little time for anything else. When his grades began to plummet, his pharmacology professor—who doubled as his adviser—insisted he come in for a chat. Joseph, embarrassed by this special attention, explained his exhausting schedule. The professor spoke bluntly. "Well, Joseph, something's got to give."

Joseph bit his lower lip and dragged his right hand through his thick, wavy hair. "I know . . . but here's the thing. I need the job to get through med school."

The professor commiserated. "I can understand your dilemma. You're not the first guy to work his way through school. It's damn hard. Give me a moment to think." He pumped his fist into his bearded chin, pondering the options. Then he addressed the issue. "Joseph, you've got a lot of potential. You're bright. Reliable. Serious. I can see you're really trying. Perhaps I can help. Our department is starting a new research project. Testing out a couple of new products for a pharmaceutical company. Our research assistant just announced he's moving to Washington, D.C. Got a better paying job with the government. Want to try your hand at research? God knows, there's plenty to do. The hours are pretty flexible."

Joseph was intrigued but cautious. "Sounds interesting. I've never done research. I'm living on a tight budget. How much does it pay?"

When he was told, Joseph quickly calculated the numbers in his head. It was slightly less money than working at the telephone company but he could still afford his shabby room at the boarding house. That private room, with the big double bed and desk was his salvation. With his taste of freedom, he was not going back to Mama's couch. For the first time all day, Joseph broke into a smile. He had gone into this meeting feeling insecure, thinking he would be scolded, perhaps even kicked out of medical school. But as he left the professor's office, he felt upbeat, like he had an advocate within the ranks who understood him and was willing to help.

A few days before Christmas, Joseph was in the university lab working on some statistics when Maureen burst in unexpectedly and broke his train of thought. On a mission, she dragged him down to the basement cafeteria insisting they get a cup of coffee.

"You know," Maureen said, "the lab will be closed New Year's Eve. And it wouldn't kill you to have a little fun."

Preoccupied with facts and numbers, he just let her jabber.

"Remember, I told you, my brother got a part-time job as a bartender at a speakeasy. Well, Sean hasn't stopped raving about the place. Says it's a lot of fun."

Always the cautious one, Joseph interrupted. "Look, Maureen, I've got no time. Besides, it's illegal. And I don't want to wind up in jail. A conviction could ruin my life."

"You know somethin', you're getting to be a real killjoy. You're not gonna wind up in jail. Prohibition's stupid. And, anyway, there's talk of changing the dumb law."

After much goading, Joseph relented.

On New Year's Eve the twosome made their way to the Beacon House, an ill-disguised speakeasy in the heart of Cleveland. Clusters of black and white balloons dangled from the high, tin ceiling. A slightly inebriated hostess stood just inside the door repeating "Happy New Year" to each new patron. From a long table filled with New Year's props, she handed Maureen a cardboard tiara.

As Maureen plopped the crown on top of her head, silver glitter fell across her face. She grabbed a silly noisemaker out of a cardboard box and twirled it around on the wooden handle. "Joseph, let's cut loose tonight."

As soon as they emptied their first tumbler of boot-legged gin, Maureen raised her hand and hollered to Sean, who was pouring drinks nearby. "More hooch. We need more hooch over here."

Joseph tried to match her drink for drink.

"Sweetie, you know something," Maureen teased, "you're really cute when you're snockered."

"I'm not snockered," Joseph chuckled, slurring his words.

Enticed by the chanteuse and the pulsating beat of the music, Maureen grabbed his arm, causing him to spill part of his drink on his only suit. "Let's dance. Can you Charleston?"

"Sure," he said dryly. "Learned in med school."

"Well, kiddo, no time like the present."

In high-spirits, they broke into spasms of laughter over his spastic efforts. Over the live band, she hollered, "Just admit it. You're having more fun tonight than you can remember."

"Yeah, you little devil . . . and some day I'm going to pay the price for it."

Three years flew by and Joseph could not stop grinning as he marched down the aisle in his cap and gown on graduation day. *It would have been perfect*, he thought, *if only Mama and Maureen were seated together.* But Mama, stubborn as she was, still refused to meet Maureen. So Joseph was careful to keep them separated. After the ceremony he took Mama, who was beaming with pride, to a local delicatessen for a late lunch.

Later that evening, Joseph and Maureen celebrated privately at a once popular steakhouse, now famous for their low prices. "Follow me," the maitre d' said, carrying thick menus as he ushering Maureen and Joseph into the lodge-like dining room. Brass chandeliers and sconces cast a moonlight glow across the mahogany panels. As Joseph closed the gap between himself and Maureen, he whispered something suggestive and slid his fingers gently down her backside.

In the red tufted leather booth, he pretended to study the menu as they snuggled together. His upbeat mood continued after dinner. "How about some brandy?" Mentally he calculated the money he had spent, well over his budget, but he figured it wasn't every day he became a doctor. Just this once he wanted to celebrate.

Since the day was so unbelievably heady, Joseph allowed himself a touch of sentiment. He brought Maureen's right hand to his lips and brushed her long, tapered fingers with feathery kisses. "Hey, funny face, I can't stop thinking about you." Then the unplanned words just flowed. "I can't make it through this internship in Chicago unless I know you'll be here, waiting for me. Will you wait for me?"

Tears moistened her eyes. Maureen wrapped her arms around his neck and kissed him hard on the lips. "Well, Doc, you know I'll wait 'til the cows come home . . . but they better come home quick."

CHAPTER 3

INTERNSHIP

INTIMIDATED BY THE hustle and bustle of Chicago, his new responsibilities, and being off on his own, Joseph put in long, grueling shifts at Cook County Hospital. He specialized in dermatology while Maureen did what she always wanted to do, teach high school English. No matter how tired or busy her day, she managed to write Joseph. Her letters, consistent with her gregarious nature, were replete with longing and humorous anecdotes about her classes. But Joseph only had time to dash off sporadic notes.

Early one February morning, two days before his birthday, Joseph found himself rushing through the hospital corridors to his regularly scheduled appointment with the chief of dermatology. Lost in his own thoughts, he almost bumped into an aide rolling a breakfast cart out of an elevator. When Joseph arrived, Dr. Highiet's office door was ajar. He overheard several male voices finishing what sounded like a serious conversation. Thankful he was on time, Joseph scanned the notices on a nearby bulletin board whittling away the wait-time. It was purely serendipitous that his eyes caught hold of the words *Budapest, Hungary* on an application for a six month dermatology research program. His heart started to race as he read more. It provided a small stipend, free living accommodations, and second-class passage across the Atlantic. He never thought of travel until that minute, but suddenly it grabbed him. He ripped the flyer from the staples, folded it into quarters, and shoved it into his starched white lab coat. *This could be the best birthday present I ever got.*

When he finally entered Dr. Highiet's office, Joseph forgot his professional reserve. After a few perfunctory remarks, his excitement spilled over. "I just found this on the bulletin board. Mind taking a look?" he said, sliding the notice across the desk.

Dr. Highiet picked up his silver-rimmed reading glasses and adjusted them on the bridge of his nose. "Ah, yes. I vaguely remember this coming through. I thought . . ."

Joseph interrupted. "I have to say, it's tailor-made for me. You've got no way of knowing, but my parents were born in Hungary. We have family there. It would be a dream come true." Then he switched his emphasis, " . . . and you know, to broaden my medical experience and do research."

Dr. Highiet smiled. "Well, I'll see what I can dig up. It's certainly worth investigating."

To share his discovery, Joseph placed a rare long-distance telephone call to Maureen. "I've got great news. I might have a chance to do research . . . in Budapest for six months. What'd you think about that?"

So engrossed in the possibility, he did not hear the tinge of disappointment in her voice. "Kiddo, it sounds perfect."

Then Joseph called Mama, reaching her on her newly installed party-line. She *kvelled*, so proud that her son, 'the doctor,' might return to Hungary to meet the relatives she left behind.

Several fellow residents questioned him. In practical terms, they saw it as an interruption in his training, a pointless detour. But one astute colleague from Brooklyn grew alarmed. "What? Are you crazy? You've got no business over there. With Hitler in power,

Jews aren't safe . . . anywhere. For God's sake, don't you read the papers?"

Joseph had a tin ear to their warnings. He thought more about the positives—the free trip to Hungary and the opportunity to collaborate on dermatology research. "What could happen?" he retorted. "I'll only be gone a short time."

CHAPTER 4

BUDAPEST

J UNE 19, 1938. The ship's turbines churned steadily, slicing through the choppy Atlantic towards the port of Le Havre, France. Bone-weary and exhausted, Joseph stood on the second-class deck of the *Ile de France*, gripping the top railing. He sought neither companionship nor conversation. The time at sea provided a rare opportunity to catch his breath and reflect on life. In a pensive mood, he glanced in awe at the canopy of stars and wondered how the ancient mariners managed to navigate.

His woolen overcoat was no match for the bitter cold. The icy mist slammed across his face, stinging his eyes. A gusty wind tousled his hair. With his steady right hand, Joseph brushed aside a tuft that landed across one eye. His left hand continued to shake. Suddenly he thought, *would his new colleagues see a cripple or would they see a doctor?* There was no place on the application calling for him to disclose his tremor.

The passenger train snaked its way across the fertile farmland and scattered villages of France, Germany and Austria. But the constant clanking of metal against metal and the herky-jerky movements wore Joseph down. By the time the train screeched to a halt at the terminal in Budapest, his head ached and he was bone weary.

Light fixtures hung from posts illuminating the beehive of people in uneven pockets of artificial brightness. A portly gentleman stood off to one side wearing a fedora, a starched, high collar white shirt, and a dark suit with a vest. He held a small, cardboard placard in front of his chest with Joseph's name printed boldly in black ink. Dr. Menyhert only knew Joseph from his three page application and several glowing letters of recommendation. Unsure exactly what to expect, he kept sweeping the crowd in search of a young American male traveling alone.

When the mob of travelers dispersed, Joseph spotted the solitary man holding up a sign. He moved closer to read the blurred letters. *I need glasses,* he thought, squinting to make out his name. After their perfunctory introductions, Dr. Menyhert, the coordinator of the work-research program, insisted on taking his newest colleague to a local restaurant for a touch of authentic Hungarian food. For the sake of politeness, Joseph acquiesced, but, in truth, it was the last thing he wanted to do. All he wanted was a quiet place to settle down, stretch out, and sleep for eight uninterrupted hours.

Dr. Menyhert parked his car on a cobblestone street not far from St. Stephen's Basilica. The brisk air and stroll somewhat revived Joseph. The host, who knew Dr. Menyhert on a first name basis, gave Joseph a warm greeting. He led them to their table as gypsy music reverberated through the room. As tired as he was, Joseph tried to take it all in. The dark wainscoted walls. The tiny black and white mosaic tiles on the floor. The lace curtains covered the lower half of a series of windows that provided a barrier separating the patrons from the world outside.

Dr. Menyhert and Joseph were seated at a table draped with a green and red checkered tablecloth and set for two. Within minutes an amicable waiter appeared. Dr. Menyhert ordered a bottle of Tokaji Slamorodni, insisting Joseph try the local wine. Over the wine, pumpernickel bread, and savory mushroom-barley soup the two doctors discussed Joseph's research experience, his residency in Chicago, and the upcoming research projects. Aware that Dr. Menyhert noticed the shaking in his left arm, Joseph wondered, *what next?* Sure enough, the inevitable question arose.

"Joseph, if I might, I can't help noticing the tremor in your arm. I'm rather curious . . ."

Joseph cautioned himself, *don't be defensive.* "Well, actually the tremor started when I was only eleven years old. My mother figured it would go away. Thought I just caught a bad cold or something. But when it didn't go away, she took me to a couple of doctors. But they couldn't help me. So here I am, stuck with the goddamn thing. Frankly I think you and I both know it doesn't matter. One good hand is all a dermatologist needs."

"Yes, of course. I didn't mean to imply that your tremor would interfere with your work. It's just second nature for doctors to explore anything health related. I apologize if my brusqueness offended you."

That night Joseph slept long and hard, knowing that that hurdle had been faced and overcome.

CHAPTER 5

THE BANQUET

WITH A TEAM OF chemists and dermatologists in Budapest, Joseph experimented with various combinations of salves and lotions for severe skin disorders. In the waning days of September, Dr. Farkas Lowenstein, the only other Jewish member of their medical team, invited Joseph to attend Yom Kippur services, the holiest of all Jewish holidays.

"I appreciate the invitation," Joseph said, "but I've got a pile of work to do."

In truth, he much preferred science, verifiable facts, over religion. He thought they were at opposite ends of a continuum. He simply did not believe that God floated somewhere up in the heavens, listening to his prayers. On the other hand, he was not dogmatic. If it gave others comfort, it was okay with him. He tried to keep his beliefs to himself.

A few days after Joseph's polite refusal, Dr. Lowenstein, an eligible bachelor, brought up the Jewish holiday again. Only this time, instead of sitting in the synagogue all day, he simply urged

Joseph to join him at a break-the-fast banquet at the fashionable Gellért Hotel that evening.

"Fair enough" Joseph conceded.

In the plush reception hall, Dr. Lowenstein ran over to say hello to his aunt and uncle. For the moment Joseph stood by himself, quietly observing the crowd. An attractive woman interrupted his reverie. "Ah . . . an unfamiliar face. I don't believe we've met. I'm Ruth Goldziher."

Joseph took her to be in her late forties or early fifties. She had regal posture and a fashionable suit that fit well on her youthful figure. Her sophistication, not quite to the point of being haughty, contrasted sharply with his mother's image: *thick build, gray hair, dowdy clothes.*

"Allow me to introduce my husband and daughter."

A short man, wearing a well-tailored suit, pumped Joseph's hand vigorously. "Unfortunately my wife neglected to tell you my name. Oskar Goldziher. And this young lady is our daughter, Leah."

Joseph noted Leah's startling resemblance to her mother in style and looks, including the delphinium blue eyes. In an effort to direct his conversation towards Leah, he asked, "Will you be joining us for dinner tonight?"

Leah patted her mother's arm gently and proffered a mischievous smile.

"Last year, when I turned twenty-one, my parents insisted I eat at the grown-ups table. They try so hard to civilize me."

Oskar, who was on the board at the Doháney Street Synagogue and a natural born salesman, filled him in on the unusual background of the chief rabbi. "If you get a chance, you ought to come to services."

Seizing the opportunity, Mrs. Goldziher chimed in. "Better yet, why don't you join us for *Shabbos* dinner. How can we reach you?"

Joseph, charmed by Leah and her parents, desired nothing more than to continue their conversation. However, the seating had been prearranged. When everyone finally sat down, he joined Dr. Farkas Lowenstein, his colleague, at another long banquet table.

The moment Joseph sat down, a surly old man with lizard eyes and a gray beard, pounced on him. "Say, I hear you're from America. Mind if I ask what the hell you're doing here?"

"Research mostly. I work with Dr. Lowenstein at . . ."

And before he could finish the old man seated across from him scoffed. "Ah, never mind. I don't want to know. These days it's better to mind your own business. Not ask too many questions. You know, you're one lucky son-of-a-bitch."

Taken aback by the old man's aggressive tone, Joseph asked, "How so?"

"The whole goddamn world's falling apart. Civilization's going to hell in a hand-basket," the old man groused. "Franco's causing nothing but grief in Spain. The Japanese are causing trouble in China. Stalin's murdering millions in the Soviet Union. And I don't have to tell you about Hitler."

Joseph, intimidated by this stranger's words, readjusted his banquet chair. "I guess I was pretty naïve before I got here. To tell you the truth, I was just trying to keep my head above water. But, of course, I agree with you. These are horrible times . . ." And remembering where he was, he added, "especially in Germany for the Jews."

"Frankly, it's not much better here," the old man groused.

His colleague, Dr. Lowenstein, jumped in. "Allow me to explain. Our troubles began after the Great War. Thousands of Jews were slaughtered. Admiral Horthy, a Fascist bastard, wanted to marginalize us."

"Can I ask you something personal?" Joseph said. "I'm baffled. If you don't like it here in Hungary, why do you stay?"

"Good question," Dr. Lowenstein remarked. "I have asked myself that a million times. I don't know. Somehow we survive. It's all we've ever known."

Joseph still believed there were few differences between people. Everyone shared the same universal needs. Now, suddenly touched by their experiences, he turned inward. "You know, I have to admit, I just don't get it. Why do you suppose Jews are always the fall guy?"

"The fall guy?" the old man asked, not sure what that meant.

Joseph explained, "Always the one picked on."

As spittle formed on the edge of his lips, the crusty old man grumbled, "Who knows? Just something we have to put up with. The damn government and churches are in cahoots. Whenever anything goes wrong, they blame us. We're their convenient scapegoats."

"Wait a second," Dr. Lowenstein pleaded, "Let me give you the framework. Not long ago the Austro-Hungarian Empire meant something. It was big and powerful. Budapest was the Paris of Eastern Europe. Artists, writers, business leaders, they all flocked here. And Jews, well, we were part of it. Even in government. But times have changed. When the Great War ended, the Austro-Hungarian Empire collapsed. They were forced to sign the Treaty of Trianon. And that's when it really got rough for us. Higher institutions cut Jewish enrollment to five percent. In essence, the damn government would rather be second-rate than engage the mind of a Jew. Don't try to figure it out." He took a quick sip of water and then continued. "It was only because of my family's connections that I became a doctor."

Joseph's dinner companions hammered away at the rampant anti-Semitism surrounding them. Realizing the extent of the Nazi's murderous actions, his long dormant Jewish soul began to awaken like a blossom budding after a long, barren winter. As a physician his belief system had always galvanized around science. But this evening, as the people at the table spoke, he gathered a deeper understanding.

Suddenly Joseph could not deny it. He realized that all his life he had been trying to slip away from the bonds of Judaism, to assimilate with his contemporaries. Fit in. As if being an American and being Jewish were two incompatible ideas. Now, at this moment, he finally understood his mother's admonition, ". . . *because you're Jewish. That's why.*"

It was no longer about the dogma. No longer cerebral. It felt primal. From the gut. He felt a link to the Jews who were persecuted. They were his kindred spirits, his brothers and sisters, his family, his *landsmen*. He connected to a submerged source that dwelt within him, that defined the core of who he was.

An emaciated looking reporter for the *Magyar Israelita*, a Jewish newspaper, interrupted Joseph's thoughts. "Everything you heard tonight is true. Mark my word, before it's over, we're going to be at war again. And this time who knows where it will end . . .

CHAPTER 6

LEAH

AT THE BREAK-THE-FAST dinner, Ruth Goldziher had asked Joseph where he could be reached. And true to her word she contacted him two days later, insisting that he join her family for *Shabbos* dinner.

Joseph felt a rush of excitement as he climbed out of the taxi in front of the imposing neo-classic apartment building. He adjusted the woolen scarf that wrapped around his neck. In the alcove, he pressed the buzzer to notify the Goldziher's of his arrival. He chuckled as he caught himself humming an Irving Berlin song. When the elevator door slid open on the top floor, his eyes lit up. Leah stood in the foyer waiting for him, looking every bit as enticing as he remembered her.

After a warm welcome she led him to her parents' apartment. In the living room, floor-to-ceiling bookcases flanked the sculpted fireplace. Leather-bound books and objects d'art filled the shelves. Several scenic paintings hung in gilded frames. Leah's father, Oskar, and another well-dressed couple were engaged in conversation alongside the baby grand piano. "Come meet Ilonka and Nathan," Oskar urged when he caught sight of Joseph. "Nathan here is an art dealer . . . and a collector extraordinaire of German Expressionist paintings."

Nathan retorted, "Well, Oskar, I must say, you're developing an impressive collection yourself, although, how should I say this, a bit more traditional."

Joseph stood there feeling uncomfortable. He knew nothing about art and hoped to avoid the subject.

Ruth swept into the room and immediately apologized. "Sorry, Joseph, I didn't realize you had come in. I was in the kitchen trying to help the cook, but she just threw me out."

Her daughter Leah turned to her father and rolled her eyes, as if it was not unusual for the cook to shoo her mother out of the kitchen.

When the last couple arrived, Oskar insisted on whipping up his new concoction, a drink he called a Blue Danube. "For anyone brave enough to try it," he teased.

After checking with the kitchen staff several times, Ruth suggested they adjourn to the dining room. A sparkling crystal chandelier hung down from the coffered ceiling. Ornate silver *Shabbos* candlesticks and matches were set out on a tray at one end of the table.

Like any Jewish mother in pursuit of a suitable husband for her daughter, Ruth was not above meddling. The doctor from America held promise. Earlier in the day she had arranged the place cards. Joseph sat to her right. Leah sat next to him. Then Nathan, the art connoisseur. After Ruth lit the candles and repeated the blessings welcoming in the Sabbath, everyone exchanged a few pleasantries. Nathan held court with Oskar and the other male guest, whose importing and exporting connections benefited him.

Joseph found Leah to be lively and enchanting. Although he succeeded in giving her his full attention, he could not help overhearing the tail-end of Nathan's dire warning. "Everything of value ought to be shipped out of Hungary. That's what I'm telling the curators. No one knows what's going to happen. Hitler can't be trusted."

Always the optimist, Oskar scowled. "Isn't that rather extreme? Besides, what place in Europe is any safer?"

The dinner guests were engrossed in an intense exchange about the possibilities of war, but Leah could not fathom the doomsayer's conversation. "So Joseph, is this your first trip to Hungary?"

"Yes," he answered, "I was born in America but my mother and father were born here. Near Miskolc. Do you know the area?"

"Sure. Wine country. Do you still have family there?"

"Aunts, uncles . . . cousins that I've never met. But before I return home, I plan to visit them. How about you? Brothers? Sisters?"

"A sister. Rose. She's four years younger and very shy. She's at a friend's house tonight. Says she needs to study for a test."

Ruth, a first-class puppeteer, pushed her way into their conversation, suggesting that Joseph might be interested in seeing the neighborhood after dinner.

Sated from dinner, Joseph and Leah strolled along an artery filled with fashionable boutiques. A three-quarter moon hung overhead like a beacon against the blackened sky. Leah proffered just enough background to make her short tour of the neighborhood sound authentic. Not far from the apartment, they approached a cobblestone plaza whose perimeter was lined with a stone church, several statues, and a succession of intimate cafés.

At that moment Leah's eyes reflected a string of Tivoli lights. "When I was a little girl, my mother often took me to this café for hot chocolate after my piano lessons. Want to go in?"

They hung their coats and woolen scarves on wall hooks and sat at an empty table near the bar. After ordering espresso Joseph asked, "Does your whole family live in Budapest?"

"Almost. Except an uncle. A Zionist. He took off for Palestine a few years back."

"Do you think your mother and father would ever consider moving there?"

"Never. We're rooted here," Leah said with conviction. "My father inherited a wine exporting business from my grandfather. Under the current regime, Jews are forbidden to trade in wine. But my father's resourceful. Now he brokers whatever he can. Mostly timber."

"I just learned about the restrictions," Joseph said. "They're outrageous." Hungary's persecution of the Jews had gnawed away his indifference. At the same time, he was beginning to understand how difficult it would be to abandon such a luxurious lifestyle.

Since they were just getting acquainted, Leah and Joseph kept the conversation alive by asking each other a series of questions. Joseph shocked her by admitting he had quit school in the 6th grade.

"You're kidding, right?"

"No, I'm serious," Joseph said, his face taking on a stern look. "Actually there's a simple explanation. That's when the tremor started in my arm. My mother took me to a doctor, rare in those days. And he sent me to a specialist. The kids at school poked fun of me, so I just stopped going. Besides, I thought I could help my mother with the doctor bills. I tried hawking newspapers, some-times cigarettes and candy. But it wasn't such a great way to make a living." Joseph got a far-away look in his eyes. "Truthfully, I got beat up more times than I'd like to remember. Hoodlums would swipe my money. But I never told my mother."

"Well, still . . . how did you get to be a doctor?"

"Finally I figured it was a losing proposition. I remembered the specialist Mama dragged me to. He had pulled me aside. Made my mother leave the room. 'Joseph,' he said, 'don't let this tremor stop you. You can do anything you set your mind to.' You know, I still idolize that man. So when I returned to school I decided to be a doctor, like him."

"Just like that, you changed?"

"Not exactly. That . . . plus I learned the library was free. When I returned to school, the kids still picked on me. So the library became my refuge, my hangout. I really loved it. After school, I'd head over there to study. Read newspapers, magazines. Over the years Mrs. Benton, the librarian, became my best friend. Actually she helped me get my first job, the one at the telephone company. Her brother was a big muckety-muck there and she wrote a letter of recommendation. She even typed my college application for me. I owe a lot to that lady."

Leah, who had led a sheltered life, was amazed with his life experiences and listened for a long time before changing the subject. "Ever been to the castle on the hill or our opera house?"

"No, afraid not."

"Have you seen any of the other tourist attractions?"

Joseph shook his head. "I guess I'm not much of a tourist. Been swamped with work."

"Well, it just so happens, my parents have two seats for Saturday night's opera. Father subscribes every year. This morning over breakfast he told mother he won't be able to make it. Something about out-of-town clients coming in. Would you be interested in going? Our opera house is famous."

For the moment, Joseph blocked out his engagement to Maureen and leaped at the chance to get to know Leah better.

CHAPTER 7

THE OPERA

JOSEPH FELT SELF-CONSCIOUS in the ill-fitting tails that he borrowed from a colleague. He sat across from Ruth in the living room making idle conversation while Leah fussed with two pearl combs in front of the dressing table in her bedroom. At the last minute, she snapped on a dainty pearl necklace her parents had given her on her 16th birthday. Joseph could barely take his eyes off her when she appeared in a muted blue gown that accentuated her tantalizing eyes and cinched in around her tiny waist.

Seated in the back of the taxi, Joseph admitted sheepishly he knew nothing about opera. Leah tried to enlighten him without appearing condescending. "Tonight's performance is Mozart's *Don Giovanni*. It's one of his best works. I'm sorry. I should have given you the *libretto*."

Joseph rolled the word *libretto* around in his brain but had to confess he had no idea what it meant.

"Opera makes a whole lot more sense if you know the story, but you really don't need to. The music is powerful enough."

At the Opera House they immediately got sucked into the arriving crowd. Joseph flung out his chest and extended his good arm. "Shall we . . ." They followed the crush of Budapest's society patrons into the rococo lobby, climbed the ornamental staircase, and were ushered down the aisle to their seats off to the right.

Within the opulent opera house, it was easy for the sophisticated crowd to block out any sense of foreboding, at least temporarily. Several days earlier, Nazi storm troopers had beaten and murdered Jews all over Germany, Austria and Poland. The windows of Jewish shops and department stores were smashed and their contents looted. Hundreds of synagogues burned while local fire departments stood motionless or simply prevented the fire from spreading to surrounding buildings. Radio commentators and newspapers were ablaze with speculation on the ramifications of Hitler's aggressions. But Leah's mother had told Leah not to worry. Hungary had aligned itself with Germany. They would be left alone. But after everything he had heard, Joseph wasn't so sure about that.

As they took their seats, Leah scrutinized the women bedecked in jewels and furs. Joseph leaned back in his seat to study the magnificent fresco on the domed ceiling. The lights flickered and then turned down to an intimate glow. When the orchestra began the overture, there was a palpable moment of anticipation.

"I love that split-second when the lights first dim and the music begins," Leah said, trying to talk over the music.

For Joseph, who had long ago dismissed opera as the fanciful domain of the upper class and long-haired men, it turned out to be an extravagant night of self-discovery. The grandeur of the opera house, the lavish costumes, the stage settings and the powerful voices and music moved him to tears. He tried to wipe them away, hoping Leah hadn't noticed.

To the contrary, Leah noticed. *Only a sensitive soul could be moved to that degree.* She leaned over and touched his arm lightly, leaving her hand there for him to hold.

At her suggestion, they capped off the evening at the New York Café, commensurate in grandeur to the opera house and frequented by the literati. She hoped they would spot somebody famous, but that didn't pan out. Nevertheless, they rehashed the opera and tried to analyze what motivated people to be creative. Leah spoke of Mozart's genius before taking a dainty bite of her Dobos torte and letting the sweetness dissolve in her mouth. "Mother started me on piano lessons when I was seven. I've taken them on and off for years."

"I'd love to hear you play," Joseph enthused, visualizing her at the baby grand in her parents' apartment.

In keeping with the gaiety of the evening, Leah offered to show Joseph the real Budapest.

Not surprising, they began seeing each other more frequently. Days turned into weeks, then into months. Leah's presence pushed aside any thoughts of his fiancée back in Cleveland, despite the fact that Maureen continued to send him perfumed letters almost daily.

Leah and Joseph walked hand-in-hand after another glorious day of sightseeing. At her suggestion, they stopped at Gerbeaud's, a well known coffeehouse, with its polished brass spittoons and turn of the century Victorian furnishings. Joseph spoke about his upcoming trip to the little village outside of Miskolc where his extended family still lived.

"Leah, you don't know how much I'd like to take you with me but for the sake of propriety, I think it best I go alone." A bit inhibited, he hoped no one at the nearby tables overheard his words.

While growing up, Mama had frequently told Joseph of her younger years in a small village near Miskolc and all the relatives she left behind. By the time he was ready for his visit, Joseph could almost picture them in his mind. He penned a letter to his uncle, his mother's oldest brother, to let him know when his train would arrive.

Joseph caused quite a stir on the first night of his visit. A flock of curious relatives—some with no recollection of Mama—gathered at the modest home of a cousin. In an effort to explain who they were, they constantly interrupted each other. America had always been good to Joseph, but being in this village—surrounded by the warmth of his extended family, their children, and their children's children—made him realize all that his parents had left behind.

What was America like, they wanted to know.

"Come. See for yourself," Joseph challenged. But for these insular people, who led a quiet, pedestrian life, the thought of traveling so far was too overwhelming.

When an opportunity arose, Joseph turned to his Uncle Chaim. "Can I ask you a favor? Could we go to the cemetery tomorrow? You know, I never met my *Bubbe* and *Zaide*. It's something I always wanted to do." He surprised himself by referring to his grandparents by their Yiddish titles. Ever since he could remember, Joseph made a point of thinking in English—substituting stiff English words and phrases for the clever Yiddish expressions of his childhood.

"Tomorrow we go," his aging uncle responded through yellowed teeth and a leathery face lined from hard work. "For tonight, let's enjoy each other's company."

Even though Joseph was bundled up the next morning, the bitter cold numbed his nose and ears. As he waited for his uncle to arrive with the horse and wagon, he spied two, small flat stones. With stiff fingers, he leaned down and clasped them, shoving one in each pocket of his woolen overcoat.

In the wagon Joseph tried to rekindle the discussion about the opportunities in America but his uncle brushed them aside. "Joseph, I'm an old man. My whole life I lived here. And this is where I'll die."

For a long time they remained silent, lost in their own thoughts, except for the clip-clopping of the horse's hoofs on the rutted dirt road that lead out of town. As they approached the cemetery, his uncle searched for the right words. "I know most everyone here— friends, family, neighbors," he said, referring to the headstones. "May they rest in peace."

After hitching the wagon, they wove their way through the unkempt cemetery. Uncle Chaim, with gnarled fingers, pointed out where his beloved wife, Dvora, and a brother were buried.

Joseph marveled at how comfortable his uncle felt among the dead and buried.

It must be reassuring to live in a tiny community and never be a stranger—even in death, he thought.

Both men tried not to step on the gravesites as they ambled towards his grandparents' headstones. They stood near an unpainted slat fence that seemed to roll away from them. Joseph shivered as his uncle swayed back and forth reciting *Kaddish*, the Jewish prayer for the dead. Unfamiliar with all the words, he fingered the small stones in his pockets. Carefully he laid a single stone on top of each tilted marker. He had no idea why he did it, but supposed it was just tradition.

Joseph surveyed the neglected cemetery. Then he asked, "Why is it that Jews are buried apart from everyone else—even in America? Why must we always be isolated?"

His uncle pursed his thick lips and thought for a moment. Then he shrugged.

On the train back to Budapest, Joseph wrestled with guilt. He ignored the scenic farmland as he tried to clarify his jumbled love life. *What have I done? I've fallen for Leah while Maureen waits for me back in Cleveland. Maureen deserves better. I've messed up my life. Have I just outgrown speakeasies and wild times? Or is it my sudden exposure to a world of culture? Or about the Goldzihers' prestige and money? Suppose Mama was right after all? Have I fallen for Leah—a nice Jewish girl— just to please Mama? Or do I simply have heroic fantasies about saving her? Think, Joseph. Reason it out.*

But he couldn't help himself. His blinding love for Leah originated in his heart, not his mind.

CHAPTER 8

FEAR

EAH HAD LED a sheltered life. She had occasionally dated the sons of her parents' friends. Though they had impeccable manners, she thought them immature—often conceited—with little direction or ambition. Joseph was different. She saw him as a man of great depth. From their first encounter, she thought he was unusually sensitive and accomplished.

Late one night Leah thrashed around in her bed, restless and unable to sleep. Like most girls of marrying age, she thought about the qualities she wanted in a future husband. In every category, Joseph exceeded her expectations. He was serious, without taking himself seriously. Leah admired his modesty and the fact that he truly wanted to be a healer. That he was a self-made man. Even though there was an age gap, he floated comfortably between her parents' generation and hers. Leah idolized him and she knew the feeling was mutual.

A few hours after he proposed, the adoring couple sat in a small, out-of-the-way café holding hands. Leah began to discuss the wedding, when Joseph's expression tightened. "Sweetheart, hold on a minute. I want you to think about coming to America *before* we get married. See it firsthand. Make sure you like it. Suppose you don't. Then what? I have to be honest. There's no way I can give you everything you've got here. Cleveland's nothing like Budapest. It's filled with a bunch of poor schnooks trying to eke out a living."

Leah's face scrunched up. "Schnooks?"

"You know, people." Joseph chuckled, realizing the word just did not translate well.

"Life in America will be good. You'll see," Leah said, with complete earnestness.

"I know I already told you," he continued, "but let me remind you again. For years I slept on the couch in the living room in Mama's tiny apartment. The only real bed I ever slept in was at the boarding house."

"I know, but look at you now. An impressive doctor," she exclaimed. "Making a life for yourself. That's what I love most about you."

As Europe's political situation deteriorated, Joseph grew more alarmed. He kept silent about his misgivings, but felt the sooner Leah left Hungary, the better. "We need to tell your parents. Let's surprise them. Invite them to dinner."

Early the next morning Joseph set his plan in motion.

That evening at dinner, the maître d' seated the four of them at a table in the elegant dining room, with a high, frescoed ceiling, marble floors, elaborately carved columns, and crystal chandeliers. Notes from a harp drifted down like soft snow flakes, creating a false sense of well-being. A waiter, with hair the color of sisal and a hint of a French accent, took their orders. Leah and Joseph eyed each other. *Who would go first?*

Leah grabbed Joseph's hand. "Joseph and I have something to tell you." And before her parents had a chance to respond, she announced their engagement.

"With your permission, of course," Joseph interjected, not taking anything for granted. "I'm asking for your daughter's hand in marriage."

The Goldzihers' faces brightened. Oskar spoke first. "I'll be damned. I had a feeling something was up when you invited us to dinner. This is wonderful news."

Tears blotted Ruth's vision. "It's a blessing you found each other."

"*Mazel tov!*" Oskar repeated. At long last some good news."

Ruth dabbed at her eyes with her white linen napkin. "So . . . tell us. What are your plans?"

"I hope this won't come as a disappointment, but Leah and I plan to live in America. That's where I've been trained. I'll be starting a practice soon. I hope to support your daughter, not lavishly, but . . . in time, I ought to do pretty well."

"I've no doubt you'll make a good husband," Oskar said. "And I've heard America is the golden medina."

Ruth added, "Leah, darling, what mother wouldn't be happy with such a fine son-in-law, such a charmer. And, Joseph, dear, I think Leah picked the cream-of-the-crop. God, how I will miss you. But America is a good place . . ." then hesitated, as if she couldn't say what she was thinking, *a safe place.*

Joseph noted that the Goldzihers did not seem unduly disappointed, considering their oldest daughter would be moving so far away.

"You'll come visit us and we'll visit you," Leah said, filled with unbridled enthusiasm for the future.

They ordered champagne and Oskar proposed a toast. "May you always be as happy as you are right here, right now." They clicked glasses, pretending all was right with the world.

Joseph laid out his vision. When he returned to America, he would organize everything and send for Leah. In the meantime she needed to obtain a visa and a passport.

That night, when Joseph returned to his room, he felt there were too many things left unsaid. *Maybe the Goldzihers have the same premonition I have,* he thought. *Maybe they are secretly relieved that Leah will be leaving Hungary, but just won't say it. There is a fine line between leaving and fleeing.*

Once again Joseph found himself aboard an ocean liner, this time steaming towards New York. Though he took his meals in the assigned dining room and mingled with a few gregarious passengers at his table, he preferred alone time to sift through his recent experiences. He had no regrets. He knew his research and medical training in Budapest would one day prove invaluable. But the pathways to his brain kept leading him back to Leah, his future bride. In her absence, he tried to reconstruct her essence: her gentle touch, her sweet voice and the way they fit together while making love.

Before Joseph left Cleveland to do his internship, he had urged Maureen, his longtime girlfriend, to wait for him. At the time, he had no idea that he would fall in love with someone else. Now Maureen, his Wild Irish Rose, seemed as distant as the Peloponnesian War. The memory of her remained but not the feelings. And her constant letters filled with yearning pecked away at his conscience and sense of decency.

In the first few days back in Cleveland, his biggest concern was getting Leah out of Europe. But he also agonized over the inevitable break-up with Maureen. He knew he would deeply hurt his dearest friend. She had encouraged him and stood by him for years. When he realized he could no longer postpone the inevitable, he waited until late afternoon before dialing her number.

"Sweet Jesus, is this really you, Joseph? I wasn't sure when you were coming home. I just walked in the door. I'm so happy you're back."

"Me too," Joseph replied, garnering little enthusiasm.

"I can't wait to see you. Come over. I'll fix us some supper. I want to hear all about Budapest."

"I'm stilling finishing up a few things. How about after dinner? Say eight o'clock." Joseph would have preferred the quick action of a guillotine to his encounter with Maureen.

As he navigated past the tricycles, buggies, and strollers in the musty lobby of the rundown apartment building, he began to second guess himself. *Maybe I should have brought her flowers or something.*

Maureen moved fast in the few hours since his initial call. She showered, changed clothes and straightened up her cluttered apartment. When she heard the familiar rhythm of his knock, she flung the door open. Without saying a word she dropped into his arms and with longing kissed him. Since Maureen's passion was thrust upon him, he grudgingly met her half-way.

"Look at you. I can tell you ate well," she teased, rubbing his bulging belly. "How 'bout a drink?"

"Sure, I could use one." While she went to the kitchen, Joseph scanned the living room. He cringed when he caught sight of several framed photograph of the two of them in happier moments.

Maureen handed him a glass and proposed a toast, "To the two of us." Almost choking on his drink, Joseph was not ready to confront her. Maureen slid an ashtray off to the side and carefully placed her tumbler on a makeshift coffee table, two wooden fruit crates covered with a thin muslin pillow case. At her behest, Joseph briefly reviewed the highlights of his experiences in Budapest, carefully omitting Leah.

"Sweetie, some days I couldn't wait to rush home and write to you, telling you all about my day. Did you get my letters?"

"I did," Joseph answered half-heartedly. Anxious to stall off the defining challenge, he asked, "How's teaching?" While she indulged in a monologue about her English classes, he nodded absentmindedly, mentally rehearsing his spiel. "Well, it sure sounds like you're happy," he said, adding a positive spin to her stories. "Listen . . . Maureen, we need to do some serious talking and I'm not sure how to begin."

Thinking they would finally set a wedding date, she said, "Sure. What do you have in mind, Doc?"

Maureen's proximity unnerved him. As he shifted his body away from her, he said, "I need to say something and it may not come out right, so try to understand, okay? We've known each other for years. We've helped each other, sometimes even clung to each other. I will always be grateful for the good times. I'll never forget them."

"Joseph, exactly what are you saying? Are you trying to tell me it's over between us?"

That question called for a yes or no answer and Joseph intended to be less abrupt. The anguished expression on her face left him tongue-tied. "Maureen, please try to understand." Backed into a corner, he had no alternative put to blurt out his thoughts. "You will always be special to me, but marriage just won't work. We need to call off our engagement."

Blood rushed to her head. "Don't say *we* when you mean *you*. *You*, Joseph, this is about *you*. *You* need to call it off. Not me. I love you." Maureen got no further. Her shoulders shuddered as she placed her hand over her mouth to muffle her sobs.

"Please don't. Come on. Don't cry. Don't make this any harder for me than it is." Joseph wove his fingers together and pressed hard. He feared holding her would only make it worse. He tried to be tactful as he stumbled over each agonizing word. "Maureen, I loved our times together, but it just won't work. I just can't marry you."

Joseph's words stung like multiple darts piercing her heart. "I don't believe this is happening. All these years I've waited for you. My knight-in-shining-armor. Now you're telling me you can't marry me. This has to do with your mother, doesn't it? Is this because I'm Catholic?"

"No, yes . . . I don't know. It just is. Look, Maureen, I can't explain it."

"Did you meet someone else?" she prodded, not content with his meager rendition of the facts.

This was the one topic he wanted to avoid, but was now forced to answer. "Yes, but . . ."

"And I suppose she's Jewish," she said, raising her voice along with the issue that had stood like an invisible barrier between them.

"Yes, but you're taking this all wrong," he protested, realizing how lame he sounded. "It has nothing to do with her being Jewish. You're jumping to the wrong conclusions."

"Am I? Let me tell you something. Joseph, you're one son-of-a-bitch. Think about it. You people call anyone who disagrees with you anti-Semitic. But in the end you stick together like glue. You're the ones that are narrow-minded. Clannish. You think the rest of us are unworthy shits. We're okay for screwing, but not for marrying, is that it? Face it, it's not me, it's you that's prejudice. I'm the one that put you on a goddamn pedestal. Like a stupid fool, I waited while you did your internship. Remember, I'm the one that cheered you on when you wanted to do that goddamn program in Budapest."

A scorned woman, Maureen shouted and screamed. She called him every name she could think of. Her anger fed on itself like flames dancing on a stack of kindling. In the end, Joseph walked out of her apartment feeling like the lowly bastard she claimed he was. At the time, he had no idea that for the rest of his life he would carry that guilt on both shoulders, always trying subconsciously to prove her wrong.

CHAPTER 9

LEAH'S VISA

HITLER HAD just challenged the world with another unspeakable event. He loaded the *S.S. St. Louis* with over nine hundred Jewish refugees and set them out to sea, daring the world to take them in. Once adrift, Cuba tentatively agreed to give the refugees safe haven. But, ultimately, when the ship docked, they were refused entry. They then sailed on to the United States, hoping to be admitted. But they were again denied entry.

America was just getting back on its feet after the crash of '29. And a covert form of anti-Semitism dictated America's immigration policies. Leah had difficulty obtaining a visa. Even though President Roosevelt had intelligence reports concerning Hitler's persecution of Jews, the United States stubbornly refused to allow any major influx of Jewish people into the country.

In Cleveland Joseph tried his best to move the process along. He banged on the doors of local bureaucrats, but they all gave him the same answer. "Gee, I'd really like to help you but my hands are tied." Terrified for Leah, he refused to give up. He hounded the consulate and immigration offices and even went to Columbus, Ohio's capital, to talk with state representatives.

One day over a quick lunch in the doctors' lounge at the hospital, his colleague asked, "How's it going?" Orrin knew of his situation and listened with rapt attention as Joseph spewed out his frustrations. "The government's stalling. All Leah needs is one goddamn visa. And all she's getting is the run around. With a country as big as ours, what's one more person?"

"It's pretty lousy," Orin sympathized.

No longer oblivious to the problems of the world, Joseph had been devouring every newspaper he could in an effort to stay abreast of the havoc being played out in Europe. "Every day Leah remains in Hungary I fear for her life. I just want to bring her over so we can get married. She needs to get out of Europe . . . and the sooner the better."

"Listen, Joseph," Orin finally said. "I've been thinking a lot about your situation. My brother-in-law, the Honorable Theodore Harrison II, is a congressman from Springfield. A real jerk, but it couldn't hurt to talk to him. I'm not making any promises, but maybe he can help."

A few weeks after meeting the congressman, and a handsome contribution to his campaign, Joseph found a crack in the revolving door. The congressman called in a favor and set Joseph up with a powerful member in the State Department. Joseph bought a train ticket to Washington, D.C. Four months later he finagled a visa for his bride-to-be. They finalized her travel arrangements via cable and a slew of back and forth letters.

Knowing how Leah was raised, Joseph realized a boarding house was not a place to bring his future bride. Besides, he presumed Leah would feel more comfortable living near Mama. So he canvassed the Buckeye neighborhood looking for a decent place. He rented a tiny apartment over a hardware store on 115th Street, in an area teeming with Hungarian immigrants. Energized by his impending marriage, Joseph bought basic furniture. He even stocked the cupboards with green glass plates like Mama's.

Six days before Leah's departure, fear rose like a flash flood in a narrow canyon. Suddenly she realized the finality of leaving Budapest, her family and everything she had ever known. Her mother was helping her set out and pack an extensive trousseau. For the moment each was left to their own thoughts. The task was nearing completion when Ruth grew teary-eyed. "I'll be back in a minute," she said. She returned from the dining room and handed her daughter one of the ornate *Shabbos* candlesticks. "Sweetheart, take this. You can squeeze it into one of your trunks."

Leah furled her brows and looked puzzled. "But mother, this belongs to you. I can't take one. The candlesticks go together."

Ruth wiped the tears from her eyes as she started to explain. "When part of the family separates, well . . . until we meet again. A reminder of your roots." She wrapped her arms tightly around her daughter and the two women hugged and wept for their unknown future.

Joseph met her ship in New York and accompanied her back to Cleveland on the train. Within days the rabbi from a nearby *shul* performed a simple wedding ceremony. Only Mama and several of Joseph's closest colleagues attended. Leah and Joseph relished a weekend honeymoon at the Palmer House Hotel in downtown Chicago. Even though he had completed his internship in the Windy City, he was delighted to see it again through the eyes of his young bride.

For Joseph the first year of marriage flew by. He was busy doing his residency.

On the other hand, all day long Leah sat in their apartment alone, counting the hours until her husband returned. Forced to rely on the radio for companionship, she pined for her parents and old school chums. Mama tried to fill in the gap, but she got up early and worked long hours at the bakery. America was far more complicated than Leah imagined and the transition to married life more difficult. She made an effort to teach herself English, but it made no sense. Just when she thought she recognized a pattern, a frustrating exception sabotaged her understanding.

She tried, but cooking was not her forte. In Budapest cookies were the only thing Leah ever made and that was with the help of the family cook. Since she only knew the metric system, she stumbled over American measurements. She grew frustrated when she tried to surprise Joseph with a new recipe. Regardless of the food, he only felt joy coming home. When he could spare the time, Joseph brought her to Mama's on Friday nights for *Shabbos* dinners. Leah invariably rallied with the familiarity of the Jewish rituals and Mama's warmth and total acceptance.

Though Joseph tried to expose her to American culture, his grueling schedule left little time with his bride. Good-natured, Leah did enjoy the Fourth of July parade and fireworks. But no matter how hard she tried, she could not figure out the baseball or football rules. As far as she was concerned, the best part of every game was the Polish hot dogs, smothered with pickle relish, chopped onions, and ground mustard. When she wrote to her old girlfriends in Budapest, she tried to explain the strange ice cream concoction called Eskimo Pie.

On the plus side, the universal language of music provided common ground. Long familiar with classical music, Leah grew to love pop music, her husband's favorite. When he could, Joseph loved to show Leah a good time. He frequently took her to listen to the big bands.

"Joseph," she would beg, "take me to the boogie-woogie again."

Joseph worked hard. He made rounds at the hospital and continued with his research. But one night, without warning, Leah greeted him with the silent treatment. His heart dropped when he tried to get something out of her. "Honey, did you hear from your parents today?"

She shook her head sidewise in response.

"What's wrong? Are you worried?"

"No," she said, not realizing how bad things were. Leah had all but given up trying to read the English-speaking newspapers.

"Why the sour puss?'

"What?"

"You know, the long face."

"What does it mean long face?"

"Why so sad?"

At first she sat silently. She averted his eyes and looked out the living room window. After Joseph's incessant urging to talk to him, she mumbled like a petulant child, "Without you, the days seem so long."

Joseph gently placed his hands on her cheeks. "Leah, look at me. I know this is hard. But one day I'll be able to give you everything you ever dreamed of . . ."

"I just want to be with you."

Her periodic mood swings drove Joseph to distraction, forcing them to have a serious heart-to-heart about their future. Leah could still remember her father's ingenuity in making a living under difficult conditions. She urged Joseph to work for himself, thinking life would be easier.

Eighteen months later Joseph got up the nerve and chanced it. He signed for a loan at the bank, rented office space, and started a solo practice in downtown Cleveland. But the plan only increased his workload. Now that he was out on a financial limb, he devoted more—not less—time to his career.

The couple gloated over their good fortune when Leah became pregnant.

"I don't want our baby sleeping in the living room," Joseph said vehemently, remembering only too well the couch he slept on in Mama's apartment.

They rented a place with two bedrooms several blocks away, but on a quieter street. Leah's moodiness lifted as she prepared for the baby. As her pregnancy progressed, Mama served as her surrogate mother. After all the years trying to assimilate, Mama became the expert. She took pride in explaining her version—not always accurate—of how things worked in America. Leah's labor was long and difficult. But once mother and daughter returned from the hospital, life settled down to a normal routine. Joseph and Leah named their daughter Ellen, after Elias, Joseph's father.

One night over thin soup and another dried out brisket, Leah beamed, "Joseph, we're a family now."

Meanwhile Hitler continued his crusade for racial purity in Germany. He attacked Jews with a vengeance no one could imagine. Jews were rounded up and transported to extermination camps, their property confiscated. Insanity and fear sucked the air out of Eastern Europe. At the start of the war Hungary signed a pact with Hitler, believing that would stave off his wrath. In their letters, Leah's parents tried to shield her from their concerns, but her old classmates spelled out their worst fears.

Every Nazi conquest was splashed across the front of America's newspapers. A noose was slowly tightening around Hungary. Joseph tried to conceal his panic as he worked the system, hoping to obtain visas for Leah's family. He played every angle—legal and illegal—to make it happen. Each refusal or dead end was a bitter defeat, but he never gave up trying.

Leah wrote her parents daily, explaining how hard Joseph was working to get them out. With a sense of foreboding, she lived for the letters she received from Budapest. Joseph pounded away at the authorities in an effort to extricate Leah's family. Mama, too, worried about her relatives living near Miskolc.

In July of 1943 Leah gave birth to their second daughter, Pauline. While Ellen had been a placid baby, Pauline was colicky and demanding. And, unfortunately, at this juncture in her life, when Leah needed to be an involved mother, she obsessed more about her family in Budapest than her two little girls. They got what attention she had, but it was not enough. Motherhood had become a chore, not a pleasure.

Joseph tried not to give in to the accruing fear floating through his head. But he knew he needed to do something to raise Leah's spirits. One Saturday, while he was helping Leah straighten up the cluttered apartment, he remarked, "You know my practice is taking off." Then he knocked on wood, an old superstition he learned from Mama. "Maybe it's time we bought a house. Wouldn't it be nice for the girls?" In reality, he was searching for something positive to distract Leah from her morose moods.

Leah's face lit up. "A house?" That was always beyond her expectations. Neither of them had ever lived in a house. For months they searched for just the right place and finally settled on a three-bedroom home near Coventry Road in Cleveland Heights.

Late one afternoon in the spring of '44, the postman delivered their mail. As soon as it was in the mailbox, Leah charged out to see if there was any word from her parents. Every day she followed the same ritual, but their letters—filled with despair—appeared less and less frequently. As soon as Leah nabbed the thin airmail envelope she returned to the living room to savor the private moments with her parents. Absent-mindedly she plopped onto the cushion in their newly purchased wing-back chair. Nothing else mattered as she ripped open the envelope and began to read:

> *Dearest Leah and Joseph,*
>
> *We received the photos of your sweet, sweet girls. They warm our hearts and we carry their pictures with us everywhere we go. If only we could see and hold all of you, our lives would be complete. Always know that you are in our hearts. We will love you forever. We don't know what will happen next. The Germans now occupy Hungary. On orders of Adolph Eichmann all Jewish organizations have been disbanded and Jews are being forced to wear a yellow badge. I have to say we are a proud lot of people. Defiantly we put it on one week earlier than necessary. Freedom of movement has been restricted and Hitler has appropriated many buildings. Rose can no longer go to school. Our people are being rounded-up and transported to certain parts of the city. We don't know how long we will be able to stay here in our apartment. Jews are constantly being sent away or disappearing . . .*

She had barely finished reading the letter when her body went limp. "NO!" she wailed as the letter glided featherlike onto the hardwood floor. Her head bobbed from side-to-side in disbelief. Her body started to tremble. She was no fool. The lights in Budapest had just been turned out.

CHAPTER 10

DEPRESSION

HER MOTHER'S LETTER, not written in her usual carefully scripted penmanship, was a chilling narrative about her family's loss of freedom in Nazi controlled Budapest. Short on details, it was what her mother did not say that caused Leah to sob into her pillow. She wrapped herself in a self-imposed shroud of mourning. For days on end, she folded into herself, refusing to eat or get dressed. Her thick hair, once meticulously groomed, remained dirty and uncombed. In her anguish, the house and children that once had given her so much joy, were neglected.

Every day when the postman delivered the mail, Leah managed to drag herself to the mailbox, praying that she would receive just one more letter from her parents. She had saved all their previous letters—those from her parents, her sister, and her friends—in a round, Marshal Field's hat box. In her shrinking universe, she sat for hours on their unmade bed and reread every letter word-for-word. She was haunted by the ghosts of her family and friends. She tried to resurrect happier memories, but grim thoughts flooded her mind: *Where are they? What happened to my family? Are they alive?*

Joseph tried to console his wife, but couldn't penetrate her deepening depression. Without uttering a word, Leah simply stared through him. Her once sparkling blue eyes no longer registered and her mind was incapable of making the most basic decisions. After three weeks of unresponsiveness, Joseph grew desperate and tried another approach.

He raised his voice, pretending to be angry. "Leah, everything's falling apart. Look at the house. It's a pigsty. The girls need you. You're their mother. Every time I come home Pauline's crying. Do you ever change her diapers?"

Leah nodded as if she understood, but the next day nothing would change. For her, one day just melted into the next. Paralyzed with fear that the letters had stopped permanently, she checked the mailbox four or five times a day. In the few hours she slept, she dreamt of gargoyle-like creatures pecking at dead bodies. On the brink of madness, she punished herself for being alive. And through her despair, she grew stubborn and unreasonable, refusing any medications.

One particularly gloomy afternoon, Ellie was playing in the living room and tripped over the laundry basket. She landed on the brick hearth, cutting her lip and knocking out a baby tooth. That was it. Joseph wasn't sure what to do, but knew he had to do something. Someone suggested he get in touch with the Jewish Family Service Agency. When the social worker picked up the phone, he explained his situation. "I need a mother's helper. Someone to look after my girls, clean the house, fix meals."

"We have a situation that might work," the social worker offered. "A seventeen year old girl just arrived. Don't ask me how, but she and her brother escaped Poland. And somehow they wound up here in Cleveland. Would you be interested in taking her in? In exchange, she would be willing to help with your children and the housework."

Joseph hesitated. "I'm not sure. Maybe I could interview her first. See how it goes."

A few days later Joseph cut his work day short and returned to the Jewish Family Service Agency. The social worker and Anna sat across from him in an airless conference room. He thought Anna looked pitiful, a puny girl with an unnatural pallor and deep bluish-black circles under her eyes. Despite his trepidations, Joseph went with his gut and hired her. He figured Ellen and Pauline could share a bedroom and Anna could have the other. He loved the girls as much as he loved Leah, but the increasing demands of his solo practice robbed him of family time.

Ellen—Ellie for short—was a precocious child. She had a little girl voice with a slight lisp, a dimple on one cheek, and corkscrew blond locks. Whenever she saw her father she demanded his attention. She badgered him with questions in an effort to make sense of her ever expanding world. Joseph playfully called her the "Why Girl."

But Pauline, a quiet child, was born in a time of stress. She needed more attention than she was getting. She fell into the shadow of her demanding sister and unresponsive mother. Between the girls and the house, Anna earned her keep. Her uninspiring meals provided sustenance, but nothing more. Yet Joseph was grateful; at least there was food on the table.

When the letters from Budapest stopped so abruptly, Joseph struggled to console his wife. He grew obsessive trying to find out what became of the Goldzihers and his Hungarian relatives. He hounded the offices of the two Ohio senators, wrote to influential people whether he knew them or not, pressed the State Department and tried unsuccessfully to connect with President Roosevelt. But all he got in return were vague letters that essentially said the same thing: We sympathize with your concern. We will look into the matter and notify you when we have more information.

On the positive side, Joseph's tremor classified him as 4–F, which meant he was unfit for service. And with war being fought in the Pacific and Europe, there was an acute shortage of stateside doctors. Without much competition, his dermatology practice flourished. He had bottled a line of skin care products for distribution and sale under a private label and the salves and creams were wildly successful. He received numerous accolades and was invited to speak at medical seminars in Boston, Philadelphia, and New York.

But, in his quieter moments, he felt a consuming guilt that he was prospering while brave, young American soldiers were fighting and dying overseas.

CHAPTER 11

SHAKER HEIGHTS

WITH ANNA'S HELP, Leah's vitality was gradually returning, although some days it still spun out-of-control. Birthdays and holidays were the worst, sending her into a melancholy spiral. It would have been her father's birthday earlier in the week and Leah was feeling empty. She longed for company. Finally on Saturday night she called Mama. "Come over for supper tomorrow. Anna will make a brisket. It's not so good as yours, but we'll be together."

Trying not to be an imposition, Mama excused herself. "No, darling. For work on Monday, you know I get up early."

"Mama, the girls want to see you. I promise, we'll make it an early evening. Joseph can drive over and pick you up."

After much cajoling, Mama finally conceded. Following dinner that night, Joseph drove her back to her apartment. Anna put the girls to bed while Leah sat on the couch listlessly watching the Ed Sullivan show on their new Motorola television set.

Joseph had no sooner walked through the door and joined Leah in the living room when he blurted out, "It was a nice night but did you take a look at Mama's legs? They're swollen like tree trunks. That damn bakery's taking its toll. She needs to stop working."

"I don't know. Except for the girls, that's her whole life."

"Leah, honey, suppose we bought a bigger house? Then she could live with us." In reality, he constantly worried about Mama and Leah. Trying to simplify his life, he figured it would be easier if they both lived under one roof and the bonus would be that Mama could stop working so hard.

Since forming his own practice, Joseph had been treating all clergy, including the nuns, *pro bono*. There was no logical reason for doing so except his lingering guilt over dumping Maureen, his first love. In his head he could still visualize that ugly scene when Maureen accused him of being insular and bigoted.

And the truth still stung.

A wealthy widow bequeathed her stately home in Shaker Heights to the Archdiocese for the nuns. One of the priests who came to Joseph for treatment mentioned it was for sale. He said the nuns did not want to live there. It was too far away from the church. Joseph jumped at the opportunity. For a fair price he bought the home, some of the furnishings, and a baby grand piano that stood near the large picture window in the living room.

The three-story suburban house rested on a knoll on a third of an acre. A mansard roof and powder blue shutters added a faux French touch. The first time Leah viewed the step-down living room, with its elegant sculpted fireplace and high-beamed ceiling, she gasped with delight. Then, remembering the elegant dinner parties of her youth, a ripple of melancholy circled her psyche.

After constant badgering, Mama finally consented to quit her job and live with them. Before they moved in, Joseph and Leah took her on a tour of the empty house. Holding tight to her traditions, Mama insisted on bringing a house warming gift: a new broom to sweep away their troubles, sugar for sweetness, and salt, to spice up their life. *"Zol zein mit mazel."* As she wished them luck, Joseph smiled inwardly. He could always count on Mama falling back on her Yiddish when her emotions got the best of her.

They showed Mama her bedroom on the second floor. When she peeked out the front window onto the street lined with manicured patches of lawn and trees, she exclaimed, *"Oy, mamanu!* In a park you're living." Mama could not believe the large closet in her bedroom was just for her clothes. Half in jest, Joseph said, "Mama, now you can get a whole new wardrobe. And just think, the girls will be so close; they'll be sleeping in the next room."

"And your bedroom . . . where will you sleep?"

When Mama saw that their bedroom and private bathroom spread across the entire back, her mouth hung open.

"Wait, Mama. There's another floor," Joseph explained.

"Another floor? Boarders you can take in."

"Upstairs, that's for Anna," Leah interjected. "Two bedrooms and another bathroom."

Eager to please, Mama doted on everyone, savoring her role as matriarch. Anna, too, counted her blessings. With Mama helping in the kitchen, Anna no longer carried the entire household burden. Suddenly she was treated like a member of the family.

It was an uphill battle, but Leah gradually regained her equilibrium. Mama, Anna, and Leah frequently sat in the kitchen. They chatted about anything that came to mind—the girls, the household, current events. Timidly Leah and Anna would ask Mama about expressions they didn't understand. "Mama, what does it mean: *It's raining cats and dogs?"*

Mama would shake her head in wonder. "I'm telling you, English makes no sense." More often than not, she didn't understand the language any better than Anna or Leah. Stumbling over words and sayings, they chuckled at their own ignorance.

Mama, whose stubborn streak mellowed with age, tried to teach her daughter-in-law how to prepare Joseph's favorite dishes, not by recipes, but by feel and taste. "Just add a smidgeon of this," she would say. "Taste it. Then throw in a *bissel* of that."

"When I grew up in Hungary," Leah confessed one morning, "we had a cook. An honest-to-goodness cook."

"A cook. *Bubeleh*, you had a cook? I was so young when I married Papa. God rest his soul. When he died, Izzy, one of our neighbors got me a job in the bakery. Truthfully, I don't know how I did it. America was to me such a stranger."

CHAPTER 12

THE SURVIVORS

PRIL 12, 1945. President Roosevelt died suddenly from a cerebral hemorrhage and plain-talking Harry Truman, his vice-president, assumed the duties of president. Less than a month later, on May 9th, the Allies declared victory in Europe. And just four months after that, America dropped atomic bombs on Hiroshima and Nagasaki, and the Japanese announced their unconditional surrender. It all happened quickly.

After four years of horrific combat, war-weary Americans rejoiced as shell-shocked soldiers sailed home. The civilized world re-emerged from the surreal nightmare of World War II. Throughout the war, news of atrocities leaked out of both the European and Pacific theaters, but none were more shocking than those committed by the Nazis. Despite it all, Americans made an all-out effort to put the insanity of war behind them.

Joseph and Leah wrote out the names of their loved ones back in Hungary. Relief and refugee agencies—Jewish and non-Jewish—were trying frantically to match-up dislocated families. Joseph hounded the Hebrew Immigration Aid Society, the Red Cross and every other agency he could think of seeking information. Joseph learned that out of all the people he had visited in the village outside of Miskolc, not one had survived. A caustic grief corroded every corpuscle in his body. Members of the Schulman household could not shake their anguish. Their only reprieve stemmed from the childlike innocence of Ellen and Pauline—too young to understand the tragedy.

Four months after that devastating news, a man from the American Jewish Joint Distribution Committee called Joseph at work. In a carefully worded conversation he explained that Leah's sister and cousin had been located in a displaced persons camp in Austria. "They're not in good shape," he said, "but they're not in bad shape either. We're trying to connect them with family."

By the time Joseph hung up the phone, a mixture of emotions shot through him. Joy. Sadness. Relief. Surprise. The sweetness of the news and the horrors of it all surrounded him. He literally shook with happiness and wept from relief.

Leah answered the phone in her usual bland, lifeless voice. "Joseph, you've already called once today. No, Joseph, I'm not sitting down. What's wrong? What? Say it again. Oh, God. MY GOD!" With an aura of disbelief, Joseph repeated the news a second time. Then Leah fell to her knees like a spineless Raggedy Ann doll and sobbed.

Anna laid down the black, cast iron pot she was drying and dashed over. "Leah, what's wrong? What happened?"

"Rose. My sister's alive! Rose is alive! Alive! And my cousin, Esther. They made it! God in heaven, they made it!" At long last, the family received *good* news.

Nothing less than a celebration was in order. Joseph couldn't wait to get home and share this momentous, unbelievable revelation with his wife. After composing himself, he found his office manager in the supply room, summarized the situation and rushed out the door.

Joseph, Leah, Mama, even Anna, sat in the living room repeating the good news over and over, as if it might dissipate like smoke on a windy day.

Trying to catch her breath through tears of joy, Leah managed to say, "They have no place to go. We've got to bring them here."

"Of course," Joseph said, trying to reassure his wife. "We'll take care of them."

Mama added, "They can share my room. It's bigger. I'll take the small room, next to Anna."

"That's the third floor, Mama. It's too much for you."

"Don't worry. It's nothing. Just one more flight of stairs."

For the moment, they let it drop. Leah's mind was reeling with plans. "Joseph, we need more beds. More blankets . . ."

"Leah, stop already. We'll get whatever we need. We'll get it done."

Leah's sister, Rose, and her cousin, Esther, were considered *Displaced Persons.* With all the bureaucratic red tape, it took over three months to secure passage for them on a ship sailing to America. The Schulman's left the girls home with Mama and boarded a train bound for New York. For a time Leah rode in silence. Finally she turned to Joseph and said, "It's been years since I last saw them. I'm haunted by the newspapers photos of the survivors. They all look like skeletons. Maybe I won't even recognize them."

"Trust me, you'll know them," Joseph said, patting her arm. "They're your flesh and blood. But I've given a lot of thought to their situation. When you first see them, don't ask anything about their past. Remain in the present. Remember, they've been through hell. Try putting yourself in their shoes. It's going to be rough for them, especially in a foreign country. They'll be confused. Scared. Distrustful. And, Leah, no matter what happens, stay calm."

Joseph bowed his head and closed his eyes. Privately he mourned for his aunts and uncles and cousins in Hungary. So full of life. So happy to meet him. When he thought about how they died, it felt as though someone gutted his soul with a rusty fishing knife. *Is it the nature of mankind to hate Jews? What kind of God can create such hatred? What kind of world can stand by and let it happen?*

Choppy whitecaps sloshed against the wooden pilings at the New York Harbor as screeching gulls swooped down from the gray sky. If one listened carefully enough, a cacophony of foreign languages could be heard. With rapt attention Leah stared at each disembarking passenger. At one point she doubted herself. She was afraid she had missed her sister and cousin.

Then it happened. "There. Over there!" Leah spotted them in the sea of humanity slowly inching their way down the ramp.

Though they looked older and much more brittle, she recognized her sister Rose and her cousin Esther. As they neared the pier, Leah pushed her way through swarms of people. She threw her welcoming arms around them, feeling their thin, fragile frames against her body.

Filled with unimaginable joy, Leah managed to exclaim, "You're home. You're safe." The emotional intensity of the three women precluded words. Afraid to let go, they simply formed a closed circle and swayed back and forth, holding each other tightly, their tears turning into sobs.

Goose bumps covered Joseph's arms as he stood back and watched. Through the observant eyes of a dermatologist, he quickly assessed their physical condition. Rose and Esther's sunken eyes and sallow faces no longer held the innocent promise of youth. He noticed their rotting teeth and made a mental note to get them to a dentist. From malnutrition, their yellowed nails turned inwards. Leah's sister Rose had a long, diagonal scar across her left cheek and Esther had what looked like a nervous tic in her right eye.

Joseph felt like an intruder until Leah pulled him into their intimate circle. "Darling, of course you remember my sister Rose. But you probably don't remember Esther."

After the brief introduction, Leah returned her focus back on the two women who were shaking with happiness. Their nightmare was over. "I'm so happy, I think I'm delirious," Leah said, her voice cracking. "I can hardly believe my eyes. You're here with us. You're here. If you gave me a million dollars, I couldn't be happier. This is my dream come true."

Since they all needed a quieter place, Joseph took charge. "Everyone, hold hands," he said softly, knowing how frightened they would be to get lost in the milieu. He led them away from the milling crowds and commandeered the first of a long line of black jitneys waiting curbside. Rose and Esther grew leery when the driver put their cloth sacks—literally everything they owned—in the trunk of his car.

"It's all right. Everything will be okay," Joseph said trying to reassure the ladies as he settled them in the back seat. Then he jumped in front and instructed the driver, "Essex House, Central Park South. This is a celebration like never before."

For a minute or two no one spoke. Then, almost like a compulsion—a need to purge herself—Rose volunteered a disjointed summation of what happened. "After we were rounded up, we were crowded into cattle cars," she explained, her face contorting in anguish. "When the train got to Auschwitz, the SS and their dogs herded us into two lines. Women and children in one. Men in another. Everyone was crying. We were very lucky," she said, referring to herself and Esther. "The SS took us from the line . . ." and suddenly her hand covered her mouth and her voice faded, unable to articulate their experiences. The twitch in Esther's eye grew more intense.

There was a long pause before Rose continued. "By the time the British liberated us, Esther was near death. The Red Cross wanted to take her to some hospital. But we refused to be separated. We stuck together and I took care of her."

As Rose continued, Leah thought her heart would break. Joseph marveled at their indomitable spirit and resilience. *Where did they find the strength?*

In fact, the displaced person camp was more humane than the concentration camps, but still only provide the barest essentials—a roof over their heads, army cots, woolen blankets, and food—those precious commodity they were denied for so long. While military doctors and nurses tended to their immediate needs, agencies worked behind the scenes to reunite the survivors with family or friends.

Rose and Esther clasped hands as they entered the Essex Hotel lobby. Always suspecting a trap, their cautious eyes scanned the lobby, studying each person. Feeling like outcasts, they gawked at the men in suits and ties and the sophisticated women in dresses, matching hats, and high heels. They had all but forgotten what civilized society was like.

In awe, Esther cried, "Everything's so clean, so beautiful."

Joseph had reserved a large two bedroom, two bathroom suite for the one night. Rose and Esther took turns taking hot bubble baths, something they had dreamt about for years. The next morning, after sleeping in luxurious bedding, the four of them boarded a train bound for Ohio. The cousins, exhausted from their travels and nervous about the unknown, rode in abject silence, barely containing the horrid memories that still echoed in their heads of the cattle cars filled with screaming human beings. Joseph and Leah had no way to gauge the depth of their fears, but knew enough to keep quiet and not pry.

Back in Cleveland, Joseph held the front door open, bowed, and gestured sweetly with his one hand. "Welcome to our home."

In the days that followed—with the whole family doting on Rose and Esther—the gradual process of healing began. Two months before their arrival, Leah had taken driving lessons. As soon as she passed her driver's test, Joseph surprised her with a gray and white Buick Roadmaster. Leah could hardly wait to drive Rose and Esther around, to familiarize them with Cleveland. But the refugees felt more secure at home. Leah—who loved to shop—constantly brought home new clothes for them to wear. When they were ready, she chauffeured them to doctor and dentist appointments.

The neighbors, touched by their plight, treated the survivors like returning war heroes, which in a crazy way they were. They constantly brought over flowers from their garden, knowing how much the colorful bouquets delighted the two women.

In her element, Mama constantly repeated, "Eat this. It *vel* put meat on your bones."

When Pauline was ready for kindergarten, Leah enrolled her two girls in Laurel School for Girls, an elite private school. In the afternoon, while both girls were in school, Leah taught Rose and Esther how to play double solitaire and gin rummy. While Mama took her afternoon naps, the women wiled away hours drinking tea, playing cards and listening to the radio or phonograph. In a light-hearted way, they bickered over who had a better voice—Frank Sinatra, Nat "King" Cole, or Al Jolson, that "nice Jewish boy."

CHAPTER 13

INDEPENDENCE

I T TOOK ALMOST two years for the extended family to settle into a comfortable routine. And by then, Leah felt pangs of guilt. She had neglected her daughters and knew she had to give them more attention. Ellie had become self-centered and demanding while Pauline, the youngest, had virtually faded into the woodwork.

Leah decided to throw a birthday party for Pauline. She invited eight little girls from her class at the private school. During supper on the eve of the party, Ellie began to whine. "I don't want to go to Pauline's party? It's for babies."

Joseph frowned. "Of course you'll go. You're her sister, aren't you?"

Ellie rolled her eyes and mumbled something under her breath.

Because he was surrounded by a gaggle of women who wanted nothing more than a peaceful supper, Joseph chose to ignore his daughter's churlish behavior.

The next afternoon parents dropped Pauline's classmates off at the house. The little girls, who looked like spun sugar, wore ribbons in their hair, frilly party frocks, and black patent leather Mary Janes. As they took turns playing Pin the Tail on the Donkey, they giggled. Joseph, the proud papa, trailed behind them snapping photographs. When they played musical chairs, Anna positioned herself alongside the phonograph, stopping and starting Leah's favorite music, *Hungarian Rhapsody*.

The entire clan joined in the celebration except Ellie, who turned up her nose. "This is stupid."

Joseph, who had been repressing his annoyance, grabbed Ellie's arm. "Young lady, behave yourself. Stop making a scene." When Ellie started to talk back, Joseph cut her off. "Keep your opinions to yourself. It often shows a fine command of language to say nothing."

That night when Joseph and Leah were lying in bed, he gently stroked his wife's hair. "The party was terrific. I never saw Pauline happier."

"I hope so," Leah responded. "I worry about her. Sometimes I think she gets lost in the shuffle. There are so many people floating around here. You know, Pauline's not like Ellie. She's a lot quieter."

"Pauline's a sweetheart. I'm so proud of her. Ellie, too." Reflecting on it a little longer, he reached for his wife's arm and whispered, "I can't imagine life without all of you.

"Joseph, this might not be the right time to say it, but do you think we take Mama for granted? All the time she's hovering over us. And, well, climbing two flights of stairs twice a day to sleep in the maid's room. Maybe it's too much."

"Remember when we took Rose and Esther in?" Joseph said. "Mama gave them her room. She volunteered to sleep upstairs. Actually those stairs are good for her. Good exercise."

Leah continued to push the point. "I know Rose and Esther need us. But do you suppose things would be a little calmer around here if we found them a small apartment of their own?"

"Maybe. But are they ready to be on their own?" he asked.

"Slowly but surely they're finding their way. Their English is improving. Besides, we'll be close-by. I could check on them every day." Leah took a deep breath before asking, "But what about the money? Can we afford it?"

"Knock on wood. The skin care products are selling like hot cakes. And my new associates are doing terrific. Truthfully, I don't know where our patients are coming from . . . but I think I've got one of the biggest dermatology clinics in Cleveland. Go ahead. Look for a place. But don't you think we should ask them first? Maybe they're not ready."

When Leah broached the subject, Rose and Esther broke into high beam smiles. Esther spoke first. "Living on our own is more than we ever hoped for."

The women scoured the adjoining neighborhoods seeking a cheap apartment for rent. Since the returning G.I.'s flooded the housing market, finding any apartment involved a stroke of luck, being at the right place at the right time. Eventually they tracked down a one-bedroom place facing an airshaft in a tired three-story building on a commercial street. The distance from Leah's to the apartment was too far to walk, so she drove over as often as she could, mostly in the afternoon while the girls were in school.

With Rose and Esther tucked away in their own apartment, the Schulman's household finally settled down. In an effort to imitate her own upbringing, Leah planned to give the girls piano lessons.

Ellie, with a growing sense of independence, challenged her mother. "You forced me to take ballet," she said, folding her arms across her chest. "Now piano lessons. No way. Mom, I'm not doing it."

Following her sister's lead, Pauline chimed in. "If Ellie doesn't take them, I don't have to."

Leah grew weary of her daughters' obstinate behavior and decided she would take the piano lessons herself. She found solace reconnecting to the classical music of her youth. And, eventually, she learned to play the music of the day: Gershwin, Berlin, and Cole Porter.

One afternoon, after her standing appointment at the beauty parlor, Leah visited Rose and Esther. They gathered around the wobbly, second-hand maple table sipping tea sweetened with sugar cubes and nibbling on coconut macaroons that Mama had baked that morning.

Rose startled Leah with her comment. "Do you remember old lady Farber? She's stooped over. You met her in the lobby a few weeks ago. She was just coming in. Walks with a cane."

Leah rubbed the back of her neck and nodded, not sure about it.

Rose continued. "Well, yesterday I saw her. Guess what? She asked if I wanted to work for her."

Leah sensed her sister's excitement.

"What do you think? You know, keeping busy helps me forget. Besides, how long can I sit and listen to the radio or play solitaire?"

Leah wrestled with a string of unasked questions. "I'm just a little surprised. But you're right. It's good to keep busy. But what about you?" she said, addressing Esther. "Will you be okay by yourself?"

"I'm fine." As an appendage, she added with a shy smile, "For a change, I could use some time alone."

Leah wanted to protect them both, but thought stepping out into the world was exactly what Rose needed.

"Mrs. Farber only needs me a few days a week. I think she's just lonely. Her son Herbie got married a few months ago and moved to St. Louis. He used to help her with the groceries. And I think the other son lives in Chicago. Works for a haberdasher."

In her job as Gal Friday, Rose sometimes ran to the pharmacy to pick up prescriptions or shopped for Mrs. Farber. And when the sun was out, she would simply accompany her on the long walk to the park where they would sit on one of the benches with the other old folks. This part-time job represented the first money Rose ever earned and it was her first step up the ladder towards independence.

CHAPTER 14

CHANGE OF LIFE

FOR THREE MORE YEARS the rhythm of the house ran smoothly. But things changed one quiet morning in late March. Mama was peeling onions for chopped liver when the paring knife suddenly tumbled from her hand. With a sickening thud she collapsed onto the hard linoleum floor.

Leah heard the noise and immediately ran to her. "Wake up, Mama, wake up!" she screamed, trying to lift her mother-in law's head. But Mama did not stir. Leah's hands trembled as she picked up the telephone. In an incoherent voice she managed to tell the operator, "It's an emergency. An ambulance. Bring an ambulance. Hurry!"

Five minutes later Leah heard the high-pitched wail of the siren approaching the house. In a state of hysterics she led the two attendants—along with their gurney and emergency paraphernalia—into the kitchen where Mama lay motionless on the floor.

One of the attendants kept checking for a pulse. Finally he stood up and touched Leah's arm. Shaking his head, he said, "Ma'am, I'm terribly sorry for your loss. I'm afraid she's expired."

Expired? What kind of word is expired? This is not a magazine subscription. This is Mama. Leah had never before seen a dead person.

In an almost apologetic voice the other attendant remarked, "Excuse me, Ma'am, may I use your phone? I need to call the coroner's office before we can remove her body."

"Her body? Her body? No-o-o. It was only an hour ago that she was cooking."

Upon hearing the news, Joseph rushed home from the office. A tug-of-war regarding an autopsy broke out. "No one's to touch her body," he protested vehemently. "According to our religion, she needs to be buried within 24 hours."

The funeral was arranged hastily. Mama was buried in the small Jewish cemetery in a plain pine coffin that was made with wooden pegs instead of nails. When it came to the final ritual—shoveling dirt over the casket—Joseph broke down and wept.

Following Mama's funeral, some friends from the bakery and old-time neighbors joined the mourners at the Schulman's house. The women sat in the living room, commiserating and reminiscing about Mama's inherent goodness. Joseph stood in the dining room next to the buffet, half-listening to the men's small talk. His mind kept returning to the same thought. *One minute you're alive, the next minute you could be dead. And, from one day to the next, you never know.* Beset with sadness, he loosened his tie, grabbed the bottle of J & B and poured himself another stiff drink.

Three weeks after Mama's funeral, Joseph's gloomy mood had not improved. In spite of himself, his neatly compartmentalized thoughts kept returning to death and dying. Just before going to bed Joseph and Leah sat in the breakfast room enjoying their last cigarette of the day. Smoke danced in the air as they took turns recalling their unfocused day.

Joseph complained, "I don't know what's going on, but my stomach's been upset. I've been fighting something for days."

"Honey, think about it. You've been under a lot of stress."

Seeming to come out of nowhere, Joseph made a pronouncement. "You know, I've been thinking, for once in our lives let's do
something crazy. You know, take a break. Do something different."

Coming from her hard-driving, structured husband, Leah could
hardly believe her ears.

Shortly thereafter, Joseph received an invitation to speak at
a dermatology symposium in Paris in mid-July. He had lectured
about his research at other conferences in his area, and as far away
as New York, but never on the continent. Without telling Leah,
he secured first-class passage for the entire family on the SS *United
States*. A colleague had put him in touch with a local real estate broker who put him in touch with an international broker. He signed
a two month lease on a villa along the Côte d'Azur.

When he confessed to Leah what he had done, she recoiled.
"Part of me wants to go. See Europe. At least what's left. But then,
when I think about it, I get upset. It will never be the same. I'm
still haunted by ghosts, by Hitler, you know, by memories of the
war."

"Leah, darling, the war's over. We've got to force ourselves to
move on."

In Paris the Schulman family registered at the swank George V
Hotel. At the dermatology symposium, Joseph planned to lecture
on the etiological factors of Tinea Pedis. When he tried to explain
it to the family, Ellie, his precocious older daughter, responded,
"Dad, why does everything have to have a big, long name? Why
don't you just call it what it is? Ringworms."

Aside from the conference, they took in the main tourist sites.
At the first opportunity, they rode on a tour bus, taking in the Arc
de Triomphe, the Eiffel Tower, Notre Dame, and the stained glass
windows in Sainte-Chapelle.

Ellie was not impressed. "How come we have to go to all these
churches?" she complained. "We're Jewish, aren't we?"

The next day as they gawked at the shop windows along the
Rue du Rivoli, their temperamental daughter insisted on calling it

the rue du Ravioli, making her sister giggle and her parents hold their breath. Ellie had taken to wearing oversize sunglasses and experimenting with a new persona. Her moods were mercurial. Sometimes she played the role of a sweet little girl but more and more she questioned and ridiculed everything.

Chapter 15

The High Life

A NOVELTY OF THE era, the Schulman's extended European vacation landed in the society section of *The Plain Dealer*, Cleveland's main newspaper. Secretly, Joseph and Leah enjoyed the notoriety. By all accounts, their stay abroad was successful and they planned to duplicate it again the following year.

When the Schulman's were away, Anna and her beau became engaged. Leah offered to host the wedding in their home. Tender memories of her own parents filtered through her head. She tried to explain herself to Joseph. "Anna deserves some happiness. Poor dear. More or less raised herself. And she's been such a big help. How will I ever manage without her?"

Joseph, always pragmatic, tried to reassure his wife. "So we'll find someone else. Remind me and I'll run an ad in the newspaper."

They interviewed and hired not one, but two people, a husband and wife. Immigrants from Ireland, they spoke with a thick brogue. They would only hire out as a team, a maid and butler or as he liked to say, "A jack-of-all-trades." With servants' quarters on the third floor of their large home, the Schulman's thought the arrangement would work.

One afternoon in the middle of March, Leah drove the short distance to Rose and Esther's apartment. As usual, they were seated at the wooden table *schmoozing* when Rose asked, "How's Anna's wedding coming along?"

"Good. I'm making lists. I swear my lists have lists. I'm working with a caterer. It's going to be a small affair, but lovely. Our living room should hold everyone."

Though reticent, Rose smiled coyly. "I have something to ask you. Have you got room for one more? Would it be okay if I brought Max?"

"There's always room for one more. But tell me, who's Max?"

"I met him when I started picking up Mrs. Farber's prescriptions. He's the druggist."

Even though her sister's revelation tickled Leah, she replied with mock sarcasm. "Oh . . . do you want to tell me about him?"

Rose blushed. "We're just friends. Max and I have just gotten to know each other. He's a nice man. You know, he's taken me to dinner a few times."

"I'm dying to meet him. Of course, invite him to the wedding."

In preparation for the mid-afternoon wedding, Leah took Anna shopping for a special dress. A fashion maven, she picked out new clothes for everyone, right down to a new pair of gold cufflinks for Joseph. She splurged on an expensive beige suit for herself. One week before the wedding she had her hair dyed platinum blond at a fashionable beauty shop.

Just before the guests arrived, a florist delivered a splashy floral arrangement of white chrysanthemums, ferns, and baby's breath and placed them in a wrought iron stand in front of the *chuppah*. Leah had borrowed the wedding canopy from the *schul*, the small Jewish congregation that met in a storefront. Everything was going smoothly until Pauline misplaced her new shoes. At the last minute

Ellie found them under her bed. No one could explain how they got there.

The only two bridesmaids, Pauline and Ellie marched into the living room ahead of the bride. Ellie seethed inwardly. She felt foolish in the high-waist pink organdy dress her mother had picked out. *It is so babyish,* she thought.

Joseph accompanied Anna as Leah played Mendelssohn's *Wedding March* on the piano. The frightened bridegroom and the aging rabbi—who had also married Leah and Joseph and buried Mama—stood in anticipation. When the last guests had said their good-byes, Leah and Joseph returned to the living room exhausted but happy. Leah sank into the overstuffed davenport and stretched her arms over her head to relax. Then she grabbed the Ronson lighter and a Gauloises blue cigarette from the silver box on the coffee table and lit up.

Joseph flipped his suit jacket over the back of one of the folding chairs. Still standing, he looked at his wife with renewed admiration. "Sweetheart, you did a great job. The wedding came off like clockwork. And you are looking pretty darn snazzy. I'm eyeing that half-empty bottle of Dom Perignon. How about we finish it off?"

"Just a little," Leah sighed, pushing her dyed to match beige heels under the coffee table. "Well . . . it's been quite a day. What'd you think of Max . . . Rose's date?"

"I took an instant liking to him," Joseph said. "I think he's a real *mensch.*"

Relieved that it was over, Leah and Joseph toasted the bride and groom and each other with flutes of champagne. *"L'Chaim.* To life."

They had no idea that Ellie had snitched another partially opened bottle. She and Pauline—who willingly followed her older sister—imitated their parents and had their own private party tucked away in their upstairs bedroom.

Leah's sister, Rose, and Max fell into a pattern of seeing each other. And before anyone realized it, Max had become an *ex-officio* member of the family. Six months later the clan gathered at the

Schulman's to celebrate Joseph's birthday. At the dining room table one conversation led to another, and before they knew it, they started to reminisce about Anna's wedding. Joseph turned towards Rose and Max. "You know, we'd be happy to throw another wedding."

From the far end of the table Leah raised her voice in exasperation. "For God sakes, Joseph, mind your business!"

With a sheepish grin Max confessed, "Well, to tell you the truth, Rose and I have been talking about getting married."

Rose's face reddened, but she said nothing.

Joseph ambled over to shake Max's hand and hug the future bride as if it was a *fait accompli*.

On a humid mid-summer day, the Schulman's hosted another gala event, the wedding of Rose and Max. Max made a decent living as a druggist and the newlyweds moved to a cozy apartment not far away.

CHAPTER 16

PARIS

NOW WITH A MAID and a butler and a steady stream of money, the Schulman's lived in high-style. Subconsciously, Leah imitated her parents' lifestyle in Budapest. Their sophisticated parties and European sojourns provided frequent fodder for *The Plain Dealer*, the local newspaper. The society editor began referring to them as the *noted or distinguished doctor and his lovely foreign-born wife* or *the Schulman's, prominent socialites in the community.*

Joseph and Leah acquired a cadre of new friends, especially wealthy Parisians who spent their holidays playing on the Riviera. The Schulman's emerged as enthusiastic Francophiles, favoring everything French: wine, cuisine, and fashions. Leah sweet-talked Joseph into renting an apartment in Paris after their lease on the French Riviera expired the following summer. She thought the experience would broaden her daughters' horizons. While the girls attended classes, Leah figured she could shop and socialize.

One evening during supper Leah announced her plan to the girls. "Guess what? This summer, when Daddy goes back to the office, just us girls are going to Paris. You can go to the American School. Won't that be fun?"

Ellie, who had grown outright rebellious, groused. "Not a chance. I just want to stay home."

Joseph lost his patience. "Ellie, get off your high horse. You sound like a spoiled brat. How many girls get to spend time in Paris with their mom?"

"Dad, I've already seen Paris. What's wrong with just spending my senior year here? I want to graduate with my friends."

Eventually Ellie's obstinate and belligerent behavior wore her mother and father down. "Ellie," Leah negotiated a month later, "let's not fight. Be reasonable, okay? Suppose we don't go to Paris this September. You can spend your whole senior year with your friends. Then the summer after you graduate, just us girls will go to Paris. How does that sound?"

The following year Joseph leased an architecturally designed villa in Monte Carlo that cantilevered off the hillside. Purple and white wisteria hung from the trellis on the terrace and colorful bougainvillea tumbled down towards the sea. This prime piece of property enjoyed an expansive view of the shimmering Mediterranean and the sailboats and yachts docked in the harbor.

Although never the leading lady, Ellie had performed in several high school plays. When she discovered the Monte-Carlo house belonged to a popular American actor who happened to be shooting a film in Mexico, her imagination grew exponentially. Suddenly she fancied herself a world-class actress.

When not insufferable, Ellie basked in the sun on the public beach where she flirted with all the boys. But she found Jean-Paul the most intriguing. The tanned young man had straight blond hair that he constantly swiped from his brow. One afternoon, after a half-hour of body surfing, Jean-Paul treated Ellie to a Coke. The son of a French diplomat, he possessed an easy-going nature. He had a decent command of English, as long as Ellie did not throw too much American slang at him. Because his family had been transferred from country to country, he knew a great deal more than she did about Europe. They spoke of many things, including their desires for the future. Ellie, so full of herself, shared her dream of becoming a movie star.

Not averse to showing off his knowledge, Jean-Paul added, "Did you know there's a special academy in London that trains actors and actresses?"

The new information gave Ellie fodder for her aspiration. She took up her new cause with a vengeance. For the remainder of the summer, as unrealistic as it sounded, she nagged, begged, and cajoled her parents to let her go to London to study acting. Her desire became all-consuming.

Leah and Joseph sat quietly at a candle-lit table in an intimate restaurant. It felt good to be away from the girls. In a hushed voice filled with worry, Leah remarked, "Joseph, this constant fighting with Ellie has got to stop. Why don't we just let her go to London? Maybe she'll straighten out if she has to do something on her own. Let her get it out of her system once and for all."

"Are you kidding? She needs to study acting like I need a *loch in kop*, a hole in my head. What she needs is a job. Some responsibilities, instead of all this mollycoddling."

After several more weeks of Ellie's constant badgering and caustic remarks, Joseph couldn't stand it anymore. "Now you listen to me, young lady, you're out-of-control. Do you ever think of anybody else? Whatever happened to *my* peace and quiet?"

Leah found herself in the middle of a tug-of-war, a power struggle of epic proportions. That night when she and Joseph were alone in their bedroom, she tried to explain Ellie's teenage angst. "Ellie's just going through a stage. You know teenagers are like that."

Still aggravated, Joseph's uncharacteristic temper flared up. "Show me one. I can't stand her attitude. She's driving me nuts. If you want to stay, stay. But frankly, I've had it. I'd rather be home . . . working." Joseph made good on his threat. He phoned

Pan Am and booked a flight the following week from Paris to New York.

As frustrated as Leah was with the constant feuding, she and the girls remained in the south of France until their lease expired. In the end, Ellie won. Her mother made arrangements to enroll her at the high-sounding Preparatory School for the Academy of Performing Arts in London. Leah believed it would force her daughter to grow up and, if nothing else, it would give the family a temporary reprieve from the constant bickering. Besides, she figured she and the girls could squeeze in some time in Paris before dropping Ellie off in London.

On their first full day in Paris Leah and the girls slept-in. After they finished a leisurely lunch at a nearby bistro, they traipsed over to the American Embassy. In addition to the changes in their itinerary, Leah needed clarification to head off any problems with Ellie's extended stay in London. As they passed through the wrought iron pedestrian gate into the embassy courtyard, they were stopped by a tall Marine in dress blues.

When Leah asked him for directions, he pointed, "Ma'am, up those stairs and through those large glass doors. Can't miss the receptionist. You'll see her desk; it's off on your left."

A slender American woman with hair the color of sunshine sat behind a curved Louis XIV gilded desk. As Leah tried to explain their change of plans, the receptionist listened with rapt attention. "Perhaps I can direct you. You'll need to see Mr. Appel. He's down that hallway, first open door on your right."

Not interested in her mother's questions or the details of travel, Ellie had her own agenda. "Mom, I'll be in the courtyard." For the short time it took Leah to clarify her travel plans, Ellie struck up a conversation with the straight-backed Marine. Flattered with her blatant flirting, he introduced himself. "I'm Barry Sanderson," he said with a winsome smile that showed a slight separation in his two front teeth. "What brings you here?"

"My mother. After Paris we're headed to London. I'm enrolling at the Royal Academy of Dramatic Arts," Ellie bragged, deliberately omitting that it was only the *Preparatory* Academy . . . not the Royal Academy itself. "Where you from?"

Enjoying this sudden attention, the clean-cut Marine asked her out for the following night. Unfortunately the next day Ellie came down with a miserable sore throat and needed to cancel the date. She wasn't sure how to reach Barry other than calling the embassy. Ellie left a short message with some assistant, hoping it would somehow reach her newly acquired Marine friend. While her mother and Pauline flitted through boutiques and art galleries, Ellie sipped hot tea and slept.

They reconnected later that afternoon. Before her mother could sit down and take off her shoes, Ellie pounced on her. "There's nothing to eat. What's for dinner? I'm hungry."

Weary from walking and the heat, Pauline plopped down on the other end of the yellow damask settee. "Me, too. My stomach's growling."

"There's not much here," Leah conceded. "I thought we'd go out and grab a bite. Ellie, honey, you'll feel better with some hot onion soup."

Still in her pajamas, Ellie begged her mother to bring it back.

"How can I bring soup back?" Leah walked over and touched her daughter's forehead with the palm of her hand. "I don't think you're running a fever. Why don't you get dressed? It'll be good for you. You've already slept away half the day."

"If I change," Ellie negotiated, "can we go to Monsieur Jean's? Barry told me they have great hamburgers and fries."

"Who's Barry?"

"Mom," Ellie sighed, positive her mother was disinterested in her life, "remember that cute Marine that I met at the embassy? The one that asked me out."

Large chestnut trees attempted to shade the sidewalk on the Champ-Élysées, but the relentless summer heat sizzled upwards from the wide boulevard. Ellie pouted all the way to Monsieur Jean's. As soon as they arrived, her face grew beet red, not from fever, but embarrassment. There sat Barry, drinking beer with three other marines at a round table near the entry.

Their eyes locked.

"Hey, Ellie," he said with *savoir faire*, neglecting the fact that he had been stood up. Flattered that he even remembered her name, she stopped sulking. "Remember yesterday I told you this place caters to Americans. Well, downstairs they serve the best burgers and fries you'll ever taste."

Barry and his buddies led the three women down the steep, narrow steps. "Be careful you don't slip," he cautioned, "especially in those high heels." As they approached the bottom stair, they could hear Frank Sinatra belting out *In the Wee Small Hours of the Morning* on the jukebox. Barry pushed two square tables together and rearranged the bentwood chairs. "We're lucky. It's not busy. This place really starts hoppin' later on."

Another Marine, one that the guys knew well, hustled over from another table. He slapped Barry on the shoulder playfully as he greeted his friend. Then he turned and flashed a smile at the ladies as he pushed his way in. "Howdy. My name's Wyatt," he announced with a mischievous twinkle in his eyes.

"Where did ya'll get that cute accent?" Ellie responded, enthralled with the hale and hearty Marine and his friendly, but unfamiliar, drawl.

"Oklahoma. A little town you ain't never heard of. Tahlequah." A fast talker, who loved to play the role of a rough-and-tumble cowboy, Wyatt turned to Ellie and asked, "Say, how about a dance, little lady?" Then he caught himself and slowed down.

"That is . . . if that's okay with Mama here?"

Ellie refused, claiming she had a miserable cold. Unfazed, Wyatt continued to be the center of attention. "I know just the thing to make you feel better." He waved his index finger in the air to grab the waiter's eye. "Bring this pretty little lady a hot whiskey with lemon."

Ellie glanced over at her mother for approval, but her mother didn't say a word. "Eww! This burns like fire!" she howled as she took her first few sips.

"Well, pretty lady," Wyatt said, "how ya feelin' now?"

She crinkled her nose. "Well . . . my throat doesn't hurt anymore."

"Atta girl. Now 'bout that dance?"

While they swayed to the sounds of the Tommy Dorsey orchestra coming from the Wurlitzer, Ellie noticed Wyatt's blue eyes flecked with specks of gold.

Leah felt out of place. Though they were well-mannered and polite, these randy young men were simply not of her generation. When one of the Marines asked her to dance she tried to extricate herself as politely as she knew how.

"I'm sorry to break away from such wonderful company, but Pauline and I have to walk back to the apartment and in a strange city we really need to get home before it gets too late."

Pauline, the voiceless one, soaked in the grown-up world filled with flirting men, drinking and dancing. Ellie, the obvious center of attention, returned to the table clutching Wyatt's hand.

The situation left Leah uncomfortable. She felt the need to remove herself. "Ellie, honey, Pauline and I will see you when you get home."

Proud of her limited French, Ellie added glibly, "*Au revoir*, Mom," and virtually ignored her younger sister. The last thing Leah wanted to do was create an embarrassing scene. So she refrained from giving Ellie a curfew.

After her mother and Pauline left, Wyatt moved in swiftly. "Well, little lady, tell me what you've seen of Paris?"

"The usual tourist sites," Ellie said, trying to sound sophisticated.

"Have you ever been to the Moulin Rouge or the Crazy Horse? Ever been to Les Halles at three in the morning for French onion soup?"

Ellie looked down.

"Well, how 'bout it?"

Loosened by the drink, Ellie felt a rush of excitement. She loved being the center of attention.

Wyatt made a quick call to borrow his soccer buddy's Fiat. He and Ellie, high on life, hopped from one nightclub to another drinking and dancing. They capped it off on a hilltop near the Sacré Coeur watching the lights disappear as the red ribbon of dawn appeared on the horizon. Ellie had never met anyone quite like Wyatt. He was a fun-loving character with such an overwhelming exuberance for life.

Of course there was hell to pay when Ellie finally returned from her night on the town. But Ellie and Wyatt became inseparable. Neither of them was inclined to put on the brakes. In less than three weeks they were engaged to be married.

When Ellie called her father to tell him of her engagement, he had an apoplectic fit. "Ellen, don't you dare do anything hasty!"

"Dad, I love Wyatt."

"Love, what do you know from love? I'm sure he's a nice enough fellow," Joseph conceded, trying to control his anger, "but marriage . . . it's a serious step, baby. It's for the rest of your life. You're impetuous. You're way too young to make this kind of decision."

"Dad, you still see me as a little girl, but I'm not. I've grown up. I know what I want."

"Do you? What happened to being an actress?"

There was a thoughtful pause. "I guess I want Wyatt more than being an actress."

"You don't know what you want. You just met him. Besides, he isn't even Jewish." Suddenly Joseph caught himself. Religion had never played a key role in his life. That remark popped into his head from an ingrained source. *Are Mama's words tattooed in my head?*

Ellie countered. "Who cares? What difference does it make? Since when did you become so religious?"

"That's hardly the point. From what your mother tells me, he's nothing but a goddamn Okie." And in his heart Joseph felt his well-educated, albeit spoiled daughter could do better than marry this stranger from Oklahoma.

Joseph's stomach started to claw like a lobster inside a pot of boiling water. He dug an antacid out of his pocket. Maureen, his first love, came to mind. Joseph knew how much he loved his wife, but to this day he couldn't help wondering if he was unduly influenced by his mother over the Jewish issue.

With Ellie, have I just traded positions—moved up the chain of command? Have I simply taken on my mother's role and Ellie taken on mine? Is that what people call tradition? Duplicating what's been done before. He never understood his mother's animosity against non-Jews or the Christian's animosity towards Jews. The divisiveness of religion always left him feeling sad and vaguely guilty.

With only Leah, her sister, Pauline, and a cadre of his marine buddies as witnesses, Ellie and Wyatt were married by a judge in the 16th Arrondissement. Joseph, disappointed and bitter, refused to travel to Europe for the wedding. Neither the groom nor the wedding was what he had imagined for his eldest daughter.

Four months later Wyatt and Ellie caught a break. He was transferred to a base near Sacramento, California. The young couple fell in love with the informality of the town, the weather and the townspeople. After serving in the military, Wyatt planned to start a used auto parts business.

Leah resigned herself to Ellie's marriage and her subsequent move across the country, but Joseph held a grudge. To a certain extent he was relieved she was now someone else's problem, but he dared not say it aloud. Pauline, who worshipped her sister, brooded over losing Ellie, her confidante, and phoned her as often as she could. Sometimes she would come home after school and dial the number, just to hear her sister's voice.

Chapter 17

Subpoena

AROUND 4 O'CLOCK in the afternoon, Joseph's office manager rapped on the door and slipped into his private office. "Sorry to disturb you but there's a guy in the waiting room. Says he's a U.S. Marshal. Needs to talk with you."

"Do you know what he wants?"

"I haven't the faintest, but he says it's important."

"Okay. Give me a minute, and then send him on in." Joseph had barely cleared his desk of patients' files when the U.S. Marshal entered. His badge looked official but the marshal showed his credentials just in case.

"What can I do for you, sir?"

The marshal wasted no time. He handed Joseph a subpoena. "I'm here to let you know the government wants you to testify regarding a Mr. John Petri. Claims he's a patient of yours."

"I'd really like to help you out," Joseph said, folding his fingers into a tepee, "but I'm not at liberty to discuss my patients."

"Well, Mr. Petri's accused of robbing a bank at gunpoint. Claims he was here at the time of the robbery." The smug U.S. Marshall continued. "What you see here is a subpoena. Now then, if you look at it carefully, it'll tell you the time and date to appear in court. You don't have much of a choice."

In his wildest dreams, Joseph could not imagine the repercussions that summons would have.

On the day Joseph was scheduled to testify, he held fast to his morning schedule. He saw a few patients, returned several phone calls and conferred with another doctor. His lackadaisical nurse and the office manager had been squabbling and he was caught in the middle, trying to pacify them both. Right before noon, he grabbed the necessary records, threw them in his briefcase, and headed for the courthouse, stopping at a nearby diner for a quick lunch.

Preoccupied with the details of his practice, Joseph was pleased when he found the perfect parking spot for his new '55 Cadillac. He had never before been in the U.S. Federal Building. Like all the other potential witnesses, he sat on a backless bench outside the courtroom. He skimmed a medical journal that he had thrown into his briefcase at the last minute. When it was his turn to testify, a burly court deputy, whose tan shirt stretched across his bulging stomach, escorted him into the courtroom.

With his hand on a bible, Joseph swore to tell the truth. The courtroom was much smaller than he imagined. Ensconced in the witness box, his eyes darted around the room, finally coming to rest on the two defendants. Blank stares masked their emotions.

The U.S. Attorney stood and reviewed his notes for what seemed like an inordinate amount of time. Approaching his fifties, the trim attorney retained a boyish look and the cocksure demeanor of his Ivy League background. He began with a few preliminary questions and then dug into the heart of the matter. "Doctor Schulman, it is my understanding that you have had occasion to meet Mr. Petri, one of the two defendants in this case?"

"Yes, sir, I have."

"Would you please tell the court where you met him?"

"In my office. I treated Mr. Petri for a fungal infection."

"And where would that be?"

"On his back." There was a titter from the courtroom observers.

The attorney waited for the courtroom to settle down. "If I might, allow me to rephrase the question. "Could you please tell the court the location of your office?"

Apparently Joseph's testimony was crucial for Petri's alibi. John Petri and Milton Grant were charged with using a sawed-off shotgun and a revolver to rob a bank in Warren, Ohio. They had allegedly taken the bank for $71,000. Petri's lawyer claimed he was not in Warren, Ohio, much less robbing a bank. He claimed that at that exact time he had an appointment with Doctor Schulman.

"Please tell the court the date that Mr. Petri first visited your office?"

Joseph had nothing to hide. "October first."

"And the year? For the record, please state the year?"

"1954."

"Dr. Schulman, I see this medical chart is stamped October 1st for the first visit and October 14th for the follow-up visit. Is that correct?"

"Yes, sir."

After giving a few more details, the U. S. Attorney, stood closer. "I would like to point out that the number 4, part of the October 14th stamp, was quite heavily written over in ink.

"That's correct."

"Could you tell me the date on the stamp—*before* it was written over?"

"The 14th."

"That's strange," the U.S. Attorney said, frowning. "How would you know that for sure?"

"Sometimes the stamp doesn't pick up clearly."

The U.S. Attorney crinkled his forehead. "Oh . . ." he said and paused, forcing Joseph to explain.

"Sometimes I forget to change the date or the ink pad dries out. When that happens, I simply write over it."

"Please tell the court exactly when you wrote over the stamped date on this particular medical chart?"

"At the time of the visit."

Not above courtroom theatrics, the U. S. Attorney leaned forward. "I'm sorry. I didn't hear that. Would you speak up?" After further questioning, it was clear the U.S. Attorney was less than satisfied. "Doctor," he said with growing distain, "do you suppose it would be possible for us to keep this medical chart for further examination? We would like our experts to review it."

"Of course," Joseph said, feeling a bit uneasy.

The unyielding prosecuting attorney gave him fair warning. "Please be aware that we may call you back at a later date."

The lengthy trial continued and the prosecutor did recall Joseph. That's when his troubles rooted like a sapling planted in the springtime. His previous testimony regarding the stamped date was eviscerated by an F.B.I. technician from Washington, D.C. He had examined the medical chart under a microscope and taken photographs of the date using ultra-violet and infra-red rays. In his testimony, he claimed the medical chart was originally stamped "8" underneath the heavily inked "4."

The U.S. Attorney concluded that the date on the chart, October 14th, the date of the robbery was falsified. And the judge concurred: *It appears the examination by the government's expert witness was impartial and scientific.* The implication was that Joseph had falsified his records to provide Petri with a credible alibi.

Yet, despite Joseph's testimony, both men were convicted of bank robbery and received lengthy sentences in a federal penitentiary.

CHAPTER 18

TRIALS

JOSEPH HARDLY GAVE any thought to his corroborating testimony at the Petri-Grant trial. As far as he was concerned, he had slipped up and made a mistake, one that any busy doctor could make. He had inadvertently mixed up the date on the medical chart.

Six months after the original trial Joseph was shocked to find himself charged with *perjury*. He had no criminal record and had never been involved in any illegal procedures. In his mind he found it almost incomprehensible. *What does all this mean? How can this be?* He believed the perjury charge against him were ridiculous and utterly false.

Several days after he received the federal summons and complaint, Leah made an attempt to divert his morose disposition. For her, shopping was a relief. She convinced him to take a ride out to the newly opened shopping center. As Joseph clutched the steering wheel, she sat pondering the recent turn of events. Drawing a blank, she finally asked, "Exactly what does it mean—perjury?"

"They claim I deliberately lied in court. But that's insanity. Can you believe it? I didn't even know those men."

"Oh, Joseph, I know you best. You'd never lie. There's got to be some mistake. Some misunderstanding."

"Frankly I'm at a loss. It's so twisted. I'm beginning to think I need a lawyer."

A colleague at the hospital mentioned R.J. Swanson, a well-known Cleveland trial attorney. Not knowing who else to call, Joseph looked up his number and set up an appointment. Mr. Swanson's office was on the top floor of a prestigious art deco building in the financial district.

Joseph stepped from the elevator directly into a large suite of offices. He spotted a young, blond woman—barely past her teens—at the reception desk. After Joseph explained who he was, she said, "Mr. Swanson is in his office. Please have a seat. Let me buzz him. Tell him you're here."

Once he got settled in the private, mahogany paneled office, the self-assured attorney tilted his padded swivel chair backward and cupped his fingers together. "Just call me R.J., everyone does. Now then, tell me what happened. Start from the very beginning."

Joseph strained his memory in an attempt to explain the sequence of events that led up to the charge of perjury.

After listening carefully and making a few notes on his yellow legal pad, R.J. responded. "That's one heck of a story. I have to be up-front. Here's the scoop. A trial ain't no picnic. For one thing, it's damn expensive . . . and it can play havoc with your psyche. But the way I see it, you don't have much choice. You've got to defend yourself."

Joseph bought into the myth that the American justice system treated everyone equitably. Six months later he went to court thinking he would get a fair shake. He believed his high-priced attorney could explain the whole misunderstand and he would be found innocent.

Joseph paled when he was found guilty of perjury. *I'm innocent. How can this be happening to me?*

His attorney, too, was stunned. "There must be some misunderstanding. Nothing like this has ever happened before. It's outrageous. Not to worry. We'll appeal."

Adding insult to injury, the next day the *Plain Dealer*, Cleveland's main newspaper, splashed a banner across the front page: "Prominent Doctor Found Guilty of Perjury."

For Joseph, time marched slowly until his case was heard by the Appellate Court. Their ruling was confounding:

"Perjury requires more than circumstantial evidence.
It requires a deliberate and willful act of deceit."

Nevertheless they remanded his case back to the lower court for a retrial.

Joseph was no longer a greenhorn. During the second trial, the U.S. Attorney actually had the nerve to bring in Mr. Petri, the man who was originally *on trial* for bank robbery. This time the tables were turned. Mr. Petri had jumped sides. Even though he was now a convicted felon serving hard time in a federal prison, he testified *against* Joseph. He claimed he was *not* in the doctor's office on the day Dr. Schulman claimed, seriously undermining Joseph's original testimony. The trial moved swiftly and the judge found Joseph guilty of perjury a second time.

His life, everything he had worked so hard for, was being torn away, like small clods of dirt under the sharp blade of a bulldozer. And once again his smooth talking attorney told him he had no choice, he needed to appeal the verdict.

By this time Joseph was constant fodder for the front page of Cleveland's daily newspaper. Overzealous reporters followed the proceedings as if they were chasing a Pulitzer Prize. Everything was blown out of proportion. Surreal.

On his second appeal, the Appellate Court ruling basically stated: *Joseph's attorney should have been allowed to question Petri's motives during cross-examination. After all, Petri was a convicted felon facing a long sentence for armed robbery. If allowed by the court, Joseph's attorney might have probed whether Mr. Petri would receive a lesser sentence in exchange for his testimony.*

But as unbelievable as it seemed, Joseph's case was once again remanded back to the lower court.

"What does it all mean?" Joseph asked, incredulously.

"Another trial," his attorney replied.

"A third trial!" Joseph tried to reconcile his predicament. But it all seemed nonsensical. Ludicrous. He was no longer enamored with his attorney. He toyed with the idea of firing him and hiring someone else. But in the end, he convinced himself that at this late date, R.J. Swanson was the only one who knew the history.

Early one morning, Joseph found himself in his attorney's posh office reviewing details for his third trial. Filled with angst, Joseph flew into a tirade. "I don't understand. What the hell's going on?"

His attorney raised his shoulders in a confused shrug. "Frankly, Joseph, I've got no idea. The U.S. Attorney is a pernicious little bastard. Obviously eager to carve a name for himself. And the feds, well, they're drunk on their own power. Troubling though it may be, it's a sign of the times."

Joseph raised his voice. "I don't get it. I've done nothing wrong. I made an honest mistake."

"Look around you," R.J. said. "McCarthy's out-of-control. The senate hearings are a goddamn travesty. Washington has grabbed hold of a couple of buzz words: *contempt of court* and *perjury*. It's like a plague infecting our courts."

"Just tell me, what that's got to do with me?"

"Nothing's fair anymore. The legal system, well, it's a mockery of justice."

"But we already won two appeals," Joseph protested. "They've already convicted Petri. I never even met the guy until he walked into my office. Give me one good reason why I'd lie? Why me? What's going on?"

"Egos, stubbornness . . . who knows." It was a specious argument and R.J. knew it. "Maybe the U.S. Attorney hates Jews . . . or doctors. Or successful people. Don't beat yourself up over his twisted motives. We have no choice but to continue. We've got to take it one trial at a time."

"We? Easy for you to say. But I'm footing the bill, remember? And I'm tapped out. For chrissakes, I just cashed in the last of my war bonds."

His lawyer tried to reason with him but Joseph couldn't stop himself. "Listen, R.J., you're not the one sweating bullets every night. This is not some abstract law school exercise. We're talking about my life. My reputation. My practice is on the skids. You and I both know this whole thing is a sham over some insignificant mistake, not some goddamn lie."

But, on his third go-round the lower court once again found Joseph guilty of perjury.

Years earlier, as an undergraduate in college, Joseph was forced to read Victor Hugo's novel *Les Miserables*. He hated the story then, and he hated it even more now. He compared himself to the protagonist, Jean Valjean—the man who spent his life being chased by the law. During this excruciating time, Joseph learned more than he ever cared to know about the legal system. The motions and hearings, the trials and appeals all blurred together. Enough was enough. He wrestled with himself trying to contain his frustration and anger.

On his third appeal Joseph nearly collapsed as the judge upheld the lower court's conviction of perjury. His attorney, who was standing by his side, grabbed his elbow and tried to steady him. "It's an outrage!" he whispered. "We'll take it to the Supreme Court."

By this time Joseph had little faith in the legal system. He knew there was only an outside chance that the U.S. Supreme Court would hear his case. But when he got official word that they refused, he fell apart.

With the exception of their extended family, the Schulman's were now pariahs. Joseph's life was turned upside-down. He was now consumed by emotions he had never felt before: anger, shame, humiliation, bitterness.

Prison was now a reality. A year in a federal penitentiary.

Sickness, even death, had crossed his mind, but never the possibility of losing his freedom. With shattered nerves he tried to refocus his thoughts on practical matters—cash and how to sustain his family. He worked out a plan, though less than ideal, for his associates to buy out his once thriving practice.

On a gloomy Monday morning, Joseph felt compelled to level with Leah. As soon as Pauline left for school, he poured himself a glass of milk to calm his stomach. Joseph pulled out a kitchen chair and sat across from his wife, who had been scanning the women's section of the newspaper. "Hon, we need to have a serious talk. I hate like hell to bring this up, but we've got to cut back our expenses. And what I'm about to say is going to be hardest on you. The housekeeper and her husband, what's his name, have to go. God, I can't remember his name. I must be losing my mind."

Without realizing the hardships she would face, Leah responded. "Don't worry. Between Pauline and me, we can handle the house. She's a trooper."

"It's more than that," Joseph said, pinching his forehead where his headache was centered. "You need to brace yourself. Life is going to get a lot rougher."

"We'll survive. You'll see. If Rose and Esther could survive the concentration camps, we can survive this," she said, twisting a crumbled tissue she found in the pocket of her housecoat.

"We've all got to stay strong," Joseph cautioned, trying to keep his lips from quivering. "Pauline hasn't complained, but with all these headlines . . . school's got to be brutal. I know how cruel kids can be." *Bad memories bubbled to the surface. Joseph could still hear the kids taunting him when he developed the tremor in his arm.* "If Pauline transfers to a public school, it will save us a heap of dough. And it might actually be good for her. You know, start fresh. Make new friends."

The Schulman's rehashed their options. With great reluctance they sat Pauline down to explain what was happening. "Pet, you're going to need to help Mom out. You're all she's got. When I go to prison . . ." Joseph shuttered, terrified by his own words. "This won't be easy on her."

"Dad, I'll help, I promise," Pauline vowed.

But underneath the bravado, she was frightened too. By the time she transferred to the public high school, Pauline had grown more introverted. The girls ignored her and the boys laughed about her jailbird father. And for good measure, they taunted her about her large breasts. She took to wearing a loose, ill-fitted jacket over her sweaters whether it was called for or not. With her eyes downcast and her arms folded across her chest, she moved from one class to another, not interested in anything but surviving. As a self-conscious teen-ager, she was slowly suffocating from the unwanted notoriety. Even though she knew her parents could no longer afford it, more than anything else, Pauline wanted to be with her private school friends, the ones she had known since kindergarten.

When a teacher asked how things were going at home, she felt like screaming, "It's none of your business!"

To take the edge off, Pauline began to sneak alcohol from the open liquor bottles her parents had on reserve.

CHAPTER 19

TEARFUL GOODBYES

J OSEPH LAID THE BLAME for his unprecedented situation on a gamut of people: the relentless U.S. Attorney who loved to see his name in the paper, inept judges, and his own bumbling attorney who he now referred to as *that shyster lawyer*. He thought R.J. Swanson's elegantly furnished law office and expensive tailored suits were a phony facade, serving only to masquerade his incompetence. "In the end, you'll win," R.J. keep repeating. "Trust me. You've got to believe justice will prevail."

Well, he did, and it didn't work.

Joseph felt duped, a patsy in some drama he didn't understand. Blisters of bitterness erupted like a bad case of the measles. Although his attorney volunteered to accompany him when he turned himself in, Joseph nixed that idea. "I'll surrender on my own," he said defiantly, thinking his attorney would make matters worse. In deference to his position, and knowing full well he was not a hardened criminal or a flight risk, the judge at the federal court allowed him five weeks to tie up loose ends before surrendering himself.

Isn't it ironic, he thought, *my parents left Hungary convinced Jews would get a fair shake in America. Whoever believes ". . . and justice for all" is a goddamn fool.*

On the home front, Leah was his greatest concern. With a propensity for depression, Joseph constantly worried that as the pressures grew in intensity, she would fall apart. Ever since they were married, Joseph handled all the financial and business transactions. Now Leah needed a crash course to gather rudimentary information. Every night after supper he explained how to sort and pay the bills and how to do the banking. On blue-lined index cards he made lists of names, addresses, and phone numbers she might need and set up files in cardboard boxes to keep it all organized.

Wide awake, Joseph would lie next to Leah, comforted by the warmth of her body. But as the sleepless hours wore on, night sweats engulfed him like a ring of fire. *What have I forgotten?* His insomnia left him ill-tempered and impatient. Their once expanded circle of friends had drifted away like pieces of balsa wood in a stormy sea. Joseph knew full well how they gossiped behind his back. Even though their absence hurt, he dismissed them as a bunch of ingrates. He did, however, make a point of saying good-bye to his closest colleagues and a handful of loyal friends.

No one knew what to say. "Hey, consider yourself lucky. I hear the federal prison's a breeze . . . like a country club," a friend kidded. When people tried to make light of his circumstance, Joseph put up a good front and simply returned their inane comments with an insipid smile

The night before Joseph turned himself in, the ringing telephone broke the glum silence that clung to the walls. Leah picked it up. "Hi, honey . . . How's Wyatt? Good. Yeah. Sure, he's standing right here." She covered the mouthpiece of the phone and whispered, "Joseph, it's Ellie. She's calling from California to wish you well." Leah recognized the momentary scowl that crossed his face. "For God's sake Joseph, let bygones-be-bygones. It's time to make amends."

Still ripped apart by his oldest daughter's defiance, Joseph could not let go of his disappointment. Though they got along superficially, he and Ellie, both stubborn and strong-willed, maintained a rocky relationship. Whenever she tried to patch things up, he held back, convinced she had thrown her life away. But, in spite of himself, he was pleased she called.

The dreaded day of reckoning arrived.

Joseph stood in the shower, letting rivulets of hot water drip down his face and body. He knew it would be a long time before he would enjoy this simple luxury again. Defiantly, he dressed as if he were going to the office on a Sunday afternoon, tan gabardine slacks and a red polo shirt.

During their flush years, Leah had surprised Joseph with a Patek Philippe watch for their anniversary. In a flowing script the back was inscribed *LOVE ALWAYS*. The watch invariably invoked a warm, fuzzy feeling when Joseph wore it. But today he deliberately left the expensive watch in an alligator jewelry case on top of his bureau. He had been warned not to bring anything of value to prison. In preparation for this day, he had purchased an inexpensive watch at J.C. Penney's. His face turned grim as he fastened it on his wrist, the symbol of his new reality.

He removed his navy wool blazer from the walk-in closet. *Screw them. I don't care if the jacket is scrunched up and thrown in prison storage.* For several days his thoughts had been irrational, but he didn't care. He slipped two identical, long, narrow jewelry boxes from his pajama drawer, shoving one in each inside pocket of his jacket. Without saying a word, he headed for the living room, gently folded the jacket in half and placed it neatly over the top of the wingback chair.

Unable to cope with the unfolding drama, Pauline had cut classes for over a week.

In the kitchen, Leah searched her daughter's face. "Are you alright?"

Slouched in a chair, Pauline gave a limp shrug. Absentmindedly, her finger played with a corkscrew curl. The corners of her mouth turned down. She fixated on the Sunbeam Mixmaster on the far edge of the tile counter, as if that held the answers to her misery. For six weeks she had barely eaten, but with everything going on, no one noticed the nine pounds she had dropped.

A tad too cheerful, Joseph tried to comfort her. "My little chick-a-dee, everything's gonna be fine."

But Pauline had learned all too well that words didn't change the fact that her father was headed for prison and their lives were turned upside down.

At the table Joseph smeared cream cheese on half an onion bagel. All eyes were on him as he tried to swallow the heavy food. Finally he pushed his unfinished plate to the center of the table, sipped some coffee and said, "I feel like a convict eating my last meal."

Neither Pauline nor her mother could eat. For a few awkward moments the family sat like glaciers frozen in time. "Let's go in the living room," Leah finally urged. "Get away from the food."

Joseph parked himself in the middle of the couch with his wife and daughter flanking him. Never before had he left them alone for an extended time—much less a year—and it was ripping him apart.

In a pathetic voice Pauline pleaded, "Daddy, please don't leave. Don't go."

Tears pooled in Joseph's eyes. "I'm afraid I have no choice. You can't imagine how much I want to be with you. But I'll be back before you know it." He crossed the room and removed the two small boxes from his jacket. "I have something for my favorite ladies. These are for you." Pauline and her mother opened the gift boxes and each found a delicate silver chain and heart-shaped locket. For fifteen minutes the discordant sound of sniffles filled the room as they tried to comfort one other. The inevitable could no longer be postponed.

"Well, the time has come." With a sense of disbelief, Joseph walked to the kitchen and picked up the black telephone.

With a jittery voice he called for a taxi. He returned to the living room with a false sense of bravado. Acting as if he were still in control, he wrapped his arm around his daughter. "Pet, don't forget to help your mom and . . ." Joseph winked, "stop playing hooky. No more excuses for cutting school. I'll be home before you know it."

Unaware of the crisis inside, the impatient taxi driver beeped his horn. Joseph kissed them on the head one last time. Then he picked up his blazer, opened the heavy door and walked outside. He did not look back. The only thing he brought with him was a well-worn leather wallet. It contained several snapshots of the family and enough money to pay the cab fare and buy cigarettes and snacks at the prisoners' commissary.

Leah and Pauline pressed against the plate glass window in the living room for one fleeting glimpse as the cab disappeared around the corner. Leah rubbed her daughter's back. "It'll be all right. Somehow we'll work it out." But the jarring emptiness hit her. "Sweetheart, it's been a tough morning. I hardly slept last night. Would you mind if I go upstairs to rest?"

Pauline studied her mother as she dragged herself up to her bedroom. Leah closed the door and fell onto her side of the rumpled double bed. She used the pillow to muffle her sobs, hoping her daughter would not hear her.

When there was nothing left but a void, Pauline tip-toed over to the liquor cabinet and poured a hefty portion of vodka into a water glass. In case her mother returned, she topped it off with some orange juice. Left alone in the lower portion of the big house, Pauline sipped her drink to calm her nerves and erase her shame.

CHAPTER 20

PRISON

A N OFFICER-OF-THE-COURT met Joseph at the U. S. Marshal's office in the basement of the federal courthouse. When he introduced himself, the officious marshal pulled a manila folder with his name from the in-box on the right side of his gray metal desk. "Take a seat," he said, plunking several government forms on his desk blotter. With no inflection in his voice, he asked Joseph a series of questions.

On the other side of the desk, Joseph sat with his right hand gripping the arm of the government-issued chair. He noticed the minutes move forward on a circular clock hanging on the side wall.

"What's with your arm?" the U.S. Marshal asked.

Here we go again, Joseph thought. "It's a tremor. Had it since childhood.

Then more questions. With several telephone interruptions, the induction process took forty-five minutes. Eventually the U.S. Marshal handed him a sheaf of papers. "Sign where the X's are."

Joseph started to peruse the papers, then thought, *what's the use?* He scrawled his full name and title, Dr. Joseph Schulman.

"Oops. Didn't catch that. Sure don't get many doctors around here."

Eventually the marshal passed Joseph along to another marshal, whose job it was to drive him to prison. Joseph winced as the new marshal pulled out his metal handcuffs and clamped them tightly on his wrists. "Just procedure. You know, we play by the rules."

The marshal led Joseph out the back door to the black and white police car parked in a secure courtyard. His gun, tucked away in a black leather holster, hung off his right hip. He eased Joseph into the backseat. There were no door handles on the inside of the back doors and a black mesh screen separated the driver from his prisoner. When the marshal pulled into traffic, Joseph cringed. Mortified, he stared straight ahead, longing to be invisible. His humiliation increased as curious strangers gawked at him. Neither of them made an effort at conversation, the marshal out of boredom, Joseph out of fear.

I'm nothing more than some cargo, Joseph thought, as he tried to massage his wrists to get his blood flow circulating.

In the minimum security prison, Joseph bottled up his anger at the system. In his rare letters home, he refused to share any details other than to say he was managing. He refused to allow Leah or anyone in the family to visit during this, the bleakest period of his life.

During Joseph's incarceration, Leah once again wrestled with depression. Since she lost her parents in the Holocaust and spent years in mourning, she recognized the all too familiar symptoms of despair. She understood what it meant to be a survivor because, in many ways, it also made her a victim.

With time off for good behavior, Joseph walked out of prison after nine months. But the injustice he experienced, the embarrassment to his family, the financial drain of his trials and losing his license to practice medicine, left deep emotional scars. His life was destroyed, with nothing to do and nowhere to go.

Leah tried hard to accommodate his sullen moods and uncharacteristic flashes of temper. She approached Joseph as diplomatically as she could. "Darling, why don't we move away from Cleveland? Go somewhere else."

Unhappy with himself and angry at the world, Joseph stood his ground. He refused to discuss it. "No, I'm not going anywhere. Mama's buried here. My father and brother are buried here. Besides, Rose and Max live here. Esther lives here. We can't just walk away. Abandon them."

But in truth, everything was gone. The good times raising the girls, helping the family, the lavish parties, his medical practice, they were all erased and supplanted with a burning bitterness that set in like rigor mortis. It was eating Leah alive to see the changes in her husband. At some level she knew that they could not continue in this tension-filled state.

Ultimately Leah pleaded with Joseph. "For a change, listen to me. We can't stay. It's impossible. All those newspaper headlines . . . Besides, there's only the three of us now. Pauline's a big help, but, honestly, this house is too big. I can't keep it up anymore. What do we need it for?"

She had a valid point, but he was adamant. Beaten-down and depressed, Joseph lacked the gumption to move. Petty irritants exploded into arguments, straining their marriage. After Mama died, Joseph had turned her bedroom into a private study filled with his old medical books and journals. Now he was content to just sit there with the door closed—shut off from everybody—thumbing through the back issues of medical journals that Leah had meticulously saved for him.

Joseph didn't know exactly what he was looking for until several articles sparked a wild idea. Physicians were advising patients with severe allergies and asthma to head west, to Phoenix, Arizona for the clean, pure desert air. Another journal had an expansive article and photographs of the newly-built clinics and hospitals. As if to underscore it, *Life Magazine* did a full spread on the opportunities and expansion of Phoenix.

As usual, after breakfast Joseph sequestered himself in his study. But he felt unusually restless. "I'll be back. I'm going to the post office," he lied, planning to research the demographics of Phoenix. At the public library he began to patch together disparate information. It just so happened that while scanning an encyclopedia, he came upon a poem about a phoenix that beckoned him.

Out of my ashes
Will rise a new phoenix.
A soaring being
Returning from death
Proving once again
life is eternal.

This is written for me, Joseph thought. *What a great omen. Phoenix. That's it. We'll move to Phoenix.* It took some cajoling on his part, but eventually he persuaded Leah that this growing southwestern community represented unprecedented opportunities to start anew.

With heavy hearts, they sold their home to a middle-aged couple with a brood of teenagers. Despite the fact that moving was originally her suggestion, Leah grew despondent and withdrawn when reality hit. She too tried to gather information about Phoenix. The hairdresser told her the west was cowboy country, like in the John Wayne movies. So Leah offered Rose and her cousin, Esther, part of her extensive wardrobe. She passed down hats and gloves, woolen dresses and coats, pure silk blouses, high heel shoes, and purses.

After so many years of gathering and collecting, the actual process of moving—sorting, discarding, and boxing—drained what was left of Leah's vitality. For weeks she had been shedding possessions, stripping away her self-confidence layer-by-layer. One afternoon, cranky from wrapping kitchen dishes in newspapers and stuffing them into waxy cardboard banana boxes, Leah climbed the stairs to see how Pauline's packing was coming along. A larger than life poster of James Dean lorded over her disheveled bedroom wall. Her daughter slumped cross-legged on the white shag carpet.

Her plastic horse and stuffed animal collections were removed from the shelves and scattered about like confetti tossed in a ticker-tape parade.

"Pauline, you can't take everything. Come on. You've outgrown this stuff. Give it away already."

Filled with anger, Pauline sassed back. "Why's it always my stuff that has to go? Why don't you give away your mink coat?" When her mother left her bedroom, Pauline turned up the volume on her hi-fi and listened to Buddy Holly sing, *It Doesn't Matter Any More* as it resonated off the almost empty walls.

In the end, two broad-shouldered men carted the remainder of their household goods away, never imagining what these possessions meant to their owners. *Our possessions possess us,* Leah acknowledged ruefully, gleaning the true meaning of the word bittersweet.

On their long, monotonous drive to Phoenix, Pauline was wedged in the backseat of the Coupe De Ville between last minute items thrown into cardboard boxes. The Schulman's sat in silence as they rolled through Indiana. In an effort to suppress the bleakness, Joseph tried to engage his morose daughter in conversation. "Pet, do you know what a phoenix symbolizes?"

"Who cares," she snarled.

Joseph ignored his daughter's belligerent attitude. "Well, my Pet, I'm going tell you anyway. It's a bird that rises from the ashes to start anew."

"That's appropriate," Leah muttered with an insincere cheerfulness.

By prior arrangement, they signed a short term rental agreement on a two-bedroom brick bungalow, figuring it would suffice until they got more settled. Several months after their arrival, Joseph's Timex watch stopped working. Leah tried to convince him to wear the expensive Patek Philippe watch she had given him on their anniversary during better years. But he couldn't bear to put it on again. It represented another era; one he knew would never return. Hoping to get out of the house before succumbing to the heat of the day, he left early to buy a new battery. On his return, he stooped down and picked up the morning paper and headed into the kitchen to pour a glass of milk, the one thing that would settle his jittery stomach. Lost in thought, he barely noticed Leah as he sat at the table scanning the Want Ads.

From the stress of the multiple trials, her husband's imprisonment, and the loss of her beloved home, Leah developed excruciating back spasms and chronic insomnia. In a constant state of agitation, she was rinsing the breakfast dishes when a soapy glass slipped out of her hands and shattered. As she tried to pick up the jagged shards, an angry outburst spewed from her lips. "I can't stand it here. It's not even eleven o'clock and already it's hot." Then for shock value she screamed, "Besides, this goddamn desert's full of scorpions and snakes! I'm afraid to walk outside. Just tell me why we ever came to this godforsaken place?"

"WHAT DO YOU WANT FROM ME? Can't you see I'm trying to find work? Take a good look. I'm a middle-aged man. A convicted felon with a tremor in one arm and I'm trying to find a job in medicine."

"That's all well and good, Joseph, but I hate it here! Why can't we live in California? Near Ellie. Every time she calls, she begs me to move there. All we do is sit around here and look at the four walls!"

"FINE. I'LL DO WHATEVER MAKES YOU HAPPY. Just tell me what you want."

In the end, Joseph gave up searching for a job in Phoenix. Two months later, the Schulman's, feeling like vagabonds, moved to Sacramento, California and were reunited with Ellie and their son-in-law Wyatt. The only thing Joseph sought for himself was a presidential pardon to clear his sullied name, even though he knew at this late date, it would amount to a Pyrrhic victory, a win that arrives too late to have any impact. Knowing himself to be innocent, he craved exoneration like a drowning man craves air.

CHAPTER 21

FAMILY REUNION

BACK IN CLEVELAND, Leah's sister, Rose, and her husband, Max, had eased into a comfortable marriage. Nevertheless Rose missed her sister—and all the Schulman's—the only *real* family she had. At first Max thought her mercurial moods would disappear, but as time went by, her feeling of isolation grew more and more prevalent.

One Sunday, after Rose made another long-distance telephone call to her sister, Max coaxed his dispirited wife into going to a movie that was up for an Academy Award. In the darkened theater, his mind drifted from the movie to a personal plan. He reviewed the details one more time, trying to assess all the implications.

They had no sooner taken their coats off and hung them back in the hall closet when Max turned serious. "Rose, can I talk to you about something? But before you say anything, hear me out."

"What's wrong? Are you sick?"

"No. Nothing's wrong."

In the living room Max began his recitation. "Suppose we move to Sacramento. You'd be back with family. And I'm fed-up working for someone else. I want to be my own boss, own my own drugstore. The other day I got to thinking. What's holding us back? We don't have kids. Besides . . ." he winked and got that boyish glint in his eyes, "sunny winters in California beats the hell out of Cleveland any day of the week."

"Max, for God's sake, exactly what are you saying? Don't say it if you're not serious."

Max and Rose hashed and rehashed the possibilities. When it all boiled down, the only thing holding them back was the thought of abandoning her cousin, Esther.

"We can bring Esther too," Max offered. In the years since Joseph lost his practice, good-hearted Max and Rose assumed the responsibility of supporting Esther, which left them on a very tight budget.

In Sacramento the trio rented a two bedroom apartment in a shabby, pre-war brick building. Max, restless and ambitious, wasted no time. Every day he scoured neighborhoods for a good commercial location. Eventually he found a vacant, corner storefront where two bus lines intersected in a densely populated district. He convinced the landlord that he would be a worthy tenant. When the drugstore opened, Rose worked alongside Max six days a week. When the pace picked up, they hired Esther to work as a Girl Friday, to stock the shelves and run to the post office and the bank.

Book Two

PAULINE
Danielle's Birth-Mother

CHAPTER 22

THE SECRET

SACRAMENTO, CALIFORNIA. 1962. At her parents' insistent, Pauline dragged herself to the fourth high school in four years. As a teenager she hungered to be part of a clique, giggling and gossiping with the other girls in her class. Instead of acceptance, she faced continuous isolation. Always feeling like an outsider, she despised school and yearned to quit. Hungry to love something, she begged her parents for a cat.

"Absolutely not. Cats give me the willies," her mother protested. As a girl in Budapest, Leah's family had a magnificent apartment in a luxurious building, but pets were not allowed.

Pauline's father tried for a lighter touch. "Actually, you're my pet. That's all we need," he replied with a nervous chuckle. For months Pauline tried to make her case. "Aw, come on. Pretty please. Just a little kitty. I promise I'll take care of it."

Pauline's guilt-ridden parents were aware of everything they had put their daughter through. After a continuous stream of badgering and begging, they finally caved-in. "Okay, here's the deal," her father announced. "You finish high school and you'll get your cat." The day after graduation, Pauline and her father drove to the S.P. C.A. and she picked out an adorable calico kitten with sorrowful eyes.

Early one morning Pauline rolled away from the light that seeped through the lower part of the window blinds near her bed. Reluctant to open her eyes, she tried to extend the time between sleep and wakefulness. She prayed the new day would somehow be different from the last. But nothing had changed. Her stomach soured with recurring indigestion. After a ten minute shower, she slipped on her tight Levis. Now free from high school—and the school bullies that teased her about her large breasts—she defiantly wore her yellow V-neck tee-shirt that showed off her cleavage. She thought, *there's no way I'm going to the beauty school today. I hate it.*

"Where's kitty?" she shouted to her parents who were in separate rooms. "Where's Fifi?"

"What?" her mother hollered from the living room. She could hardly hear her daughter over the advertisements on *Good Morning America*.

Short on patience, Pauline repeated the question.

"Fifi's behind the curtain . . . snooping out the window," her mother said. Pauline's disheveled father, still in his striped pajamas and terry robe, stood over the stove stirring oatmeal. "Pet, come have some mush."

"Dad, not now," Pauline responded, trying to disguise her foul mood. "I've gotta feed kitty."

No one had to remind her to perform that chore.

Sure enough, she found Fifi spying on the neighbors. Pauline cradled her beloved cat in her arms, rubbing her face against the soft fur. After feeding Fifi, she secluded herself in the bathroom, the only place in the house that offered a modicum of privacy. She quickly brushed her teeth and her thick, curly blond hair. *Forget the make-up,* she thought. *I just wanna be out of here.* No talk. No questions. No answers. No lies.

As she dashed out the front door, she was purposefully vague. "Mom, I've got a lot going on today. I'll be home late."

In a woe-is-me frame of mind, she lamented, *what's the use of going to beauty school? I've got no future.* She wanted to take in a matinee, but with only a few bucks in her wallet, she decided against it. She made an impetuous decision to head downtown. The bus jostled and rumbled through the streets. The stench of sweaty bodies and strong perfume assaulted her sensitive nose.

Pauline had no interest in academia, and even if she did, money would have been an issue. Her first priority was to earn her own keep and, if possible, help her parents financially. As a high school graduation present, Auntie Rose and Uncle Max had paid for the course at Betty's Beauty School. From their perspective it was a practical gift, but Pauline attended the classes with little enthusiasm or passion. It was merely a place to hang-out. In her fantasies, she envied her sister. She thought Ellie and Wyatt led the charmed life with their own apartment and good jobs. Making money. Buying what they wanted.

Out of a desperate need to unburden herself, Pauline located a telephone booth on a downtown corner, across from a women's ready-to-wear shop. She fished two dimes out of her purse, plunked one in the slot, and placed the other on the triangular metal shelf, just in case she needed to talk longer. She did not want the operator to cut her off. Mentally she braced herself before dialing her sister's work number.

CHAPTER 23

DRIFTING

WHEN PAULINE'S SISTER Ellie answered the phone, she assumed it was one of the usual family interruptions in her busy day.

Pauline tried to hold back her tears. "Ellie, I need to talk to you. It's *really, really* important."

"You don't sound right. What's wrong?"

"I'm in trouble."

Growing alarmed, Ellie asked, "What happened? You sound weird. Are you stoned?"

"No," Pauline said indignantly, "I'm not stoned. But I've got a real problem. And I can't talk about it over the phone. Can we meet . . . at your apartment?"

"Well, kiddo, it's Monday. Our phones have been ringing off the hook. I'm really busy. Is it a real emergency or can it wait?"

"I wouldn't be calling unless it was important."

"Okay, okay. Listen up. Wyatt flew down to L.A. this morning. On a buying trip. Won't be back 'til late Friday. Meet me at the apartment at six, okay?"

"Can't you make it any sooner?"

"You know I can't just knock off any time I want. See you at six. It's the best I can do." When Ellie hung up, she collected a few telephone messages for Cheryl, her boss, and sauntered down the corridor to her private office.

Cheryl O'Connell, Ellie's boss, was the O'Connell in O'Connell, Sorensen, & Hubble, Attorneys-at-Law. An unconventional woman with a forceful personality, Cheryl blazed her own trail as a divorce lawyer. In less than ten years, she earned a reputation as a tenacious litigator, a battering ram. She understood family dynamics more than most people. As the oldest and brightest of four children, she was constantly straightening out her own family's jams. Once, when Ellie explained the Schulman's troubles, Cheryl even volunteered to write a letter on Joseph's behalf to the Internal Revenue Service regarding a dispute over the deductions for his legal fees.

"Can I talk to you?" Ellie asked.

"Sure," Cheryl said, absent-mindedly thumbing through the pink call-back slips. "Sit down. Take the load off your feet."

"My sister's having some sort of crisis. Would it be okay if I left promptly at five?"

"No problem. Do what you have to do. Nothing serious, I hope."

"I don't know. She seemed pretty disturbed."

After the call to Ellie, Pauline had the rest of the day to kill. She drifted over to the Greyhound Bus Depot, just a few blocks away. Inside the air-conditioned terminal she sat among strangers as she mulled over her situation. *What would happen if I just hopped on a bus and took off? No one would even care?*

Pauline scrutinized a wafer thin woman with deep purple circles under her eyes trying to placate a screaming infant. A scruffy lad, maybe two or three, crouched on the floor alongside her. Deep in concentration, the boy played with a metallic blue Matchbox car, running it back and forth on the dirty floor.

An obese man, whose belly hung below his belt, carefully lowered himself onto the seat alongside Pauline. He was juggling a bottle of orange soda and a paper container with two hot dogs and fries from the adjacent diner. "Say, by any chance are you going to Frisco?"

The man and the stench of the greasy food turned Pauline's stomach. *I don't need this*, she thought and scooted outside. A few blocks away, she wandered over to the capitol. For a moment the high dome reminded her of the neoclassic buildings in Paris. Once ensconced in the impressive rotunda, tiny beads of perspiration accumulated on her nose and between her breasts.

"Excuse me, where's the water fountain?" she asked someone who looked like they belonged.

Pretending she had a reason to be roaming the marbled hallway, she let the icy water roll off her parched tongue. She glanced at the lighted displays of California's gold rush history, but quickly grew bored. She wandered back outside and plunked herself down on a bench under a canopy of fully grown elms that left a lacy shadow on the walkway.

"Ah, it feels good to sit down," Pauline groaned, hoping to strike up a conversation—any conversation—with the deeply wrinkled Asian woman who sat at the far end of the bench. Except for her sister, she hadn't spoken to anyone since she left home that morning.

The old woman with rounded shoulders and a honey-colored satin mandarin jacket did not respond.

"Pretty flowers," Pauline continued, not sure if she was talking to herself or the elderly woman.

The woman offered up a half-smile showing a gold-rimmed front tooth. "Very pret-tee. Me come with granddaughter every day," she said, motioning to a four year old girl that resembled a little cherub playing on the grass close-by. The little girl was scooping handfuls of leaves and tossing them over her head. For a brief time the two strangers sat side-by-side relishing the tranquility.

Finally, it was time for Pauline to head out. The crowded bus sputtered along in the commute traffic. Pauline had to transfer once, but arrived at her sister's in less than an hour.

CHAPTER 24

CONFESSION

I N THE MOTEL STYLE apartment complex, Ellie saw Pauline approaching through the large, plate-glass window in the living room. Before her sister had a chance to knock, Ellie swung the door open. Pauline, wearing a doleful expression, looked like a little kid about to be scolded. For a girl that loved nothing more than playing with make-up, Pauline's paleness was unusual.

"You look like crap," Ellie remarked bluntly. "Are you okay?"

Pauline offered a noncommittal shrug and stared down at her shoes.

"Well, come in. Don't just stand there."

They sat on the second-hand couch with a new brown cotton slip-cover. Ellie offered her sister something to eat.

In an angry voice Pauline said, "I'm not hungry."

"What about something to drink? Iced tea? Scotch?"

"Scotch. Make it a double," Pauline snapped.

After making drinks for the two of them, Ellie persisted, "What's going on? Wanna tell me what's on your mind?"

Teary-eyed, Pauline said nothing. She took a few sips and held on to her glass. Ellie caught her sister's hand trembling.

Pauline made an off-handed remark about the heat and humidity.

"Yeah, it's hotter 'n hell. Our air-conditioner can't keep up. Remember when we lived in Cleveland, how we bitched about the bitter cold? Now it's the heat." On edge, Ellie grabbed a package of Benson and Hedges that rested on the coffee table, pulled one out for herself and asked her sister if she wanted one.

Pauline shook her head from side to side and looked away.

Ellie lit up, taking a deep drag and exhaling in one smooth stream. Then she tried in earnest to extract some information from her sister. "For chrissakes, what's going on?"

All hunched up, Pauline clasped her hands into a ball and her body shuddered with silent sobs.

Ellie found herself growing impatient. Partway through her drink she pleaded with her sister. "Pauline, let's not play games, okay? You have something to tell me. So talk."

Pauline's tongue finally loosened. "All right. Do you really want to know?"

"Uh-huh, I do. What the hell's going on?"

"If I tell you, you got to promise to keep it a secret."

"I promise. Now tell me."

"I'M PREGNANT!" Pauline managed to spit out through a steady flow of tears. "Okay. There . . . are you happy?"

"You're pregnant! Oh, shit!" Ellie's mind froze. She was searching for the right tone and the right words. She wrapped her arms around her sister in a comforting hug, rubbing her back to soothe her. "Oh, honey, I don't know what to say. But it isn't the end of the world."

Now that the word was out, Pauline tried to get control of herself. She wiped her eyes and sniffed. "Easy for you to say. You're not the one who's preggie."

Ellie was stalling for time when she asked the usual question, "Who's the father?"

"Gil," Pauline whispered, almost ashamed to say his name. "You know, that cute guy I met at Tower Records. God, Ellie, I still can't believe it. I got pregnant the first time I ever did it."

When Ellie and Wyatt—the no-nonsense ex-marine—were married, he insisted that Ellie drop her pretensions and silly teenage tantrums. Torn from the bosom of her protective parents, she was forced to mature. She actually developed a down-to-earth practical side. "Listen, Pauline, maybe the two of you can get married."

"Well . . . that isn't gonna happen anytime soon."

"Don't be so hasty. Would you at least give it some thought?"

A torrent of vitriolic words shot out of Pauline's mouth like bullets from a machine gun. "I can't. He lied to me. How can I marry him when he's already married? Would you answer me that?" She wiped her runny nose with her sleeve.

"Okay. Okay. I get it. Just calm down. Let me get you some Kleenex." Ellie dashed into the bathroom and grabbed a half-empty box from the top of the toilet tank. "Here. Blow your nose."

Between intermittent sobs, Pauline lamented, "Now everyone's gonna think I'm a slut."

"Pauline, that's not true and you know it. Did you at least tell him you're pregnant?"

"Yeah. And he wasn't too thrilled about it. Said it was my problem. I needed to take care of it."

At that moment, as if listening to their conversation, Archie, Ellie's cat, jumped up and plopped on Pauline's lap. The cat purred sympathetically as Pauline stroked his soft fur.

"Gil drove me over to Chico's apartment. He told me his friend had some quinine. Made me drink it. He said it was supposed to cause a miscarriage."

"Well . . . what happened?"

"NOTHING! I puked my guts out. That's what happened. Gil and Chico just sat there watching a stupid football game on T.V. They could care less."

Ellie found it tough to visualize, but she allowed her sister to ramble on, purging the humiliation from her mind.

"My head was in the toilet for hours. But nothing happened. Gil's a bastard. If I died tomorrow, he wouldn't even care."

Not sure how to handle the situation, Ellie hesitated. She simply wanted to defuse her sister's anxiety. Calm her down. In truth, she didn't know whether to scream, admonish her, or offer comfort. Either way, she reasoned, a little food couldn't hurt. "I'm starving. How 'bout something to eat?"

As they sat at the kitchen table facing each other, Ellie was not fooled by Pauline's little charade, shifting her small portion of scrambled eggs from one side of the white melamine plate to the other. Ellie studied her sister's troubled face silently. Without make-up and teased hair, she looked like an innocent teenager. "Want some toast?"

"No. What I want is an *abortion*."

When they returned to the living room, they continued to explore Pauline's predicament. "Did you know Catholics are against abortion?" Ellie pontificated, not sure why she even brought it up.

"Who cares? We're Jewish," Pauline retorted, reducing Ellie's argument to its lowest common denominator. "Besides, I—don't—want—this—baby." She enunciated each word individually, as if each told its own story.

In the early 60's, abortions were illegal. Ellie, like most women, had some inkling that an underground network existed if one dug beneath the surface. She promised her sister she would explore that option. "Listen, sweetie, come back tomorrow night. I'll fix us some supper. In the meantime I'll do some investigating."

Early the next morning, before the office grew hectic, Ellie approached her boss. "Can I speak to you . . . alone?" She had a hunch that Cheryl, being an attorney, knew how to get things done.

"Close the door, sweetie. What's on your mind?"

"Remember when I was talking to my sister yesterday?"

"Uh-huh. Aren't families wonderful?"

Ellie rolled her eyes. "Well, to make a long story short, she needs an abortion."

Cheryl rubbed her long tapered fingers back and forth over her mouth, as if her hand was an eraser. "As an officer of the court, this conversation didn't happen and being Catholic, it goes against my faith."

Ellie swallowed hard, thinking it was a mistake to confide in her boss.

"But as a woman," Cheryl chimed in, "I understand completely. The law against abortions is wicked. It ought to be thrown out. Look, I can't make any promises, but if I have time this afternoon, I'll make a few calls. If I find anything helpful, I'll let you know."

It was encouraging, but not definitive.

At the end of the day the work tapered off. In a hurry to get home, Ellie started to clear her desk when she heard the familiar clip-clop of Cheryl's high-heels on the hardwood floor. Without saying a word, her boss raised her eyebrows and broke into a smug smile. On a yellow sheet of paper folded into quarters, she dropped a name and telephone number on Ellie's desk.

CHAPTER 25

MIRACLE HILL CHURCH

THE LAST call the law offices received that day was from Pauline. She came right to the point. "Well . . . what happened? Did ya get a name?"

Ellie felt like the cat that just swallowed the canary. She was doodling little circles on a notepad as she talked. "I got it. The number's right here in my hot little hands."

After putting down the receiver, Ellie realized there was more than one problem. The man that performed abortions lived in Portland, Oregon. One state away. She thought, *how is Pauline going to get there? And how is she going to pay for it? Geez, life would be a whole lot simpler if I didn't have to solve everyone's problems.*

Pauline arrived at Ellie's apartment a few minutes after her sister. "Good timing," Ellen commented. "Take off your shoes, stay awhile."

"El, I need a drink."

"Okay, okay. Come, sit at the table. Keep me company and I'll fix us both a drink."

After she handed her sister the Scotch, Ellie placed two cereal bowls on the Formica counter, divvied out what was left of an open carton of cottage cheese, and threw in some canned peaches. She scrounged through her half-empty food cabinet—she had been meaning to get to the grocery store for days. She found some stale soda crackers and tossed them on a separate plate.

Pauline could hardly wait to throw out the question she had been worrying about all day. "D'ya think I can get an appointment this week?"

"Sweetie, it's late now. After hours. But I promise I'll call first thing tomorrow. From the office."

"I'm really scared, Ellie. I'm afraid to go by myself."

Ellie laid her fork down and rubbed her forehead. She tried to hold back her frustration, knowing that meant two airfares instead of one. Money—or the lack of it—was a real issue. Finally, in a noncommittal voice she said, "Look, Pauline, I'd really like to go, you know, be with you and everything, but it all hinges on money. Let me check the airlines. See how much it costs to fly to Portland."

Pauline had a panicky expression. "I don't know what to do. You know I don't have any money."

Ellie tried to reassure her sister. "Wyatt and I have a few bucks tucked away. And if we need more, I may be able to get an advance on my next few paychecks."

Dismissing the financial matters, Pauline appeared relieved. "Does that mean you'll go with me?"

"No guarantees, but I'll try and swing it."

After dinner Ellie scanned the yellow pages of her telephone directory and found the twenty-four hour reservation numbers for United and PSA. The cost of the abortion was still unknown.

In the four years Ellie worked for Cheryl, they enjoyed an easy-going and casual work relationship. Ellie closed the door to Cheryl's office and sat down. "Do you remember yesterday? You handed me a name . . . ?"

Cheryl had a way about her that made everyone think they were the most important person in the world. "Of course."

"Well, I'm about to make that call," Ellie announced with great trepidation. "But here's the thing. My sister's too scared to go alone. I hate to ask this, but I'm going to need a day off . . . and, if you can swing it, an advance on my salary. I promised I'd fly up to Portland with her."

"Look, Ellie, the day off isn't a problem. We're kind of busy, but we'll manage. No one's indispensable. About the money, well, that's a different story."

Ellie's heart dropped. She thought she had pushed her boss too far.

"Maybe it would be better if I loaned you the money personally. That way no one else will know."

A wide smile broke across Ellie's face. "What can I say? You're the greatest."

"I'm headed for a deposition. Call from my office. It's private. No one needs to hear your business. You know how fast gossip spreads around here."

Ellie waited until the door closed behind her boss, and then dialed the number.

A woman with a Midwestern twang picked up the phone. "Ruby, here."

Ellie explained who she was and her sister's predicament.

"Well, Hon, you know only God can redeem her sins. But we can absolve her problem."

"About the price, how much?"

"Two hundred . . . cash," Ruby replied, being careful never to use the word *abortion*. When asked, she gave the address and explained that they worked out of a church.

"A church? That's the last place I'd expect to go," Ellie exclaimed, feeling as if she was swimming in uncharted waters.

"Ain't that the point, sister?"

Early the next morning the two sisters hopped a PSA flight to Portland, Oregon. Pauline practically choked from the stagnant air and second-hand smoke on the plane. Ellie tried to engage her sister in conversation but Pauline was not in the mood for chitchat. Nervous, Ellie lit one cigarette after another.

Black thunderclouds filled the sky as the plane bumped along the tarmac. Ellie and Pauline—never thinking it could be cold and rainy in Portland—were in light-weight summer clothes and sandals. Ellie took charge. She handed the cab driver a piece of notepaper with the address scrawled in pencil.

"Ladies, we'll be there in a jiff," the cabby said. "It's not too far away."

A few minutes later Ellie screamed at the taxi driver as he wove in and out of traffic on the wet streets at breakneck speed. "Hey, Buddy, slow down. We're only going to church." She nudged her sister as if it was one big joke, but Pauline looked straight ahead and sat in stony silence.

On the western edge of Portland, not far from the Hare Krishna temple, the taxi finally pulled to the curb. "Here we are," he announced with a burst of pride.

Painted a flamingo pink, the decrepit clapboard church was nestled between a used book store and an empty building that once sold furniture. A large white cross mounted on the front of the church protruded outward towards the sidewalk. A shadowbox— protected by a cracked glass—was fastened on the right side of the stairs. Even with a few missing letters, Ellie and Pauline could still make out the words:

Miracle Hill Pentecostal Church
All Sinners Welcome

This was the moment of truth.

Ellie sensed her sister's trepidation and tried to make light of it. "Hey, kiddo, let's go in. I know enough to get out of the rain."

The church vestibule separated the sanctuary from the office. Soft, diffused light filtered through the orange, pebbled glass windows. Pauline's eyes darted around like a hummingbird in flight. She could not help but notice the few seedy stragglers. They sat listlessly in the wooden pews watching a woman with flabby flesh dangling from her arms playing the organ.

"Can I help you?" a middle-age woman with penciled in eyebrows and concave cheeks asked as she stepped out of the untidy office.

"Uh-huh. I'm looking for Ruby," Ellie sputtered, thinking the lady was a little too flashy for church in her low-cut dress and red patent stiletto heels.

Thinking herself clever for being able to quote from the Bible Ruby responded, "Seek and ye shall find. Look no further. Say, who are you, anyways?"

Ellie did all the talking. "Remember, uh, I spoke with you on the phone yesterday. My sister, well, she's the one with the problem."

"Oh, yeah, now I remember. Hon, go on upstairs."

Ellie hesitated, not sure she should go along or whether those instructions were specifically for Pauline. Almost as an afterthought Ruby glanced at her. "Sister, if you like, you can tag along."

Even though it was daylight, the fluorescent lights projected a bluish-white cast. The upstairs hallway and the large, glass partitioned office smelled from cigarette smoke and accumulated dirt. A plaid beanbag ashtray filled with cigarette butts and a half-empty cup of coffee were plopped on top of the disorderly desk.

An emaciated looking man with greasy hair that hung over his soiled collar stood up. Devoid of warmth, he said, "For today's purpose, call me Sven."

"Nice to meet you," Ellie stammered, although she wasn't so sure. Something about his impersonal eyes disarmed her. "Yesterday I called and spoke to Ruby."

"Uh-huh. She told me. Come, sit down." He cleared his throat. "About the finances . . ."

"I brought money," Ellie said anxiously, fumbling through her straw purse for her wallet. "You know . . . um, this is for my sister."

"Very good," he said, counting the bills. "You can stay here. Smoke if you like. Everything's gonna be fine." Then he turned his narrow eyes towards Pauline, who was too frightened to say a word. "Sister, how far along are you?"

"Around two months."

He hitched up his pants and gave a smarmy smile. "Two months. Good . . . that's good. Let's take care of your problem. Follow me."

Pauline glanced at her sister, searching her face for reassurance.

"Go on. Go with him," Ellie urged. Not once did Sven ask their names or addresses or write anything down on paper.

Pauline trailed behind Sven slightly as they proceeded down the hall to another room. Left alone with this strange man, she felt disoriented, as if this was all a nightmare. She desperately wanted to wake-up and find herself warm and snuggly under the covers in her own bed.

"This won't take long," Sven said, reaching for the light switch. Feeling discombobulated, Pauline scrutinized him carefully, judging him to be in his fifties or sixties. "Throw your clothes over there," he ordered, pointing to a twin bed sorely in need of a bedspread. The bed had been pushed up against a wall adjacent to two windows draped in musty royal blue velvet. One rotted drape had a long slit, permitting a sliver of light to seep through.

Still standing, Pauline asked, "All my clothes?"

"From the waist down." Completely preoccupied, he added, "If you like, you can leave your brassiere and blouse on."

From a cupboard he took down several instruments, a pair of rubber gloves, and several brown bottles and placed them on a hospital tray next to the stirrups on the examining table.

While the solemn, but unfamiliar organ music wafted through the floorboards, Pauline spotted the crucifix nailed over the bed, a bleeding Jesus lashed to a plastic cross. Tiny dabs of red paint represented dripping blood. In a daze, she slipped her huaraches off and started to step out of her skirt. Partially undressed, the blood suddenly drained from her face and her heart began to race like an out-of-control metronome.

"Sorry. I, I, I just can't do this."

Sven replied coldly, "Suit yourself, sister. It's between you and the Lord."

In a near panic, Pauline threw her clothes on. A bit disheveled, she retreated through the narrow hallway to the office where her sister was waiting. Visibly shaking, she cried out, "Ellie, let's go. Let's get out of here. I don't want to go through with it. I want to go home. NOW. "

CHAPTER 26

TWO CHOICES

ELLIE AND PAULINE scurried away from the wacky church like mice being chased with a broom. They followed the heavily traveled street, dodging the sporadic puddles left by the intermittent rain. At a Texaco station in a telephone booth decorated with dried out wads of chewing gum, Ellie fumbled through the directory secured by a cable under the grimy metal shelf. When the taxi dispatcher answered, she did her best to explain their location. Pauline stood on the other side of the folding door, fixated on the noise the cars made swooshing along on the wet pavement. As they waited for the cab to take them back to the airport, they paced back and forth like refugees preparing to cross an illegal border.

Ellie looked over her shoulder as they approached their seats on the plane. "Honey, want the window or aisle seat?"

"Aisle, in case I puke."

Ellie slid into the window seat, fastened her seatbelt, grabbed an airline magazine and pretended to read. But mentally she was weighing the pros and cons of Pauline's plight. She knew returning home would merely compound the problem.

Lost in the *what ifs* of life, Pauline silently berated herself. *I'm a failure.* She repeated it over and over, like a mantra. After the second drink, her mind and body began to relax. And by the third drink she was smashed.

"If it's any consolation," Ellie finally said aloud, "you did the right thing. That guy was a first-class weirdo!" When there was no response, she continued. "Listen, Pauline, I love you. So don't get mad, okay? But the way I see it, you've got to tell Mom and Dad."

Terrified by this suggestion, Pauline snarled, "Are you crazy? No way."

"For once in your life, just listen to me. They won't be thrilled, but they won't throw you out of the house either."

Pauline crossed her arms. "NO. It's not gonna happen."

"Don't get stubborn. You've got to do something." Finally, what had been rummaging through Ellie's head crystallized. "You only have two options. One is to have an abortion. And two is to have the baby. Look, your problem is not going to go away by itself."

Pauline glowered, as Ellie stood firm.

As the plane landed in Sacramento, Ellie said firmly, "I'm staying for dinner. You have to tell them . . . or I will."

Arriving home, Pauline climbed out of the car and entered their duplex, paralyzed with fear and wishing she were dead.

"Pauline, honey, is that you?" her mother hollered from the kitchen. "You're home early."

"We're both here, Mom," Ellie explained from the small entry hall.

"Oh, hi, Ellie. Did you take care of your business?"

Pauline needed to be alone and retreated to the bathroom. Ellie wandered into the kitchen, kissing her mother on the cheek. "Yummy. What smells so good?"

"Garbage can soup. You know how I throw everything in but the kitchen sink."

"My favorite. Did you add the barley the way I like?"

"Of course," her mother said, wiping her hands on a nearby dishtowel.

"By the way, where's Dad?" Ellie asked as casually as she could.

"Out back. Moving the sprinklers. Funny how things work out. Ever since we got to Sacramento, Daddy loves fussing in the yard."

Ellie tried to hide the tension that ran through her. "Mom, Pauline and I have something we need to discuss with you and Daddy. I'll go get him." After she urged her father to come in, she called Pauline, who by then had fled to her bedroom and closed the door.

While her father rinsed the dirt off his hands at the kitchen sink, Ellie practically dragged her sister into the kitchen. Her mother reached for a pack of cigarettes and the black ashtray with the Hotel Monte Carlo logo in gold. Finally the four of them gathered around the kitchen table like serious players in a high stakes poker game.

Reluctantly Ellie started the conversation. "I need to clear something up. I didn't travel to Portland today on business. I made that up." Then she hesitated, trying to organize the sequence of events bobbing around in her head.

Pauline knew what was coming and masked her personal feelings like a Kabuki actor. Her ears still buzzed from the drinks on the plane and her tongue felt like it was buried in a sandbox. Apprehension rapped to a staccato beat as she slumped in the chair.

Ellie took a deep breath. "This isn't going to be easy, but I have something I need to tell you. But please don't get upset, okay?" She momentarily paused and glanced over at her sister who refused to make eye contact. "Pauline's pregnant. We flew up to Portland because she wanted to have an abortion."

"*Oy vey es mir!* You're pregnant?" her mother gasped. She turned toward her youngest daughter. "I don't . . ."

Ellie cut her off. "Ma, Pauline didn't have the abortion. That's a whole other story. The important thing is . . . well, I guess, to let you know she's pregnant. There, it's out." Instinctively she knew Pauline's pregnancy would cast a black mark of shame and humiliation over the entire family but they needed to know.

Visibly shaken, Pauline tried to hold back her tears as she recounted the whole litany, including her ugly experiences trying to abort the baby. Questions and explanations flowed back and forth. In the end, Pauline felt neither good nor bad. Just empty.

By the time dinner was over, her father, too, looked beat. He directed his comment to Pauline. "Pet, it sounds like it's been an ugly day. You must be dead tired. And your mother and I've been caught off-guard. Let's give it a rest. Sleep on it. We'll sort is all out in the morning."

Ellie recognized her exit cue and rushed home.

That evening, before turning in, Joseph draped his good arm over Pauline's shoulder in an attempt to calm her. "Tomorrow's another day, Pet. I'll ask around. Get us some help. This is way too much for you to handle by yourself."

CHAPTER 27

EPPIE'S

PAULINE, TOO DISTRAUGHT to sleep, tuned in to a late night movie starring Humphrey Bogart after her parents went to bed. The telephone rang unexpectedly and she ran to the kitchen to pick it up. "Wyatt, why are you calling so late?"

"Listen, Pauline, I had a long talk with Ellie tonight. She told me everything, okay? Do me a favor. Set-up a meeting with Gil. But don't tell him I'm coming. I just want to have a little man-to-man chat with that bastard. That's all."

"Wyatt, stay out of this. My dad's gonna make arrangements for a, you know," and she lowered her voice, "an abortion."

Undeterred, Wyatt continued. "Tomorrow afternoon, when I get through with my meeting, I'm cutting out. Set it up for Saturday, okay?"

"I'm not sure that's gonna happen."

"Goddamit, Pauline, make it happen. For once in your life stop being a wimp. Call me back. Collect. I'll be in the hotel for the rest of the night and in the morning 'til ten. I expect to hear back from you."

Pauline called back. "Okay. I did it. He's meeting me at Eppie's on Saturday at two o'clock. But, Wyatt, there's really nothing more to talk about."

"Oh, don't be too sure about that."

Saturday afternoon Pauline met Wyatt at the coffee shop. "Where is he?" Wyatt asked, scanning the few patrons left in the restaurant.

Forty minutes later Pauline spotted him through the plate glass windows. She tapped Wyatt's arm. "That's him . . . coming in now. That guy in the black Grateful Dead T-shirt and jeans."

Gil offered a half-assed apology for being late but Wyatt wasn't buying it. Gil could handle Pauline, but wasn't prepared for the *tour de force* sitting alongside her. Wyatt immediately took control of the situation. "Gil, listen to me. I'm gonna give you some free advice. When someone says they're gonna meet you at two, be there . . . on time."

"Look, man, I'm sorry. I couldn't get here any earlier."

"Cut the crap. Let's get down to business. I just want to know one thing. Are you the father of Pauline's baby?"

Not knowing what else to say, Gil shrugged. Then he roared back belligerently. "Who in the hell are you? And what's it your business?"

Bathed in anger, Wyatt refused to be badgered. "Don't try and jerk me around. I'm Pauline's brother-in-law and, just for the record, an ex-marine. Let's get one thing straight, asshole. Where I come from, men honor their commitments. You need to stand by Pauline."

"But, but . . . I can't marry her," Gil stammered. "I'm already married . . . with a baby." So disarmed, he started to crack his knuckles, a habit he had been trying to break.

Wyatt's hands balled into fists. He couldn't remember ever being so mad. "This is gonna cost Pauline big bucks. You need to pony up so she can take care of things. Know what I mean?"

Pushed to the limit, Gil blurted out, "Man, I don't have any dough. I'm already paying for some goddamn twins." After he said it, his hand shot up and covered his mouth, regretting the slip-of-the-tongue.

"Twins . . . you got twins with *another* woman?"

Gil's head drooped down and he remained speechless.

"What's with you?" Wyatt asked, his finger poking the lettering on Gil's T-shirt. "You can't keep it zipped?"

Gil averted Pauline's eyes. "Look, I know I screwed up, man. But what you're asking is fuckin' impossible."

"Don't tell me what's fuckin' impossible," Wyatt snarled, flying into a rage. Veins popped out on his forehead. "Just how many lives have you screwed up?" His bad temper mixed with a show of force. He pulled a small caliber pistol from his jacket pocket.

Pauline was stunned. It was way more than she bargained for. "Wyatt, for God's sake, p-p-put that damn gun away," she stuttered. "Stop it! Please. And Gil, if you know what's good for you, you better leave right now."

Not one for backing down, Wyatt continued to threaten Gil. "You know something, you're a loser. Get out of here before I kill you," he yelled, shoving Gil sideways.

Gil recoiled as he slid out of the booth and almost tripped over his own big feet as he fled.

"Wyatt, put that thing away!" a shaken Pauline commanded. "Don't be stupid."

By Monday afternoon, Pauline's father offered a glimmer of hope. He let his daughter know he had the name of a man who performed abortions in San Francisco. "Pet, don't worry. Tomorrow we'll drive down there together and deal with it."

Pauline reverted to her *little girl* ways, relishing the warm, comforting feeling of letting daddy take charge.

As they approached the Bay Bridge, Pauline's self-absorbed attitude was momentarily transfixed by a few driftwood sculptures—a semblance of a primitive Trojan horse, a stylized man that resembled Don Quixote, and an artist's rendition of Noah's ark—all set on the mudflats. In San Francisco, the one-way streets befuddled Joseph, but ultimately they reached their destination.

This notorious neighborhood, known as the Tenderloin, resembled a seedy paradise for the disenfranchised. After circling the block several times and giving his sheltered daughter an eyeful of the truly rejected, Joseph gave up looking for a curbside parking spot. He pulled into the small parking lot on the northeast corner of Eddy and Taylor Streets.

Uncertain what to expect, the pair crossed the busy intersection with the signals. Curious about the surrounding, Pauline eyed a Rexall Drug Store that featured incongruous window displays—a hot water bottle, an assortment of aluminum canes, a canvas port-a-potty, an enema bag, along with Revlon beauty products and perfumes. Five buildings down from Lisa's Delicatessen Joseph spotted the address he was looking for above a wooden door with ornamental grillwork over the inserted glass. He surveyed the list of names on the unpolished brass mailbox in the bleak, recessed entry filled with yellowed throwaway newspapers.

With a sense of purpose, he pressed the buzzer for Mr. Leroy Lewis. Not knowing what to expect, Pauline trembled slightly as she and her father rode the graffiti-filled, wood-paneled elevator up to the third floor. Joseph rang the doorbell at apartment 3C, the third door from the garbage chute. A young, muscular Afro-American woman, a head taller than Joseph, slid the door open. A black plastic comb with a long thin handle protruded from her frizzed out bulb of hair.

"Excuse me. Is this the Lewis' apartment?" he asked.

"Who wants to know?"

"I'm Doctor Schulman. This is Pauline, my daughter. We're from Sacramento." Then Joseph, unsure of himself, began to stumble over his own words. "Well, uh, a colleague told me someone here performs abortions."

"That so?" she shot back.

A powerfully-built black man with dark, blazing eyes came up behind the woman. "Hey, man, why you be here?" Then he commanded the snarling Doberman pinscher alongside him to back off.

Joseph stepped back, intimidated by the menacing dog. "Excuse me. I just was wondering if you're Mr. Lewis?" When there was no answer, Joseph continued. "Look, if you're Mr. Lewis, I've been given your name by a colleague. Doctor Rodino."

"I ain't never heard of no Doctor Rue-dean-o."

This was definitely not the welcome Joseph expected. "Give me a minute to explain. My daughter, well, she's looking for an abortion."

"I don't know nothin' about no abortions. You best be leaving."

Joseph was aghast. "Honey," he said, turning to his daughter who had been standing behind him the whole time, "I think we better go."

The sour smell in the hallway nearly gagged Pauline as she followed her father.

"I'm so sorry, Pet. I don't know what I was thinking. Being a doctor, I should've known better. Let's get out of here. Maybe grab some lunch and think things over."

In Berkeley, Joseph followed the directions on a billboard and headed for Spanger's Fish Grotto on Fourth Street. Neither of them wanted to discuss their surreal experience. When the waiter came, Joseph ordered New England clam chowder and filet of sole with fries. Except for the oyster crackers on the table, Pauline ate nothing.

Afraid to make a scene in the restaurant, Joseph addressed his daughter as gently as he could. "Pet, first and foremost, your mom and me, well, we don't want anything to happen to you. Illegal abortions are way too risky. Look what happened today. Why don't you put the baby up for adoption? And before you respond, I want to make one thing perfectly clear. You're not the first girl to get pregnant, and you won't be the last. I'm going to let you in on a little secret. If I could make it through all those trials and prison, believe me, you can make it through this. Everyone's busy with their own life and their own problems. In the final analysis no one will care but you."

"Yeah, but Mom cares."

"She'll survive. Trust me, she's gone through a lot and she'll make it through this too."

When the check finally came, Pauline excused herself. "Dad, I'll meet you outside."

What's wrong with me? Pauline lamented while she dawdled in the front of the restaurant waiting for her father. *I tried three times to abort. Once with quinine, once at that crazy church, and this morning. Three times. And I'm still pregnant!*

CHAPTER 28

THE HIDEAWAY

PAULINE AND HER FATHER sauntered through the restaurant parking lot. Pauline was tossing around her father's suggestion about adoption silently when she almost got hit by a car starting to back out.

"Watch it!" her father scolded, grabbing her arm. "Pauline, you need to be more careful."

No kidding, she thought with a touch of irony. Until her father broached the subject, Pauline had never considered a real live, crying baby, one that smiled and wet and suckled milk. But something clicked. She remembered the cute little Asian girl playing in the park outside the capitol and the little boy running his car over the floor in the Greyhound Bus Terminal. *But that was different,* she thought. *Those children belonged to someone else.* She didn't know anyone who had a baby, and in truth, didn't know the first thing about them. But suddenly a new stream of thought began to bubble up. *What would it be like to have a baby? Could I bear the labor pains?*

Would it be hard to give my baby up? What then? Would I go through my life wondering? Feeling guilty?

As they drove off, Joseph kept glancing at his daughter, hoping to continue their previous discussion about the baby. "You know Pet, this abortion business is risky. But, on the other hand, if you gave the baby up for adoption, you could get on with your life. Do whatever you want."

"Uh-huh." *Do what I want,* she repeated to herself. *What exactly do I want?*

"You know, giving your baby up for adoption is a *mitzvah*, a good deed. Just think, the baby will get a good home. And you'll make some couple very happy. I know we can somehow work this out." Her father droned on and on as if he were selling hot watches on a street corner.

No matter what he said, Pauline did not respond. She was grateful when he got the message. "Okay. I know you want to think about it. Pet, want me to turn on some nice music?"

Without looking at her father, Pauline simply leaned over and flipped the shiny dial on the radio. She fiddled with the stations until she heard the familiar voice of Don Sherwood, the rebellious disc jockey.

The mindless scenery—rolling hills, sparse clusters of scrub oaks and eucalyptus, and a couple of dairies—provided a brief reprieve, an opportunity for Pauline to dig deep within herself. When they neared the Nut Tree Restaurant in Vacaville, she rolled down her window to let in the warm air, but the pungent smell of onions growing in the fields assaulted her nose.

Leah had just started to mop the linoleum floor in the kitchen when she heard the garage door open. In an effort to economize, the Schulman's were down to one car, having sold Leah's Buick to a neighbor in Shaker Heights before they left. Financially strapped, Leah had been juggling all the cleaning chores others used to do for her. She couldn't rationalize it, but, in a strange way, the physical effort—mopping, ironing, and vacuuming—kept her mind from their trouble-filled life.

"Okay Pet, we're home," her father announced, as he turned off the motor. "Do you have everything?"

"Oh, yeah," Pauline grimaced. "Everything . . . and then some." The ugly experiences of the past few weeks were gnawing at Pauline like hungry termites attacking a piece of rotting wood.

As Pauline and her father entered the kitchen from the garage, Leah slid the cleaning bucket filled with water out of the way with her foot. "So . . . how did it go? I wasn't expecting you 'til later."

"Don't ask." Joseph responded. "It's been one heck of a day. We've got plenty to talk about; just give me a few minutes to unwind. My stomach's acting up. Would you pour me some milk?"

Leah could read between the lines. "Would someone please tell me what's going on? Both of you, sit down and tell me what happened?"

Joseph gulped down half a glass of milk and then began. "Okay. Want the bottom line? It was a disaster. I think the guy we were supposed to meet was a Black Panther."

"A what?"

"A Black Panther. You know, one of those black militants you see on television with the ferocious dogs. Anyway, he brushed us off. Pretended he knew from nothing. Even if he let us in, I had second thoughts. The trip was a waste of time."

"Well, what's Pauline supposed to do now?" Leah asked, nervously rubbing her thumb with her other hand.

"There's still a few options. If Pauline decides to have the baby, there's always adoption. And she can go to a home for unwed mothers 'til the baby is born."

"*Oy vey es mir!*" Leah dragged out the Yiddish words of despair that rose from the depth of her soul.

Pauline grew panicky. "NO. I'm not going anywhere. I want to stay here . . . with you guys."

"Honey, no one's forcing you to go anywhere," her mother said, sickened by the deep circles she just noticed under her daughter's eyes. "Of course you can stay with us."

Joseph tried to calm his daughter. "Pet, remember, no one's going to force you to do anything you don't want to do."

Sensing her daughter's abject misery, Leah suddenly did an about-face. "Maybe we could just raise the baby ourselves."

"Don't be silly. With me still out of work, you know how tight money is."

Leah felt trapped. "Well, maybe we could give the baby to Rose and Max. They don't have any kids."

"There's a reason they don't have a kid. The drugstore's their life. What kind of parents would they make?"

After listening to their ridiculous options, Pauline blurted out, "I want this baby to have a *real* home." No one noticed but this was the very first time Pauline thought exclusively about the baby's well-being and not her own.

Concerned about his daughter's reputation and mental health, Joseph proposed another possibility. "Suppose we rent an out-of-the-way house? Then Pauline doesn't have to see anyone 'til after the baby's born."

"You must be *meshuga*, crazy, out of your mind," Leah exclaimed. "Ellie slips us food money and Rose and Max help with the rent. And you're thinking of moving again. We're not gypsies."

"Just calm down," Joseph said, raising the flat on his hand in the air. "Tell me, who says we have to stay here forever?"

"Joseph, what's with you? For one thing, money doesn't grow on trees. We don't have two nickels to rub together."

That was only too plain. Joseph simply ignored his wife's comment. "There's a new housing development . . . in Citrus Heights. The homes are advertised constantly. I doubt the builder's setting the world on fire. Maybe I could make a deal to rent one. You know, shill for the builder." Almost as an afterthought, Joseph threw out another suggestion. "Maybe the builder would even be willing to absorb the down payment and we could buy one."

Leah scoffed. "You must be dreaming. Besides, we can't just pick up and move again. This would make the third move since we left Cleveland."

"So . . . people move all the time."

"Moving's not cheap."

"I'm sure Wyatt and Ellie would help us out," Joseph said, offering his kind of logic.

"Wyatt and Ellie, Ellie and Wyatt. You can't keep asking your kids for help."

"This out-of-the-way neighborhood would give Pauline some privacy. At least let me try. We've got nothing to lose. Remember, those homes have three bedrooms and *two* baths," Joseph said, extending two fingers. He turned to Pauline, who had been sitting quietly during this give-and-take. "Tell me, wouldn't you like to have your own bathroom, Pet?"

Joseph met with the struggling builder and negotiated a deal to his liking. The Schulman's moved into their new home on the outskirts of Sacramento, far away from Max and Rose and Leah's cousin, Esther. Although the house had a botched up floor plan, its newness boosted their sagging morale—fresh carpets and new appliances—and symbolized another new beginning. Several partially-framed houses had been left unfinished. The development resembled a ghost town—only the builder's married daughter and her husband and three other families lived there. The Schulman's kept to themselves, deliberately avoiding any personal contact.

Joseph took charge. "No booze," he warned Pauline. "That's an order. It's not good for the baby. And no smoking." A stickler for proper nutrition, every morning he faithfully prepared hot cereal for Pauline and insisted that she eat it.

On the advice of a former colleague, he turned to the Catholic Church for help. Not believing in abortion, the church had built a network of homes for unwed mothers. One of the Sisters suggested that Pauline sign-up for the county's free pre-natal care program. Leah accompanied her self-conscious daughter to the overcrowded clinic for all her appointments, praying she would not run in to anyone she knew. Except for her visits to see an obstetrician, Pauline remained shielded from the probing eyes of the outside world.

"For the baby's sake, you've got to get some fresh air and exercise," her father insisted. "You can't mope around the house night and day reading movie magazines and watching television."

Leah and Joseph took Pauline outside for a walk every night, like a thoroughbred that needed to be exercised. In the early part of the fifth month, she started to show noticeably. Her ample breasts filled out even more and she had taken to wearing loose fitting tops and baggy cotton pants. At first, Pauline wasn't sure if the flutter she felt was the baby kicking. But it happened again the next day and the next, and then she knew. Now that her morning sickness had subsided, she focused on her changing body and the life growing inside her.

Is it a boy or girl? Will the baby look like me? Pauline was advised not to pick a name or she might get too attached. But it was only natural that she rolled names around in her head.

Max and Rose were grateful the drugstore had started to eke out a small profit. Though they were on a tight budget, they were helping the Schulman's financially. After another long day standing on her feet, Rose slid her shoes off as soon as they got in the car. "My feet are on fire. If you paid me, I couldn't shop and cook now. What would we do without Esther? She's like a substitute wife."

"You have an odd way of putting it," Max said, stopping for a signal.

"So . . . smarty pants, how would you put it? She does the laundry, the shopping, she cooks. She's the one that takes care of us. She even works in the drugstore when we need her."

Without a job and a car, Esther was dependent on Max and Rose for everything. Although they were still a tight-knit clan, they saw the Schulman's less often than they had in Cleveland. They only got together for prearranged occasions. In the midst of the busy holiday season, Leah phoned and invited them to see their new home and stay for supper the following Sunday.

On the drive out to Citrus Heights, Max grumbled to himself more than to the ladies, "Where in the hell do they live? There's nothing but orchards out here. Are we still in Sacramento?"

When Max, Rose, and Esther finally found the modest house in a nearly deserted subdivision, Leah insisted on giving them a house tour. The entourage feigned enthusiasm for the modern kitchen appliances and bathroom fixtures, but no one had to remind the guests that it was a far cry from the grandeur of the Schulman's former home in Shaker Heights.

The pretense of it all made Esther uneasy so she quickly changed the subject. "Where's my favorite niece?"

"Out," Leah responded tersely, plastering an artificial smile on her face.

"Oh, yeah, she's out with some friends," Joseph interjected, also shaving the truth. In fact, they had made arrangements for Ellie and Wyatt to pick Pauline up earlier in the day and keep her hidden away.

CHAPTER 29

IMPETUOUS REQUEST

ALTHOUGH HER PARENTS had the best of intentions, isolating Pauline only magnified her shame and diminished her self-esteem, foreshadowing future problems.

Leah, familiar with private medicine, was disappointed by the impersonal treatment her daughter received through the County Department of Health. They waited for hours in the tacky reception room teeming with pregnant mothers and screaming babies. The doctor varied with each appointment. Leah wanted her daughter to have a personal doctor, someone who would be sympathetic to her situation.

Frustrated by the bureaucratic system, she complained to Joseph. "Can't you find a private doctor that won't charge us?"

"I'll try, but I don't have a lot of pull around here." When a contact referred him to Dr. Sockolov, Joseph immediately followed up. As a professional courtesy, the obstetrician offered to see Pauline.

On her first visit, Pauline noted a genuine gentleness behind the thick lens of his glasses. Although he practiced in a three-man office, he promised to see her personally throughout her pregnancy. He would listen to the baby's heart beat, give her advice on nutrition, and patiently respond to her concerns. A warm, old-fashioned doctor, he knew just what it took to gain her confidence. On a routine visit, Pauline and her mother were sitting in the waiting room when they bumped into an old neighbor. Leah caught the neighbor giving Pauline's bulging belly the once over. And without so much as a blink of an eye, Leah faced her former neighbor and whispered, "Poor thing. You know her husband was recently killed in Viet Nam."

Too stunned to say anything, Pauline froze, unable to believe her reserved and proper mother would create such a wild tale.

"I can't believe my mother said that," she confided to the doctor.

"She was only trying to protect you. Forgive her. We live in such hypocritical times." During the course of his practice, Dr. Sockolov heard the most bizarre stories spewing from his unmarried patients or their parents. Their lies and subterfuge invariably invoked his sympathy. He understood the women's fright and how these incidents could destroy their shattered egos or worse, their lives.

Joseph worked out a financial arrangement with Mercy Hospital. The Sisters of Mercy believed strongly in the sanctity of life and did everything they could to accommodate unwed mothers. In her ninth month, Pauline was barely able to get around. She spent her time indoors surrendering to life's *what ifs*. Foremost on her list, she wondered if she would have made a good mother.

When Pauline's water broke, the labor pains started gently but gradually increased in intensity. Her white plastic overnight case had been standing by the front door for weeks. After several stressful calls to Dr. Sockolov, Joseph drove his wife and very pregnant daughter to the hospital. Young and inexperienced, Pauline was frightened. Without a husband and the grace of a marriage to soothe away the pain, she prayed the nightmare would be over quickly. With each contraction, she hunkered down and gripped her mother's hand.

Pauline tried to watch the birth through a mirror in the sterile, well-equipped delivery room. For a first delivery, labor went relatively fast. Grinning from ear-to-ear, Dr. Sockolov patted her shoulder gently. "It's a girl. And she's a real cutie," he crowed, as if this was the only baby he ever delivered. "You did great." Working as an efficient team, the delivery room nurses wiped the baby and weighed her—8 pounds, 2 ounces.

Immediately following the delivery Dr. Sockolov notified Pauline's concerned parents that she had given birth to a healthy girl. He purposely refrained from using the common phraseology: *mother and daughter are doing well.*

Pauline had just witnessed the miracle of birth and tears of joy rolled down her cheeks. For the moment, the humiliation of being an unwed mother and the pain of childbirth were forgotten. To the staff's credit, they dealt with her precarious situation with more tact and diplomacy than she would have received beyond the hospital doors. The experienced nurses—aware the baby was going to be put up for adoption—treated her with kindness and sensitivity. To spare her the anguish of being placed in a ward with excited new mothers fawning over their babies, she was quickly rolled from the maternity floor to the surgical wing.

Pauline rested comfortably, grateful for the emotional support her parents had given her. That evening Ellie and Wyatt—the only other family members aware of her pregnancy—came to the hospital to visit. The following morning, after the breakfast tray had been cleared, Sister Catherine, a middle-aged nun wearing a black habit and a dangling wooden cross entered Pauline's private room. "Good morning, young lady. How are you feeling?"

"Okay, I guess."

"And each day you'll feel better and better. May God bless you. Pauline, dear, I apologize for bringing this up now," Sister Catherine said with compassion, "but if you're still interested in putting your baby up for adoption, there are some papers you'll need to sign."

"Uh-huh," Pauline said indecisively.

Being an old hand at this delicate job, Sister Catherine parceled out information judiciously—neither too much nor too little. "Let me make it perfectly clear," she stated, "if and when you sign these documents, the baby will become a ward of the state. She'll be placed in a foster home first. That is, until we arrange for her adoption."

"But will she be put in a *loving* home?" Pauline blurted out, suddenly as protective as a mother lion.

"Absolutely. You needn't worry about that." Sister Catherine said, looking her square in the eyes.

"You know . . . not just the foster home. I mean for good."

"Yes, of course. We work closely with the County Welfare Department. They carefully screen prospective couples." Using her most intimate voice, Sister Catherine continued. "But, dear, I want you to understand. If you decide to go ahead with the adoption, there's no going back. There will be a protective wall separating you and the adoptive parents. They'll never know who you are . . . and you'll never know them."

It was all too much for Pauline. Everything seemed so final. Through it all she had matured. She realized this wasn't some childhood game. And it was no longer about her. It was about *her* baby. "Could I make a request?" she asked meekly.

"Yes, of course," Sister Catherine said, patting Pauline's hand. "We'll try hard to accommodate your wishes."

"Could you place her with a Jewish family?" Despite the fact that Pauline's father had a lifelong ambivalence about religion, in one of their discussions he suggested the baby be permanently placed in a Jewish home. She wasn't sure why, but somehow that idea alleviated part of her guilt.

Sister Catherine paused, "Well, that's an unusual request under the circumstances. No one has ever made that request before. But I'll check into it." She jotted down a few words on her clipboard. "Pauline, if you like, I'll fill out the necessary forms for you. But, of course, you'll have to sign them. Does the baby have a name?"

Pauline nodded her head. Her face resembled the quintessential Greek tragedy mask.

"Would you like to give her a name, dear?"

Once again the room expanded with silence. Secretly Pauline had picked out a name, but was afraid to say it aloud.

"Then I'll just put down Baby Doe."

Before Pauline left the hospital, the final paperwork relinquishing the baby to the state had been completed.

From the day she was released, her feeling of emptiness turned to self-pity. And to alleviate her pain, she began to carouse and hang out in bars. Her anguish turned to anger and she lashed out at everyone. One evening after Pauline took off, Leah discussed her daughter's downward spiral with her husband. "This can't go on. I've got to call Dr. Sockolov. Maybe he can give us some advice."

Over the telephone the obstetrician diagnosed Pauline's dark moods as post-partum depression and prescribed a sedative and an anti-depressant. But Pauline only grew more despondent and her excessive drinking spun out-of-control. Finally, in desperation, her mother called the County Adoption Agency. "Pauline's having a hard time letting go," she explained to the social worker. "I think she needs to see the baby one last time."

"Well, it just so happens she's still in foster care. But I have to tell you, I think it's a real bad idea. The more time she spends with the baby, the harder it's going to be to break away. But we'll go along with whatever you want. After all . . . we're not baby snatchers. If Pauline doesn't want to give the baby up, it isn't too late to change her mind."

Leah talked it over with Joseph. While conflicted, they didn't know what else to do. In the end, Leah accompanied her grieving daughter to the home for a final good-bye.

Vera, the foster mom, opened the door and invited them in. Compelled by the circumstances, Pauline managed to disguise her anxiety.

Vera guided them into the drab, but tidy living room. "Have a seat. I'll go get the little one. I've just bathed and fed her."

Pauline couldn't help herself. "Can I just go back and peek at her?"

"Sure. I can't see any harm in that. You can come along, too," she said, acknowledging Leah.

The three women tippy-toed down the straight hallway towards the tiny, straw-colored bedroom. In a white wicker bassinet, Pauline's two-and- a-half month old daughter lay on her back fast asleep. She looked like a cherub all snuggled up in pink feety pajamas.

Vera rolled up the plastic window shade to allow more light in the room.

"Mom, isn't she precious?"

"Wanna hold her?" Vera asked.

Pauline's eyes brightened. "Oh, can I?" The exchange was made and she cradled her daughter with both arms. "Look. Her eyes are opening."

"Hon, sit here in the rockin' chair. It'll be easier."

Leah restrained herself. She was eager to hold her granddaughter but did not want to deprive Pauline of these last magical moments. *The agency was right,* Leah admitted to herself. *The emotional bond is just growing stronger.*

Pauline inhaled deeply. "She smells so sweet." Then she rubbed her cheek against the baby's soft skin.

Vera chuckled. "That's baby powder you're smelling. I just gave her a good dousing after her bath."

"When's she going to her adopted family?" Pauline asked with more than a touch of sadness. In truth, she wanted and didn't want to know the answer.

"Hell's bells. I was afraid you'd ask that question. Now don't be getting all upset. But when I took her to the doctor, he had some concern about her heart. He told me it's probably nothing, but I heard the couple who was supposed to adopt her backed out. I think the woman is a nurse at the hospital."

"Oh, my God. My poor baby." Hearing about the potential health issue only compounded Pauline's feeling of remorse as she pumped Vera for more information.

But Vera didn't know any more than she had told them. "She's gonna be fine," she said, patting Pauline's shoulder gently.

I'm sick of everyone's reassuring phrases, Pauline thought resentfully. But in the end, all she could do was brush her daughter's forehead with feathery kisses. She closed her eyes as if in prayer. *God knows, my precious one, I'd like to buy you frilly little dresses and dolls and hear you giggle with friends. Maybe even wipe away a tear or two. I'll never stop thinking about you. Never. I'll alway be wondering if you're happy and healthy.*

The final farewell did not leave Pauline with a sense of closure. It simply left her with an overriding sense of guilt and a gigantic hole in her heart.

CHAPTER 30

GIL

IN AN EFFORT TO escape her emotional turmoil, Pauline's heart shriveled up like a houseplant in need of water. Nothing pleased her. To avoid her parents, she slept in every morning. Then she would prop herself up with two pillows, listen to her favorite rock music on the clock-radio, smoke, and thumb through *True Confessions* and other tawdry magazines.

Every day was predictable. Her father would holler in, ""Pet, stop smoking in bed. Come out here. Let me fix you something to eat."

And at least once a day her anxious mother would remind her of the beauty course. "It's already paid for. Don't waste it, Sweetheart. Don't waste this opportunity."

For the most part Pauline ignored them.

In the evenings she stood in the shower until there was no more hot water. Then, in nothing but her underwear, she would wipe the steamy mirror until she could see her reflection. She would backcomb and tease her hair and toy with make-up. After she lost the weight she gained while pregnant, she favored her skin-tight Levis or her low-cut, lavender sheath. Like an owl or raccoon, she preferred the cover of darkness. *New Faces,* a dark, funky bar at the far end of Arden Way, was the center of her universe. One of the regulars usually picked up the tab for her drinks. The rough-and-tumble crowd flirted, drank, and danced to music from a freestanding jukebox in the knotty-pine side room. Robbed of a normal high school experience, Pauline craved nothing more than the party atmosphere and the illusion of total acceptance.

Her parents were convinced that once she returned to beauty school and interacted with her peers, things would normalize. Neither of them realized that when she tried to sleep without drugs or booze, a host of demons goose-stepped across her psyche, taunting her about every slip-up, embarrassment, and blunder she ever made. To appease her parents, Pauline finally re-registered at the beauty school and reluctantly showed up every day.

Almost a year later, Gil, the father of her child, resurfaced.

In his flashy red and white Chevy Impala, he waited like a hungry predator in the parking lot of the rundown shopping center for Pauline to leave the beauty school. To pass the time he listened to the radio, tapping the tips of his fingers on the steering wheel to the jazzy Latin beat. When he spotted her, he took one last peek at himself in the rear-view mirror and ran his tapered fingers through his slicked-back hair.

"Pauline," he shouted, "Wait up." Gil, with a lithe, athletic body, wore clothes gracefully. There he stood, as handsome and full of himself as ever. "Hey, Pauline, I've been waiting for you."

"I can see that," she said with a mixture of curiosity and anger. "Gil, whata'ya want from me?"

"Can we talk?"

"Are you serious?" she said, furling her forehead to mock his sincerity.

Gil was hoping for a bit more encouragement. "Let's go somewhere, you know, just to talk. Come on . . . you know I'm not gonna hurt you."

"Right," she said with more than a trace of bitterness. "Look, Gil, it's been a long day and I'm beat. I want to get home." Her head throbbed and her mouth felt parched from some heavy drinking the night before. That morning one of her instructors had chewed Pauline out about her careless handling of supplies. And, right after lunch, a gray-haired old biddy, who found the world a miserable place, complained that her perm was too curly.

"Come on. Just a cup of coffee or a Coke. By the way, I have to tell you something. I can't take my eyes off you. You look sensational in that pink sweater. Really sexy."

A year ago Pauline would have fallen for his effusive line, but now she could see through his glib talk. "Gil, cut the bullshit, will you."

A contrite expression crossed Gil's face. "I know I've made a few mistakes. I'll go so far as to admit that. But I'm ready to settle down. For real." They had been standing in the aisle in the parking lot and had to step aside as a mother and a brood of rambunctious kids cruised by in a tan Ford Country Squire. "This really isn't a good place to talk. Can we go somewhere private?"

"Not a good idea," Pauline said firmly, noticing his new signet ring and gold watch.

"Come on, lighten up. Let's go to Heidi's. You used to love their lemon meringue pie. It won't kill you to go."

After much cajoling, Pauline caved in. "Well . . . all right. I'll only go if we take separate cars." *I'm never again going to let you lead me around,* she thought to herself.

"Great." Gil grinned, flashing a mouthful of teeth, white as paper against his almond-colored skin. Self-satisfied, he sped ahead, making sure he arrived first. As she passed through the front door, he beckoned her to join him in the next-to-last booth. Too late for lunch and too early for dinner, a few loners sat at the counter nursing mugs of coffee and pie.

As always, Gil, the consummate salesman, controlled the conversation. "Hey, you'll never guess what I did?"

"No, Gil, I can't imagine." Her enthusiasm was underwhelming.

"I enrolled at Sac State."

"Good for you."

Gil wasn't sure if she meant that sarcastically or not so he continued talking. "Taking psych and lit classes."

"I thought you hated school."

"I do, but I hate the draft more. Who wants to go to 'Nam? Since I gotta choice, I might as well hit the books. You know how I love to read."

"Didn't your dad serve in the military? The navy or something? What does he think of your patriotic attitude?"

"He hasn't said much." As usual, Gil dodged the question. "Anyway, the timing works out. I go to class in the morning and sell cars at night."

"Oh, you're my hero."

He ignored her comment and continued. "Bigger commissions and better hours than the jewelry shop." Almost as an afterthought, he got around to asking about her. "By the way, how's beauty school?"

"Crappy. It's not my thing. I don't wanna do hair for the rest of my life."

Not really listening, Gil continued. "You know what? I've really missed you, Pauline. Let's get back together."

"Uh-huh. Just like that. Snap your fingers and I'll come running."

"I'm divorced now. We could get married."

"Big wahoo! Whoop-de-do. Now that the baby's gone and my life is in shambles, you want to get married." Pauline reveled in her anger, poking fun of him every chance she got. "You're unbelievable."

"Shush. Not so loud. You're making a spectacle of yourself. Lower your voice," he commanded, patting her arm lightly. "We can start over. Wipe the slate clean."

"Don't touch me. Move your goddamn hand." Then it happened. Pauline exploded with rage. Somewhere in the depth of her soul, Pauline found a kernel of her own self-worth. Free from his gravitational pull, she finally found her voice and herself.

"GIL, GROW UP. Take a close look in the mirror. You're the father of, let's see, how many children? Never mind. Don't tell me. Let me count: one, two, three, four that I know about. According to a rumor I heard, maybe more. And divorced. Do you ever think about those kids? Look at you. YOU'VE SCREWED UP MY LIFE AND EVERYONE ELSE'S!"

He deflected her anger as if he were Superman repelling a speeding bullet. "To tell you the truth, I can't stop thinking about you. I think I love you."

"It's always about you, Gil. Do you want to know something? You only love yourself. Have you even once asked me about the baby, our baby?"

"Listen to me. I'm doing good now. I'm a different person."

"Yeah . . . and I'm Marilyn Monroe."

After her showdown with Gil, Pauline made up her mind to complete the cosmetology course, not because it thrilled her; it was more about taking control, an attempt to give her life structure and direction. Her Aunt Esther showed up at the beauty school every Friday at noon. She would bring a shopping bag with deviled egg sandwiches on pumpernickel bread, some sweets, and two bottles of Dr. Pepper. Pauline savored those few carefree hours. Actually it was the most wholesome fun she had all week without booze. Following lunch, Pauline would show her aunt the trendy beehive, artichoke, and bouffant hair-dos in the beauty magazines. Esther would pick out a style and Pauline would set her thick hair.

Her Aunt Esther had recently married. While working part-time in the drugstore for Rose and Max, she had met her husband. Nathan, seven years her senior, practiced dentistry in a suite of offices directly over their drugstore. When his wife was diagnosed with cancer, he frequently ran downstairs to pick up her prescriptions. And Esther, always so compassionate, offered him encouraging words and a sympathetic ear. Nathan was a lost soul after his wife died. He despised going home to an empty house. Out of habit, he would show up at the drugstore after working just to schmooze. Their friendship flourished into romance. A year later, he and Esther eloped to Reno, Nevada, where they were married by a justice-of-the peace in a small, non-denominational chapel.

CHAPTER 31

PRESIDENTIAL PARDON

J OSEPH HAD BEEN bombarded by so many humiliations and set-backs that when he finally received a presidential pardon from President Kennedy in 1963, he was delirious with happiness. Even though it arrived nine years after the fact, that single document—that one official piece of paper—virtually expunged his felony record. It meant exoneration and redemption. The siege, the scourge, the hex on his life—that began with his innocent testimony in a bank trial and ended with him serving time in a federal prison—finally ended.

In practical terms, he could reapply for a license to practice medicine, a steady source of income and self-respect. However, the residual effect—the frustration and bitterness, the loss of his good name and successful dermatology practice, and what it did to his family—had eaten away his peace of mind and corroded his health.

Nothing was simple any more. Joseph knew he was in trouble when his family doctor referred him to a neurologist. After a series of expensive tests, it was clear that he not only had the tremor, he had Parkinson's disease.

Despite his deteriorating physical condition, Joseph studied diligently from morning until night and passed the State of California Medical Board exams, an absolute requirement if he planned to practice in California. A proud man, who endured more humiliations than most people could imagine, still saw himself as the breadwinner. He held out hope that he could find a job in research or the field of dermatology, two familiar fields. However, his spirits plummeted as he trudged from one unsuccessful interview to the next. Under constant stress, his mental health also began to slip. At one point, desperate to earn a few dollars, he resorted to a pathetic job selling greeting cards door-to-door.

A mediocre, low-paying job offer materialized as the on-site physician for a private boys' school outside of Carson City, Nevada. As part of his compensation, the school provided a dreary but functional studio apartment on-campus. Joseph returned to Sacramento every other weekend—but his isolation only magnified the family's problems.

Leah adapted to the routine, but Pauline was miserable.

Her father was gone again, reviving the dark memories of his time in prison. Except for her mother, Pauline was the only one home. She felt pressured to be supportive and help out financially. To keep the money flowing in, she worked as a hairdresser fussing over ladies' hair even though her heart was heavy. Under the cover of darkness, Pauline prowled the bars in search of emotional support. At several local bars she hooked up with a fast, raucous crowd that drank and partied to excess. They temporarily filled her time and satisfied her inherent loneliness, but underneath that facade, she was deeply disturbed.

One sleepless night, when the ugly demons clashed in her head, she threw back her blanket and climbed out of bed. She tip-toed down the darkened hallway to the bathroom and closed the door. In a haze that she didn't remember the next day, she opened the medicine chest, removed a razor, and slashed both wrists.

Her pathetic screams for help awakened her mother. When Leah rushed in, she discovered her hysterical daughter on the floor half-leaning against the bathtub. "OH MY GOD! MY GOD!" What have you done to yourself?" she screamed as she instinctively grabbed a pink towel off the rack. "Here. Press this against your wrists. Hard. No. Press harder."

In the emergency room a triage nurse and an orderly attempted to calm Leah. They tried to reassure her that her daughter would be okay. An efficient clerk behind the admitting desk managed to elicit Ellie's telephone number and immediately called to tell her what happened. Twenty minutes later, her daughter Ellie and Wyatt, her son-in-law, dashed through the automatic doors to join Leah's vigil in the waiting room.

Leah's hands shook and her voice trembled. "If only I could have reached Pauline."

Ellie grabbed her mother's hand. "Mom, it's okay. You did everything you could. What happened isn't your fault."

"I thought finishing beauty school and working would straighten her out . . ." Leah's mind froze and she couldn't finish her sentence.

"Ma, Pauline's had problems for years. She needs professional help."

"I know. I just don't know where to begin." Over the intercom they heard a doctor being paged.

"Ellie," Wyatt said, "go peek and see if Pauline's awake?"

When Ellie popped her head into her sister's room, she found her lying on her back, eyes shut, her honey-colored hair splayed across the white pillow. Pauline looked angelic, Ellie thought, until she caught sight of her wrists thickly wrapped with gauze.

Hours later the sedative wore off and Pauline found herself in a private room. Exhausted from the stress, Leah sat in the one straight-backed chair while Ellie and Wyatt stood at the foot of the metal hospital bed making innocuous conversation. It was obvious that no one wanted to bring up the episode of the previous night. A doctor rapped on the open door. With his mop of tousled brown hair and well-tanned, boyish face, he looked like he just returned from sailing. Doctor Sorenson was embroidered in blue above the chest pocket of his starched white lab coat.

"Good afternoon," he said in a cheery voice. Since no one was sure who he was addressing, they just stared. "I'm a staff psychiatrist. Pauline, how are you feeling?"

"Fine," she whispered, embarrassed to be the center of attention.

"Would you mind excusing us? I'd like to speak to Pauline privately."

Wyatt offered his bone weary mother-in-law a hand and practically yanked her out of the chair. "Angel, we'll be back later," Leah commented. "Can we get you anything?"

Even though the doctor was solicitous, Pauline felt uncomfortable. He was an excellent listener, but when he asked her probing questions she clammed up.

"Pauline, there's really no reason to keep you here. You'll be fine. But you need professional help. I'll release you today if you promise you'll make an appointment with a psychologist."

After meeting with Pauline, Dr. Sorensen accompanied Leah to a small, sparsely furnished conference room. Completely distraught, Leah tried to explain the problems leading up to her daughter's attempted suicide. Dr. Sorensen listened carefully, and then summarized the situation. "Pauline has a festering wound in her mind. A lesion that won't heal itself. This event was Pauline's cry for help. I've got to be honest. The sooner she gets professional help, the better off she'll be."

Distraught, Leah wanted to get her daughter some help but threw in a roadblock. "But we're in no position to pay . . ."

To reassure her, the doctor pulled a page from his clipboard and handed it to Leah. "The county provides assistance for troubled patients. The fee is on a sliding scale. You pay what you can. This paper explains it all. And there's a number to call, right here on top."

The following Monday Pauline returned to work—with less conspicuous bandages covering her wrists. When her colleagues asked what happened, she lied. "I went hiking and klutzy me, landed on some barbed wire."

CHAPTER 32

DR. MILLER

D R. MILLER, the psychologist, was in his late sixties. He looked distinguished with his neatly trimmed beard and snowy-white hair that hung over his collar. His bushy eyebrows almost ran together, like two caterpillars crawling across his forehead. Even though Pauline saw him every Thursday, her downhill spiral continued unabated. Fired from one beauty shop, she would simply drift to another, hung-over and miserable.

Dr. Miller and Pauline had another one of their slow-going sessions the week before Thanksgiving. After her usual evasions and excuses, he removed his silver framed glasses, laid them on his desk, and rubbed the bridge of his nose with his fingers. Her lack of insight stymied him. As a psychologist, he realized that nothing would change unless he intervened. "Pauline, I've got to be frank. Have you ever thought of joining AA?"

She turned her face away from him and stared out the window.

"Pauline, do you know what AA stands for?" Before she could respond, he answered his own question. "Alcoholics Anonymous.

It's a successful organization that helps people. It's nothing to be ashamed of."

Acting indignantly, she protested. "But I'm not an alcoholic."

Dr. Miller nodded, more to acknowledge that he heard her, than to agree with her point of view. "Let me be frank. We've had a number of sessions but don't seem to be getting anywhere. Pauline, you're a sweet person," he uttered, showing his softer side. "In many respects, quite remarkable. And, no doubt, you've had a heck of a lot to deal with. Would you say that's a fair assessment?"

She lowered her eyes and shrugged, remembering some of the more unpleasant events.

He had been trained never to chastise his patients, but he rationalized that a non-judgmental review of their behavior was sometimes in their best interest. "If I might, let me ask you a few questions, okay? Are you taking anti-depressants to get through your days?"

Pauline avoided his gaze.

With no response, he pressed on. "Would it be fair to say that at night you've become dependent on alcohol and a few recreational drugs?"

"Yes, but . . ." Pauline's body language told the story as she nervously fingered the locket her father gave her.

"Frankly, Pauline, we're at an impasse. I can only help you when your mind is clear." With that, he opened the bottom drawer and his fingers flipped through the neatly spaced folders until he spotted the file with the green tab. "This little brochure and paper will tell you all about AA. Look it over. Give it some thought."

In the end she simply folded the brochure and the blue mimeographed paper in half and shoved both of them inside her purse without as much as a passing glance.

The holidays were the worst. Pauline made a half-hearted New Year's resolution to try AA, but made one excuse after another not to go. Her life-style was growing more extreme. She had blacked out a few times and there were huge gaps in her memory. After one particularly rowdy night, she did not return home until mid-afternoon the following day. Her mother paced the floor, debating whether to call the police.

When Pauline finally staggered through the door without her shoes, her hysterical mother was both frantic and relieved. "Where've you been? I've been worried sick about you."

"Mom, would you leave me alone." All Pauline wanted to do was sleep off her hang-over. She could not remember which bar she had gone to the night before and with whom she left. After several more blackouts, she vowed she would take Dr. Miller's advice and see for herself what the AA meetings were about. Apparently the fear of blackouts trumped the fear of being labeled an alcoholic.

Just after closing time, Pauline hung back as the last patrons were leaving Patty's Bar. She faced the bartender who had become a close friend. "Mario, do you have a few minutes to talk? I need to ask you something . . . and I want a straight answer."

"Sure, twerp. What's up?" he said, unplugging the neon sign and locking the entrance.

Barely crossing the five foot mark, Pauline's feet dangled from a high bar stool as she explained her dilemma about going to an AA meeting.

"I know a lot of people who joined. Hell, what'd ya have to lose? If you don't like it, you can always quit."

CHAPTER 33

TURNING POINT

AFTER SEVERAL MORE blackouts, Pauline gathered her courage to check out AA. The weather had turned vicious but she felt too enclosed to stay home. A little before seven-thirty she threw on her black turtleneck sweater and a pair of jeans. She searched through the pile of clothes heaped on the floor and found her Levi jacket with all the patches. "Bye, Mom, I'll be back," she announced cryptically.

Pauline hid in the shadows of a large ash tree outside the Presbyterian Church. Lost in her thoughts, she did not hear a woman approach from behind. "Excuse me," the stranger in the heavy parka said. "Are ya'll looking for someone?"

Spooked, Pauline jumped.

"Oops! Sorry if I scared you," the plump woman remarked in a distinctive southern drawl. "You just looked a little lonesome standing out here all by yourself. I don't think I've seen you before. Are ya'll a friend of Bill W's?"

"Huh?"

"What I mean to ask, are you a member of AA?"

"Well, no, but I'm thinking about joining."

"Hey, darlin', see for yourself what the fuss is all about. Oh, by the way, everyone around here just calls me Auntie Dee. My real name's Delores, but it got shortened way back in high school. Say, it's colder an' hell out here. Why don't we go on inside where it's a whole lot warmer?"

In or out. Yes or no. What am I supposed to say? Ultimately Pauline released herself to the inevitable.

The two women descended the poorly lighted stairwell into the social hall. Men and women, young and old, mingled in little cliques, chatting as if they were at a cocktail party. A large aluminum urn of coffee and some pitchers of water rested on a countertop against the far wall. "If alcohol or drugs don't get you, the coffee will," Auntie Dee joked. "Wanna try some? It'll warm your gizzards."

Pauline yearned to make herself as unobtrusive as possible. "Okay," she replied meekly, thinking that was what everyone did.

"What about a doughnut?"

"Uh, no thanks." Her stomach was already turning somersaults.

Auntie Dee scrutinized the tray, picked out an old-fashion glazed doughnut and grabbed a couple of thin paper napkins. "Can't resist 'em. Will power ain't my strong suit. I eat one of them damn things every time I come to a meeting—and I come here five or six times a week. Doughnuts replace booze. Not a bad trade-off. But since I've been dry, I must of gained thirty pounds." She introduced Pauline to a few friends, explaining that she was new to AA. They found two gray folding chairs towards the back of the hall.

"Honey child, let's talk. For starters, why don't you tell me about yourself?"

At exactly eight fifteen a slight, middle-aged man, with thinning hair combed across his shiny pate, stood to quiet the room. His fringed western jacket, bolo tie, and scuffed up tan and black cowboy boots stood out. His welcoming smile was replaced by a quiet intensity.

"Please join hands and join me in the *Serenity Prayer*:
God, grant me the serenity to accept the things I can not change.
The courage to change the things I can,
And the wisdom to know the difference."

Those simple words wrapped around Pauline's emotional pain
like mentholated ointment on an open sore. And, for the moment,
they comforted and soothed her broken spirit.

"Are there any newcomers tonight? If this is your first AA
meeting, don't be afraid to raise your hand."

Auntie Dee nudged Pauline's arm. "Go on, hon. Hold your
hand up."

Out of a crowded social hall—with well over thirty-five people—seven raised their hands, most reluctant to call attention to
themselves. "We welcome you," Milt smiled, glancing around the
room trying to make eye contact. Pauline felt his sincerity. "You're
our life blood and we're here to help."

When the meeting ended, Auntie Dee and Pauline lingered
in the downstairs social hall while volunteers cleaned up. Above
the clamor of the folding chairs being restacked, Auntie Dee
explained that she had been sober for four years, two months,
and seventeen days. "I mean to tell you, I was a wicked woman
before I landed here. Let me give you some free advice. For people like us, there's no such thing as cutting back. Nope. It's all
or nothing." She tried to go into more detail about the program
but recognized the confusion on Pauline's face and recognized
her inner turmoil. "Why don't you give me your phone number,
and I'll give you mine. That way, maybe later, we can talk some
more."

Under Auntie Dee's tutelage, Pauline started attending AA
meetings, fighting hour-by-hour to take control of the demons.
Her withdrawal was painful physically and psychologically. With
the best of intentions, like a nun in an abbey, she would repeat
her vow: *Just for today I will not drink.* But temptations germinated
like weeds after a rainstorm. All too frequently her depression and
unquenchable cravings caused her to fall back.

A little after four o'clock on a Thursday afternoon Leah heard the phone ring. A nurse who assisted Joseph at the private boys' school in Nevada was on the other end of the line. Obviously uncomfortable, and stammering as she identified herself, the nurse explained her reason for calling. "Mrs. Schulman, I don't quite know how to tell you this, but, well, your husband really shouldn't be practicing medicine anymore."

"I beg your pardon, Leah said indignantly. "What an awful thing to say." *This woman, this perfect stranger, had no idea how hard Joseph worked to get back into the medical field.*

"Well . . ." the nurse paused, "for a time I thought your husband was just forgetful. I had to continually remind him of things. But recently I've noticed his confusion. At times he's even disorientated. Frankly I'm concerned for the boys. One day he could make a tragic mistake. After all, these are just young children. I'm so sorry, but I had to tell the headmaster about several incidents. And, as you might imagine, he is extremely concerned. You know the school would face a huge liability problem if he screwed up."

Shortly after he left his position at the private school, Joseph's Parkinson deteriorated and he was also diagnosed with Alzheimer's.

Book Three

NANCY
Danielle's Adoptive Mother

Chapter 34

My Dad's Illness

At the time, Pauline had no way of knowing that I—the adoptive mother of her child, someone whom she had never met—shared similar emotional scars growing up. As vulnerable children, raised by loving parents, we both stood by helplessly as pockets of illness, unexpected, life-changing circumstances, and hard times decimated our families, molded our thoughts, and abruptly altered our way of life.

San Francisco. 1951. Sometimes on Sundays the San Francisco Seals—a minor league team—played a home game. My dad, an ardent baseball fan, and his buddies—along with their kids, me included, could be found in the wooden bleachers that gave everybody splinters unless you rented a cushion. While the men were enthralled with the game, it was the foul balls that held the interest of our gawky gang consisting of a bunch of boys and me.

I loved to hear the bat crack and watch a foul ball sail past the third base line. Then I, along with the rest of the gang, would run helter-skelter as the baseball ricocheted from bench to bench. Once in a while, if I was really lucky, I would leave the stadium clutching one of those treasured baseballs—a trophy more revered than a gold nugget. And when that happened, no one could wipe the proud, self-satisfied smirk off my face.

Sometimes when the baseball games slowed or I inevitably grew whiny, my dad diverted my attention. Refusing to call me Nancy, he would say, "Lala," as in Lala Petunia, "are you hungry?"

Of course I'd shake my head up and down. I always had one eye on the popcorn, cotton candy, and Cracker Jack vendors. During the fall, the same motley gang switched ballparks. Just three miles from our house we headed for Kezar Stadium to watch the San Francisco Forty-Niners play football from the cheap seats behind one of the goal posts.

Basically I learned to love sports just to be near my dad, although I remembered times when I excelled too much. When the boys on the block started knocking on our front door, asking if I could come outside to play baseball or football, my dad grew protective. He feigned disgust with my tomboy antics. "You don't need to be out there playing with the boys," he would admonish half-heartedly. When I would come in all dirty and red in the face, he would invariably kid me. "Well, if it isn't Lucille Sweeney," although I never did discover who she was. Just before my twelfth birthday, my dad made the mistake of asking, "What do you want for your birthday?"

It was an easy decision. "A football," I replied.

Concerned that I had taken my love of sports to an unlady-like level, he fought back. "Girls don't need a football."

I thought I was pulling the wool over his eyes. That year for my brother's 8th birthday, I bought him the football that I wanted.

Though we lived in the Sunset District—a misnomer if ever there was one—it was a rare day to wake up to anything but piercing cold weather, a cocoon of fog or overcast skies. But when it happened, when the sun popped out on a Sunday, my dad would drive my brother and me to Playland-at-the-Beach, a modest, west coast version of Coney Island. Or to a hokey circular corral across from Fleishhacker Zoo to ride sedated Shetland ponies and pretend we were Tom Mix or Hopalong Casssidy.

That's how it was until my father's forty-second year. That's when my happy-go-lucky dad suffered back-to-back heart attacks and my childlike sense of security dissolved like honey in a hot cup of tea. In the 50's, medicine was light-years away from angioplasty or by-pass surgery. Doctors believed patients recovering from heart attacks needed six weeks of complete immobilization in a hospital and another six weeks at home of solid rest to recuperate.

Gravely ill, my father remained at St. Luke's Hospital for six weeks. The impoverished men's ward, with six beds on each side, resembled a setting straight out of *Farewell to Arms*. From the moment you walked in, a pervasive antiseptic smell assaulted your nose. The hospital lacked color. Everything was white: the floor tiles, walls, sheets, nurse's uniforms, patients' faces, right down to the flaking white painted metal bed frames. The sick patients appeared small, silent and still, only separated by white wraparound privacy curtains.

Sadly, this childhood memory has never faded.

I can still see my dad's face under the clear plastic oxygen tent. Less than twenty-four hours after he returned home, my dad suffered another serious heart attack and an ambulance carted him back to the hospital for another six weeks. At twelve years old, I understood the seriousness of his health problems, but was too young to help out.

Never a titan of industry, my father owned an unpretentious, nondescript neighborhood bar on Pine Street. It was a small, marginal business and he had no health insurance. Another six weeks had gone by when his doctors allowed him to return to work. The bartenders that handled things during his recuperation had skimmed off most of the money. I overheard my parents discussing the situation, but I felt powerless to do anything about it. I longed to barge into the bar and tell the men to stop stealing from my dad. In the inglorious end, my dad wound up selling the bar to one of the bartenders. I believe he actually paid for it with the money he swiped from the cash register.

At that point, my father, too sick to switch jobs, worked as a bartender, barely eking out a living. "We may have to borrow money this month to make ends meet," I heard him tell my mom in a hushed voice as they commiserated at the kitchen table about their mounting bills.

Two years later, after the third serious heart attack, my good-natured and gentle dad grew despondent. Sapped of any realistic hope of conquering his failing heart, he could see the Angel of Death slow-dancing on our rooftop. Now instead of a cheerful, teasing father, I would find him brooding at the kitchen table. I could only imagine his bleak thoughts for the future.

During his siege of poor health, I tried to boost his crushed morale. I don't know why I felt it was incumbent upon me to change the tenor of the house, but I assumed that responsibility. Sometimes as I got up from the table after dinner, I would playfully run my fingers over the top of my dad's thick wavy hair, prematurely gray with worry. I tried to joke with him, hoping to rekindle the spirit he once had. "How come I didn't get your wavy hair?" And when a momentary smile crossed his face, I was happy.

"Dad, would you draw me a picture?" I sometimes pleaded, feeling the need to flatter what had become an empty shell. If the mood struck him, my artistic father would sketch a sports figure on a napkin or a piece of paper that I tore from my school binder.

Circumstances made our situation what they were. Proud and honorable people, my mother and father were too honest and unsophisticated to ignore their bills or declare bankruptcy. In order to settle the doctor and hospital bills, they sold their most prized possession, a two-bedroom row house on 27th Avenue. Gone were my carefree tomboy days. Gone were my neighborhood friends. Gone was our warm, cozy home—our family's only security. This modest house, that my mother had just started to decorate, had been her pride and joy. The impact of losing our home ran deep. For years I actually had reoccurring dreams of buying the house back for her.

We moved into a no-frills two-story flat built after World War II, when building supplies were scarce. The flat was squeezed on a short block between five other flats that looked exactly like it. The building, painted flat pink, faced Judah Street, a busy thorough-fare along the N streetcar tracks. Whenever a streetcar rumbled past—and they came every five minutes—the front windows in our living and dining rooms rattled in protest. The front landscape consisted of a hole cut in the sidewalk separating the garage doors from the tunnel entrance. Every few years the optimistic landlord would plant another bush in the three by three foot space. And I would watch the plant slowly wither away from car fumes, the frigid air and lack of water.

I would frequently sit at the kitchen table with my icy toes rubbing the heat register.

"Get your feet off the heater vent," my mother would scold. "You'll get chilblains."

"I don't care what I get. I'm freezing," I would protest, refusing to remove my frozen toes from the only source of warmth. "What are chilblains, anyhow?"

We lived on the first floor with no window coverings except wood slatted blinds, yellowed from cigarette smoke. Our living room carpet and furniture were tattered and grew shabbier by the year. It still causes me pain to admit I was ashamed to invite my more affluent friends to our house. I felt like an imposter, a poseur.

Mrs. Benetto, a heavy-set woman lived in the flat above us. When my brother and I started to get boisterous in the bedroom we shared, our upstairs neighbor, whose bedroom was directly above ours, would pound the handle of a broom or shoe or something on her floor. In her not so subtle way, she would tell us to shut up.

From time to time my mother would tell me, "Dinner's ready. Go wake your father up."

I would tip-toe into their bedroom and whisper gently, "Dad, it's time for dinner." If he didn't stir immediately, I would choke-up, terrified that he had died in his sleep. An unspoken fear hung in the air, as if we were all waiting for the inevitable.

One Saturday after lunch I was sitting on my bed, lost in a library book. I heard my mother holler, "Nancy, come quick!" When I heard her emphatic tone, I suspected something important was happening. "Hold your dad's hand while I call an ambulance." That was heart attack number four.

My dad's face was ashen. Propped up with two pillows, he sat on their bed quiet and very still. With childhood innocence I tried to comfort him. "Dad, you'll be all right." I held his hand as if I alone could give him the gift of life. Silently I pleaded with God: *Please don't let my dad die.*

My father must have been reading my mind. "Don't worry, Petunia, I'll be fine," he said, his lips turning a bluish-purple.

CHAPTER 35

MY MOTHER'S ILLNESS

FROM MY EARLIEST recollections, my high-strung mother suffered from headaches, not just the usual ones that kids give their parents, but debilitating migraines. It would be difficult to figure out what came first—the constant stress or the headaches. But it was a vicious cycle. The migraines defined her life—often immobilizing her for days on end. The pain got so bad that she sometimes landed in the hospital for an intravenous dose of Demerol.

If my brother and I bickered over something, she would scream, "Don't do that. It makes me nervous. It'll give me a headache!" Between my father's heart condition and my mother's migraines, I was forced to bottle up any emotions. No temper tantrums, no outbursts, no questioning of authority, no teenage angst. I did not want to upset them for fear of making either—or both—sick.

Despite adverse conditions, my mother was a self-effacing, generous woman, who could always be counted on to do the right thing. She never asked anything for herself and, most remarkably, never complained about what life had dealt her. She tried hard to be a good parent. Every night she prepared dinner for the family, but never had much of an appetite herself. With money so tight, sometimes I worried that she starved herself so we might eat. A bundle of kinetic energy, she weighed less than one hundred pounds. Coffee, prescription drugs—sleeping pills, tranquilizers, painkillers for the migraines—and cigarettes were her life's blood. She smoked between two and three packs a day, nervously lighting one from another.

I remember one elementary school conference she attended when I was in the fifth grade. Before she got out of the building, she started to light up. "Don't do that," I begged, embarrassed that she couldn't restrain herself until she got outside.

A dirty ashtray filled with cigarette butts sat on the counter near the kitchen nook, the hub of our flat. We were like the odd couple. I had an aversion to cigarettes, smoke, or dirty ashtrays and my mother had an aversion to clutter. Except for the cigarettes and smoking, my mother, God rest her soul, was obsessively clean. In her whole life, she never left a dirty cup or glass in the sink, a bed unmade, or an extraneous newspaper lying around. No report cards with sloppy little magnets hung on our refrigerator. She was compulsively neat and tidy.

"Hang up your jacket," or "Pick up your shoes," were all she demanded from my brother and me.

Once in a while I would ask, "Have you seen that paper I left on the dresser. I can't find it."

I soon grew familiar with her response. "Oh, I didn't know you wanted it. I threw it out when I cleaned your room." What could I say? She was the one cleaning the room, not me.

Even though money was scarce, her largess knew no bounds. Her heart weighed more than she did. Invariably she would open her purse and give money to a street person. One incident stands above the rest. We were in downtown San Francisco, in the pedestrian crossing at Fifth and Market Streets, when a raggedy man walking in the opposite direction stuck his hand out. Right then and there, in the middle of everything, my mother stopped, opened her purse, and gave the bearded beggar a dollar. Always the practical one, I questioned her. "Why are you giving money to a beggar when we need it ourselves?"

I can still hear my mother's philosophical comment: *Because it won't make me any richer or poorer.*

One particularly damp morning, a thick carpet of fog hung in the air. I could hear the fog horns as I was preparing for another day at school. "Where's my coat?" I asked. "It's not here." I knew I had hung it in my half-empty closet just a few days earlier.

"I gave it to a poor family," my mother explained, feeling she had done a *mitzvah*, a good deed, despite the fact that there wasn't another coat waiting for me. One of my mother's more affluent friends had just given me four hand-me-down wool blazers, at the time the *in*-fashion at Lowell High School. "Let someone else use the coat," she said. "You have all those beautiful new jackets to wear." I think my mother kept her pride by playing the role of Robin Hood.

As a teenager, I tried to shield myself from the oppressive layers of tension. I spent countless hours involved with my youth group. I mooched rides to evening meetings and got involved in the leadership program. The organization expanded my horizons exponentially. After dinner, I would spend countless hours on the telephone talking to youth group and high school friends. When there was nothing else to do, I read. I would wrap myself around books, biographies—especially Horatio Alger's type stories—poetry, and quotations. Mostly I was searching for hope and direction. Luckily, I was born with an insatiable curiosity. I posed more questions than Socrates. I raced through books passionately, trying to make sense of an unfair world. One day I happened to pick up a powerful maxim that has always stuck with me:

I cried because I had no shoes, until I met a man without any feet.

It summarized the essence of my situation.

I would have been humiliated if I thought anyone felt sorry for me. Like my mother, I was too self-contained and proud. I preferred to meet my peers on their turf. But a split-personality is damaging. During school hours I was naturally gregarious and fun-loving. But at home, where the tension picked up, I internalized my anxiety and withdrew. I felt boxed in with no way out. Now, as I reflect on my unpredictable moodiness, I'm sure I drove my mother and father crazy. At one point I just clammed up. It got so bad that for months I would only respond with a yes or no answer.

Not knowing what else to do, my mother made an appointment for me to see our family doctor. He gave me permission to talk and listened sympathetically. So, sitting across from his desk, I poured my heart out. I confessed my frustration with my life, my sadness and overwhelming sense of responsibility. It felt good when he simply told me to take care of myself.

Invariably the morning sky was a sad, gloomy gray as I waited for the streetcar on 38th and Judah. *The Examiner*, the San Francisco daily newspaper, ran a series called The *Power of Positive Thinking* by Norman Vincent Peale. Although I have felt guilty ever since, I would steal a five cent newspaper off the open rack and sop up his advice. I was also hooked on *Reader's Digest*, a magazine that ran short stories about people who succeeded against all odds. On reflection, those two series, written in language that I could understand, plus my participation in the youth group, helped stabilize and guide me through my teenage angst.

My mother was inherently a classy lady.

If circumstances had been different, she would have been a perfect match for the Junior League. I had a sparse wardrobe but thanks to her impeccable taste, what clothes I had consisted of classic styles and quality fabrics. Meticulous to a fault, she even ironed my pajamas. Every night she was the one who did the dinner dishes and polished my white buck shoes, while I piddled away hours with other pursuits.

Once in a while, motivated by guilt, I would volunteer. "Can I help you iron?" or "Want me to dry the dishes?" Looking back, my attempts at helpfulness were infrequent and not offered with much enthusiasm. Apparently that didn't matter to her. She would beam if I got on the honor roll or was elected to some position at school or my youth group. For her, being a *good* kid was enough and, in that respect, I tried hard.

With no money, no work skills, and no one to fall back on, I can hardly imagine how frightened my mother was if and when something happened to my father. Because of my parents' precarious financial situation, I grew unusually practical by teenage standards. That strand of common sense, etched into my psyche at an early age, has become an integral part of my being. Like a vein of ore, it has penetrated so deep that even if I wanted to, I could not shake it loose. Early on, I learned to distinguish between the *I need, I want* syndrome and found there was not a whole lot that I needed.

We are all a product of our childhood circumstances and experiences. My early years were forged with equal amounts of love and insecurity. And that was not all bad. Self-reliant to an extreme, I grew circumspect and appreciative of any material things. Except for a Brownie Hawkeye camera and a tennis racquet, I never asked my parents for another thing.

Even then, I felt lucky growing up in San Francisco. In the 40's and 50's San Francisco had a sophisticated panache, elegant ladies shopping downtown in high-heels and gloves, debutante parties, and private men's clubs. *The City*—as true San Franciscans call it—is only seven miles by seven miles. Being so compact, the metropolitan area provided infinite possibilities to its less wealthy denizens, especially the young people. It offered a cornucopia of activities, from the mundane to high culture—from catching pollywogs in Mason jars at the nearby reservoir to free concerts in Sigmund Stern Grove.

In my early years as a city kid, I was easily amused. Our whole block was filled with a motley gang of kids. We played ball, made coasters, put on shows, sold lemonade and swapped comic books and trading cards. My girlfriend and I would often swim at the Y.W.C.A., Crystal Plunge, or Marine's Memorial on Sutter Street. Afterwards, with our hair still dripping and clothes askew, we would stroll down to the Kress Building, the *five and dime* on

Market Street, to buy a chili dog from a vendor on the landing between the basement and main level. Feeling like hotshots, we would wander through Woolworth's perusing all the counter displays. Once in a while we would buy a card of black bobby pins, but most of the time, with no more than ten cents in our pocket, we just fantasized about the merchandise.

Golden Gate Park was my playground. Sometimes a friend and I would traipse through the Japanese Tea Gardens to climb over the arched wooden bridges or stand for hours watching the remote controlled sailboats at Spreckel's Lake. Everything was free, including visits to the de Young Museum, Steinhart Aquarium, and the Museum of Natural History.

As I got older, I burnished my volleyball, ping-pong, and tennis skills at Sunset Playground and took fieldtrips all over the city with the playground director. A complete urbanite, I mastered every variation of the Muni—San Francisco's amazing network of public transportation. For a fifty cent car ticket that I bought at school, I could travel on any streetcar, bus, trolley or cable car for five cents.

My mother, never one to mince words, used to tease me, saying: *I was like horseshit; all over the place.*

At age fifteen-and-a-half I got a work-permit and starting working part-time in the summers and during Christmas breaks. In school I willed myself to get good grades. If I didn't know anything else, I knew times would not always be good. Life had already provided that lesson. Intuitively I knew that getting a college education and having a career to fall back on would be my passport to a decent life.

CHAPTER 36

MEETING RUSSELL

S AN FRANCISCO BAY AREA, 1956. Without cars, teenagers in San Francisco were confined to the city, our invisible boundaries. But at the age of seventeen I met a new friend at a B'nai B'rith Youth Organization convention. And her friendship expanded my horizons. Cynthia lived in Piedmont, across the bay bridge in an upscale suburb of Oakland. From San Francisco to Oakland was a toll-call, charged by the minute. I was too conscious of money to initiate those calls, but she assured me that her father, a dentist, didn't mind footing the bill. When she called, we jabbered about everything and nothing.

"Next Saturday I've got a date with Russell, a real nice guy," she announced during one of our long-winded conversations. "He invited me to a dance. Want to go?" Before I had a chance to respond, she added, "I'll fix you up."

"Sure," I said, always looking for a new adventure.

The following Saturday morning I set out for Cynthia's house in the East Bay. Somehow I made my way over the Bay Bridge to

Oakland, by far a warmer city, and managed to find my way to the right trolley. Alone in my thoughts, I strolled through Piedmont's upscale neighborhood hunting for her house. Of course I noticed the spacious two-story homes separated by large manicured yards. Not for the first time, I made comparisons. It seemed like everyone I knew lived in elegant homes in more imposing neighborhoods, and not one of them had to share a room with their brother. Most of my friends had high-powered fathers—mostly professionals or owners of major businesses. They had money and social status. Thankfully, coming from more modest means, bothered me more than it bothered them. No one seemed to care what my father did or why I never invited them to my house.

Cynthia's girly-girly room was swathed in pink and white. Dotted Swiss curtains matched the canopy draped over her bed. On her private telephone line, we took turns chit-chatting with mutual friends. It wasn't as if telephones were a big issue with me, but I can still remember comparing her white Princess phone to the clunky one that my family shared. If I wanted privacy, I had to drag our old-fashion black telephone into the bedroom, being careful to slip the long, heavily tangled cord under the door. Thankfully my brother watched a lot of television, because I could only talk to my friends while he was in the living room.

As our unstructured afternoon drifted towards evening, Cynthia and I sat cross-legged on the wall-to-wall shag carpet in her bedroom with the door closed. We thumbed through *Seventeen* and a few movie magazines. At random, we picked out tiny 45's scattered helter-skelter around her phonograph. Each song had to be played one at a time. Eventually her mother stuck her head in the room and announced they were off to Trader Vic's, an expensive and trendy Polynesian restaurant of local renown. She gave us permission to eat whatever we wanted. So, in the absence of parental supervision, we finished off a rich chocolate cake, something I never got at home, and milk. Giddy from sugar and life, our thoughts turned toward our dates and the dance. Except for the *Pixie Pink* lipstick that we shared, neither of us wore make-up, although we did rub Vaseline on our eyelashes and used an eyelash curler.

The two boys rang the doorbell punctually at seven-thirty. Cynthia's date was a tall, charismatic guy named Russell. Marcus, my blind date, was shorter, had a buzz cut, a slight build, and poor posture. To get acquainted, we sat in the living room for a few minutes and joked around before heading to a youth group dance at Lake Merritt in Oakland. After the dance, like a scene out of *Happy Days*, we stopped at Edy's, a popular creamery. Halfway through our hot fudge sundaes, I asked no one in particular, "Who's your favorite singer?"

Russell, who was then regional president of the boys' division of our youth group—quite an impressive position in those days—responded first. "Elvis," he said with exuberance, strumming on an imaginary guitar as he sang: *"You ain't nothing but a hound dog . . ."*

Cynthia and I picked up the slack, *". . . and you ain't no friend of mine."*

Our laughter annoyed an older gentleman who was sitting at an adjacent table with his family. In an effort to tone us down, Marcus changed the subject quickly. "So . . . Nancy, where in San Francisco do you live?"

"The Sunset," I explained, not sure people from the East Bay knew the difference.

Russell immediately piped in, "Really. My family owns a restaurant in the Richmond District. Just across the park. The Ranch House. Ever heard of it?"

"I've been there," I replied. "My dad used to take me to Forty-Niner games. After the games there were Ranch House flyers attached to the windshield . . . offering a discount."

"Well, guess who put them there?"

And so it went . . . four wholesome teenagers out on a Saturday night. I had gone out on many dates, even had a few crushes, but there was something about the chemistry that night that clicked. There was only one problem, it wasn't for my date . . . I was infatuated with Russell.

A few weeks later, on a Sunday afternoon, I found myself pleading with my dad for the car.

"What for?" he asked, curious to know where I was going.

"To visit a friend," I replied, mindful never to give out any more information than necessary.

After a bit of cajoling, he handed over the keys to his navy blue '50 Ford with the stick shift. I called my girlfriend Bonnie, and within fifteen minutes I was zipping through Golden Gate Park, thankful to be out of the house for a few hours. I beeped the horn when I pulled in front of her flat on 14th Avenue, just off Lake Street. Within minutes, she ran down the stairs. At my suggestion, since we had no prearranged destination, we cruised by the Ranch House Restaurant just a few blocks away. I wanted to get to know Russell, Cynthia's date, and I didn't want him to forget about me.

To find a parking place in the Richmond district takes more patience than I had. After circling the block four or five times, I grew frustrated and pulled into a red zone, blocking a fire hydrant.

"Bonnie, wait in the car," I said. "I'll just be a minute. I want to see if Russell's working tonight. Warn me if a cop comes by."

"Okay, but hurry. This is a lousy place to park. It can be an expensive ticket," she warned, giving me some practical advice.

Ignoring her admonition, I strutted down the block to the Ranch House Restaurant and swung open the door like some gunslinger in *Rio Bravo*. "Is Russell here?" I asked the bartender standing behind the long, empty bar. How was I to know that he was Russell's uncle?

"He's in back. Want me to get him?" he asked with an amused grin. I sensed that he understood what was going on.

Even though it was daylight, and the restaurant hadn't officially opened, I was uncomfortable. The bar reeked of stale cigarette smoke and whiskey. A multi-colored Wurlitzer jukebox stood alone in a dark corner near the brick fireplace. A popular Frankie Laine song, *I Believe*, played to an empty room.

"Tell him I'll be outside?"

"Who should I say is here?" As our perfunctory exchange took place, he filled the stainless steel containers atop the bar with the green olives, maraschino cherries, and tiny cocktail onions.

"Oh, sorry. Nancy. Tell him it's Nancy."

"I'll check. If he's not busy, I'll send him out." His mischievous brown eyes twinkled.

I skedaddled back to my friend. "He's here. Just leave the car alone for a minute. It'll be okay. I want you to meet him." Not bothering to lock the doors, we hustled back to the restaurant. In our plaid skirts, button-down blouses, bobby socks, and white Spalding shoes, we resembled two wide-eyed groupies waiting backstage for Frank Sinatra.

Within minutes Russell emerged. After I introduced Bonnie, he asked coyly, "So what brings you here?" as if he didn't know why we tracked him down.

I side-stepped his question. "We were just out cruising. I thought we'd drop by to say hello."

"What do you do at the restaurant?" Bonnie asked.

"Clear tables and bring dessert. It's a hofbrau. Sort of like a cafeteria. Everyone helps themselves."

Even though San Francisco is out west, it is not a western town. Russell looked outlandish in his plaid cowboy shirt, carved leather belt with its big silver buckle and bolo tie and I had to tease him. "Hey, partner, where'd ya get those cowboy togs?"

"I have to wear 'em. You know, ranch house . . . cowboy theme."

I couldn't let it rest. I continued to play the part of a smartass. "So, Roy Rogers, where's your horse?"

We bantered and flirted for a few more minutes, oblivious of the people getting on and off the buses and the cars swooshing down Geary Boulevard. When Russell claimed he needed to get back to work, Bonnie and I scurried back to the Ford and cruised over to Mel's Drive-In, a popular teenage haunt. We ordered fries and cherry Cokes and giggled about our flirtatious foray.

CHAPTER 37

DATING

F LIRTING WAS NOT ENOUGH; I wanted a date with Russell. As luck would have it, our youth group was having a once-a-year Sadie Hawkin's dance, a girl-ask-boy affair. For the most part I was shy and reserved around boys. Afraid of rejection, I devised a fail-safe scheme. I sent Russell a telegram that read: SADIE HAWKINS DANCE COMING SOON. WILL YOU GO WITH ME?

Within four hours I got back a telegram accepting the invitation. It was a pivotal moment in my life. It turned out that Russell and I both adored similar things and basically responded to the world in the same simplistic manner. Our backgrounds were in perfect sync, right down to being delivered by the same obstetrician in the same hospital just three months apart. Russell, a precocious child, had skipped an entire year in school. So, at the time we started dating, I was a junior and he was a high school senior.

Russell and his family now lived in Richmond, California, a small town just across the bay. But in the early years, they had also lived in San Francisco. In the 40's and 50's the city had a tightly-knit Jewish community and our parents—even our grandparents—were acquainted. The ironic part is that as infants in baby buggies, we were both sunned by our grandmothers in the same schoolyard on Golden Gate Avenue.

Russell's parents, now far more affluent than mine, never complained about paying his long-distance telephone bills. A teenager with a car was a rarity. Russell owned a turquoise '54 Mercury coupe, enjoyed free reign of a Standard Oil credit card, and, from my point of view, had an endless supply of money. In addition to parties and dances, we explored the nooks and crannies of Marin County, the East Bay and the jagged Pacific Coast as far away as Carmel and Monterey. Puffed up on the joy of living, we were like two little bluebirds tweeting our way through each day. Russell led the way and, love-struck, I followed.

It was as if someone had removed my chains. For the first time, I felt light-hearted and carefree. There was an inexorable sweetness to our time together. I loved getting out of the city—away from the streetcar tracks and the cold weather. We generally topped off our dates in the Marina district at O' Solo Mio's, an intimate Italian restaurant with red and white checkered tablecloths and Chianti bottles with melted wax candles. We would order Cokes, our favorite drink, and share a mushroom and pepperoni pizza and play records— Fats Domino, The Everly Brothers, Little Richard, and Enrico Caruso, five for a quarter—on the small jukebox attached to the wall at each wooden booth.

Right after World War II, Russell's dad grew wealthy buying land in outlying areas and building tracts of homes, primarily for G.I.'s. For a time he had the Midas touch. As a side business, he started the Ranch House and magnanimously employed his extended family. But as we dated, Russell's father's financial situation imploded. His father's uncontrollable gambling habit, rogue behavior, and a sudden shift in the housing market left him broke. Like my family, they too were forced to scale back their lives and sell their cozy little home. They returned to San

Francisco and moved into an even more modest apartment than my parents had.

Russell attended my junior and senior proms and I, his senior prom. Even though we graduated from different high schools, we were both accepted at the University of California at Berkeley. For a short time, we went to the same university. We even managed to schedule a few classes together. With his potential, I begged Russell not to drop out of college. But after his freshman year, much to my regret, he left the university to help his struggling parents.

Impetuous and eager to move on with our lives, Russell and I got married when we were only twenty years old. He actually needed a note from his parents before we could obtain a marriage license. Eager to get ahead, he held down three jobs: sold real estate, worked as a desk clerk at his uncle's hotel, and on weekends worked at the Ranch House, now owned by another uncle. I continued with my education, more determined than ever to graduate and obtain my teaching credential. As newlyweds we lived in San Francisco in a one bedroom apartment on the second floor of a relatively modern four-plex on 14th Avenue in the Sunset District.

I was always fearful that my father would not live long enough to walk me down the aisle, but fortunately he did. Death finally caught up to him two years later. It was an exceptionally warm night for San Francisco and my parents had just driven home from visiting his cousin in Westlake. My mother and father were conversing in the kitchen when he keeled over. My mother never did overcome the shock of seeing his limp body fall off the chair or hearing the clunk it made as it hit the linoleum floor.

During our first year of marriage, I had a miscarriage in my sixth month. And from then on, I had trouble conceiving. The longer I went without getting pregnant, the more anxious I became. I darted from one specialist to another and endured test after test and all the humiliating procedures that went along with it. My identity—or lack of it—became inextricably bound in my desire for a baby. All I longed for was a toddler to hold my hand and call me *mommy*.

We were barely past the honeymoon stage when Russell and his parents—backed by a wealthy uncle—bought a large restaurant in Modesto, a farm community with a population of 44,000 people. It was tough to leave behind my widowed mother and everything familiar and head for the unknown ninety miles away. However, Russell and I were full of adventure and searching for opportunities to make our way in life. Russell's father, like my father, had serious heart problems. So the burden of making the restaurant a success landed on Russell, just twenty-one years old, energetic, ambitious, but completely inexperienced. He put his heart and soul into it while I finished the units I needed to graduate at Stanislaus State College, known then as Turkey Tech since they met at the fairgrounds.

Two years passed quickly. One Sunday night, Pete Seegar, a popular folk singer that embraced the civil rights movement, landed in Modesto for a fund-raiser. Russell and I headed to the concert in a high school auditorium. Real life tragedies left me stoic, but I always was a pushover for social justice. I have always wanted to remake the world. Give people a chance. At the conclusion of the concert, everyone joined hands and sang *We Shall Overcome*, the anthem of the civil rights movement. Overcome with sentiment, tears streamed down my face. Along with a huge mob of invited guests, we gathered afterwards at a private home for a wine and cheese reception and the opportunity to rub elbows with Pete Seeger.

That night driving home Russell and I rehashed the evening. Eventually the conversation drifted to our plans for the following week. Without enthusiasm, I remarked, "I think I've got another doctor's appointment." With a single glass of white wine under my belt and a barrelful of raw emotion, I was finally able to express my true feelings. "God, Russ, I just can't go through another round of tests. I'm sick of the charts, the thermometers and driving up to

U.C. Hospital. If I can't get pregnant, let's adopt." *There . . . it was out. What I had been mulling over for the past six months.*

Without hesitation, Russell responded. "I've got no problem with adopting. Kids are kids."

Since Russell and I openly broached the subject, I felt empowered to call our friend and personal physician's office. Knowing that they had just adopted a baby boy, I schedule an appointment to discuss the ramifications of adopting. Three days later his receptionist led me in to his sparsely furnished office. I couldn't help noticing one shelf devoted to framed photos of his son.

Lukas, a tall, broad-shouldered Swede with piercing blue eyes and a starched white lab coat sauntered in and sat down a few minutes later. "What's up?" he asked.

From the looks of his crowded waiting room, I assumed he didn't have time to chit-chat. So I got right to the point. "Well, you did it, Lukas. You and Karina finally convinced us to adopt."

"Good for you," he said, breaking into a genuine jack-o-lantern smile.

"But I don't know the process. Exactly how do you get the ball rolling. What'd we do?"

"Well . . . there's a couple of ways to go. You can adopt a baby directly through a professional, like a doctor or lawyer. Or . . ." and he paused, "you can go through the County Welfare Department, like we did."

"What's the difference?"

"If you go through a doctor or lawyer, the *biological* parents will know who adopted their baby. And if they wanted to, somewhere down the road, they could track you down."

For once I knew what I wanted. "I can't imagine anything worse than someone popping into our lives."

"Yeah, it's risky. But it's different if you go through the County Welfare Department. The *biological* parents turn the baby over to the state. Only after they sign a waiver relinquishing their parental rights, the state turns the baby over to you. Essentially the state is the go-between. They protect both sides."

There was something weird, too clinical, about using the word *biological parents*. To me it seemed more natural to use the word *real parents*. But I was forced to make that distinction. "But what about the baby's birth certificate? Won't the *biological* parents' names be on it?"

"No. The state will issue you a completely new birth certificate. You guys would be listed as the mother and father. You'll never know the biological parents and they won't know you. Why don't you call the County Welfare Department? See what they have to say. They're great to work with."

Still afraid to take that first step, I invited Jackie, one of my closest friends, over for coffee the following Saturday. Russell was at the restaurant preparing for a wedding reception. I needed my friend's feedback. We sat in the dining area at the end of the long galley kitchen nibbling on her home-baked banana-nut bread. When I told her what we planned to do, she began drilling me. She tried to couch her concern in politesse, but the word *welfare* nagged at her. "Why are you going through the Welfare Department? You won't know a thing about the birth-mother or birth-father."

When I explained the risks of going through a private adoption, she quizzed me. "Isn't going through the Welfare Department just as risky?"

"Even if you have your own baby," I said defensively, "there are *what ifs*."

CHAPTER 38

ICE LADY

S EVERAL WEEKS AFTER my fact-finding appointment with our doctor friend, I feigned sleep as Russell bent down and kissed me good-bye. In order to get ahead of the breakfast rush, he invariably left for work at the crack of dawn. When I heard the garage door slam shut, I shoved the blankets back and slipped out of bed. I had a secret mission. Just after the seven o'clock news began, I dialed the secretary at the junior high school where I was teaching art.

"I've got the flu," I fibbed. "I can't come in today. I'll need a sub." A sense of relief overshadowed the guilt I felt for telling a little white lie. I didn't want to tell anyone—not even Russell—what I had in mind. I wasn't sure I had the nerve to go through with my plan.

While I showered, hot beads of water bombarded my body, and I fantasized about the possibilities of becoming a mother. *What would the baby be like? Would the baby be smart? Cute? What would we name him . . . or her?*

If everything went as planned, it was going to be a memorable day. I threw two pieces of raisin bread into the toaster, took out the butter, and filled my blue and white striped mug with fresh, steaming hot coffee. I retrieved the newspaper from the porch and scanned it section by section. Although my eyes focused on the printed words, random thoughts tumbled around like marbles in my head. Constantly glancing at the clock on the wall, I nursed one mug of coffee after another, trying to bide my time until nine-thirty. By my calculations, the key players would be at work, but not yet on a coffee or lunch break. Although I was not particularly superstitious, if anything extraordinary happened, if I stubbed my toe or accidentally broke a glass, I would have taken it as an omen *not* to call.

The telephone number for the Child Welfare Department felt electrifying in my hand. Ever since I was a young girl, I had memorized inspiring quotations, creating my own guidebook to life. *The journey of a thousand miles begins with a single step.* As I dialed the number, bubbles of fear welled up in my stomach like a carbonated soda.

An anonymous female voice answered the phone. "Child Welfare. May I help you?"

Here goes. "I would, that is . . . uh, my husband and I would like to make an appointment to talk to someone about adopting a baby." *There, it was out, and there was no turning back.*

"Your name?"

"Nancy. Nancy Zimmer."

"Mrs. Zimmer. It is *Mrs.* Zimmer, I assume."

"Uh-huh," I mumbled nervously.

"Well, before you go any further, you and your husband need to come in. Fill out some paperwork."

To the voice on the other end of the line it was another routine call; to me, my life hung in the balance. Normally I had an aversion, perhaps even a fear, of bureaucracies and their intimidating forms. This time, seeing no way to circumvent it, I listened obediently. I settled on a date and time to fill out the forms, figuring that one way or another, we would be there.

After I hung up the phone I felt self-satisfied, as if I had sailed solo across the Pacific. With no time for reflection, I dialed Russell at work, eager to share my news.

As I started to talk, Russell interrupted. "Is everything okay?" He had assumed I would be at school.

"Couldn't be better," I said with a lilt in my voice. "I stayed home 'cause I wanted to call the Child Welfare Department. You know, about adopting a baby. And I couldn't really do that from school.

"Really? You called them. Who'd you talk to?"

"Just some lady who answered the phone. The receptionist, I guess. She told me the first thing we have to do is come in and fill out some papers. That's why I'm calling. I made an appointment for next Tuesday."

"OKAY! I'll check the calendar, but it sounds great. I really want to hear all the details, but I can't talk now. We're getting ready for two lunch banquets. One of the waitresses didn't show and we're already behind."

"Fine," I said, feeling brushed off.

The following Tuesday Russell and I drove to the Stanislaus County Welfare Building, nestled just around a curve on Scenic Drive. As luck would have it, it was a breeze to park the car. *That's another good omen.* I smiled inwardly. *I must be getting superstitious.* Within the red brick building, the Child Welfare Department offices resembled a montage of gray and black, duplicating the monotony of the Department of Motor Vehicles and the post office. Florescent lights threw out a cold, impersonal light. As we faced the receptionist, social workers were tucked away behind a maze of impersonal metal cubicles on the left.

"Good morning. I'm Russell Zimmer," my husband said, an earnestness spreading across his face. "This is my wife Nancy. We have an appointment to fill out some paper work."

"I'll be right with you," the receptionist mumbled, barely lifting her head, as she continued typing. We froze, not sure what to do next. A minute passed before she pointed to an alcove. "Just take a seat over there. I'll call you."

Chrome-framed, black leather chairs were strung together in a U-shape in an alcove. Above one set of chairs was a large bulletin board with two simplistic posters, one of puppies in a basket and one of a kitten with a red ball of yarn. On both sides of the corkboard were pastel-colored flyers listing classes in childcare. I hunted for something to read but there wasn't a single magazine or newspaper lying around. So I stood there absent-mindedly reading the outdated notices.

"These ought to be taken down," I commented, unsure why they disturbed my sensibilities. But since I taught art, the job of updating the junior high hall bulletin boards was mine. I was in high-gear for new and original ideas.

"It's not important," Russell scoffed, giving me an impatient look. "Why don't you just sit down. Relax."

"I'm just a little fidgety," I admitted. "You know . . . when I get nervous I talk a lot."

Russell didn't bother to answer.

I took a seat kitty-corner from him. Fortunately, we were the only people waiting. *This place is inhospitable. It lacks warmth, color, a sense of coziness.* I distracted myself by attacking the problem. *It could really use some fresh green plants, maybe a spiffy area rug, for sure softer lighting . . . even some original children's art.*

We both shifted from side to side, crossing and uncrossing our legs, trying to disguise our restlessness. From where I was sitting, it didn't look like the receptionist was working with anyone else, although the phone rang several times. "What's holding us up?" I whispered.

"Would you just calm down."

"What do you think I'm doing?" Knowing my peevish attitude towards bureaucracies, before we parked the car Russell had warned me to refrain from making any smartass remarks.

When the receptionist called our name, we rose to meet her as if we had been summoned to the Pearly Gates. "Now then, how can I help you?" she asked, finally offering an artificial smile.

After all that, I felt shy, almost at a loss for words. Russell handled it. "We're interested in adopting a baby."

"I called last week and made an appointment to fill out some paperwork," I added, trying to act very business-like.

"Ah, yes," she said, as if she recalled the whole conversation. "You probably talked to me. You'll need to complete this packet of forms. You can fill them out over there," she said, indicating a gray metal table and two folding chairs in the corner of the room.

Why didn't she just hand us the papers when we came in? I tried hard not to show my exasperation.

On top of the table someone had thoughtfully placed a telephone book, helpful in looking up local telephone numbers and addresses. A master of efficiency, Russell quickly divvied up the job. "I'll hunt the numbers and addresses. You can fill out the forms. Your teacher handwriting is more legible than mine."

A little nerdy but always prepared, Russell invariably carried a clean white handkerchief and a pen in his pocket. He forked over his ballpoint pen and I diligently attacked the forms. Box after box asked for basic information: city of birth, education, employment history, name and address of present employers, religion, hobbies, personal recommendations. We had no idea how crucial that information would be. Eventually we returned the completed forms to the receptionist, who reviewed them to make sure we hadn't left anything out.

There it was, our lives summarized on a few sheets of paper. Now we were reduced to nothing more than government abstractions.

"A social worker needs to verify all this information," she explained. "Someone will call you sometime soon."

Just how long is sometime soon? With nothing left to say, we practically genuflected as we said our good-byes. We headed home, our confidence shaken, reliving everything that transpired.

"I think it went pretty well," Russell said. "At least we filled out every slot on every form."

"I don't know," I said shaking my head. "That receptionist went out of her way to be noncommittal."

"Don't worry. She doesn't make the decisions. She's just doing her job. Probably sees hundreds of people like us every day."

Ultimately we convinced ourselves that it would all work out. "Hey, look on the bright side," Russell said. "We finished the first hurdle without any mishaps."

"Don't tell anyone where we went today. I don't want them to jinx us," I said, totally insecure about the whole process.

CHAPTER 39

THE INTERVIEW

FOUR MONTHS ZIPPED by since Russell and I had completed the adoption forms at the Child Welfare offices. Even though we were preoccupied with our busy work schedules, we feared our application was unacceptable or, worse yet, buried in a stack on someone's desk, all but forgotten. Out of enlightened self-interest when I attended college, I developed a pit bull mentality dealing with bureaucratic procedures. Russell called it *nagging*, but I preferred to call it *persistence*. I debated whether I should contact the adoption agency or let the process unfold at its own pace. Not able to withstand the pressure, I convinced myself a little nudge couldn't hurt. So I called the adoption agency from a telephone booth at a Standard gas station on a lunch break.

I prayed Ice Lady wasn't on the other end of the line. "This is Nancy Zimmer. Umm . . . well, my husband and I came in awhile back and filled out some adoption papers." In the sweetest voice I could project, I asked, "I'm wondering how the process is coming along?" I tried my hardest to keep the inquiry from sounding aggressive or hostile.

"Mrs. Zimmer," the receptionist said with an edge, "our office is verifying your application. Someone will be contacting you *soon*." Her indifference cut me off at the knees.

Soon. What's soon? There she goes again. I swallowed hard. "Thanks for your time," I said, trying not to sound sarcastic.

The slow pace of the adoption process haunted me. Like a bicycle chain—it rotated through my mind in the middle of reading a book, while teaching a lesson, eating breakfast, or in a movie. I could not get away from it. *Why aren't they calling; did they forget about us? Did we give the right answers?*

Months passed before a designated social worker contacted us. And when she finally did call, I was caught off-guard. "Is this Mrs. Zimmer?"

"Yes," I said, wondering who was calling.

"This is Mrs. McMurry."

"Who?" The name sounded garbled.

"I'm a social worker at the County Welfare Department. I understand you are interested in adopting a baby."

When I realized this was the connection I had been waiting for, I practically shouted, "YES."

"I've got your application right here on my desk. I've had an opportunity to check out the information," she said cautiously. "Everything seems in order. Would you and your husband like to come in for an interview?"

Hallelujah! Joy seeped into my bones like rainwater into the porous sand. Who was she kidding? Of course we wanted to meet with her. "Sure. Tell me when and we'll be there."

"How does eleven o'clock next Thursday sound?"

"Wonderful," I said, searching for a pencil to jot it all down. If we had to crawl on our hands and knees, we would somehow manage to get there.

The second I hung up, I dialed Russell at the restaurant. "Guess what? I've got fabulous news. The social worker called." Then I repeated everything Mrs. McMurry told me . . . word for word.

At six-thirty in the morning on the day of the interview, I called the secretary at school, feigning yet another reason she needed to call in a sub. At twenty-three, I was the youngest teacher on the staff. And with my multitude of excuses for not showing up at work, I feared I'd be labeled a hypochondriac. I loved my job, but felt I had no other choice but to fib again.

Relieved of my usual morning rush, I tried to read the paper while sipping a mug of steaming coffee. But butterflies accumulated in the pit of my stomach. I worried about everything. I wanted to make a good impression, to project ourselves as the perfect couple. As I waited for Russell to return home, I began talking to myself. *Sit down, read a book, turn on the radio, do something.* But I could do nothing but think about our impending meeting with the social worker and run to the bathroom.

At nine-thirty Russell pulled up and hurried inside. "I've got to change. There's sweat marks on my shirt." Before I could say a word, he headed for the bedroom and grabbed a starched white shirt and black shoes that he had shined the previous night. He fussed with the knot on his knitted maroon Ernst tie. "How does this look?"

I gave him two thumbs up. "Want something to eat before we go?"

"No. I already ate. Are you okay?"

"Yeah. Fine. How was your morning?" I was trying to avoid thinking about the interview. "What's happening with the theater? Is it still closed?"

The local district attorney and his views on censorship had become a contentious issue in our small farm town. The previous week he closed down the movie *Not Tonight, Henry,* located in the theater adjacent to the restaurant. A number of irate townspeople thought he overstepped his bounds. All week the debate had been front page news in the *Modesto Bee.*

Eventually we focused on the interview and tried to anticipate the questions. Russell glanced at his watch. "We better get going."

Once we pulled away from the house I continued jabbering; actually it was more like a stream of consciousness than a conversation.

Russell pulled into the parking lot behind the Stanislaus County Welfare Department building. "Well, here goes," I said, taking in a deep breath. "I wonder what the social worker's like?" I realized that a perfect stranger, someone we had never met, was going to decide if we were qualified to be parents.

"Well, you know, she'll ask a bunch of questions." Russell's clipped manner of speech indicated he wasn't as relaxed as he wanted me to believe.

My high heels created a clacking noise every time they hit the pavement. For a person only comfortable going barefoot, walking in heels presented a challenge. By the time we reached the Child Welfare Office, I felt overwhelmed. *I'm glad we didn't tell anyone. Suddenly the adoption process seemed risky. Suppose she doesn't approve of us. Then what? My life hung in the balance.*

We collided head-on with the same unfriendly receptionist we met on our first visit. Russell took the initiative, reintroducing himself. "Good morning," he said, in a bouncy and cheerful voice. "I'm Russell Zimmer. Mrs. McMurry is expecting us at eleven." I preferred to stay out of the receptionist's way. This time, however, the sterile office appeared less ominous.

I tried to make eye contact when Ice Lady graced us with a thin-lipped smile while sorting a stack of file folders on her desk. "Yes, she's expecting you, but you're early." It sounded as if she was chastising us. We retraced our steps to the now familiar alcove.

A scruffy looking woman in her late thirties arrived five minutes later. Dark roots showed from her bleached blond hair. Shifting from one foot to the other, she too stood waiting to get the attention of the receptionist. *Where is her husband? Is she trying to adopt a baby? Does she want to give up a baby? What is she here for?* When the receptionist finally acknowledged her, my ears perked up trying to overhear her conversation.

Shortly thereafter, a middle-aged woman in a stylish navy dress with big white buttons left her cubicle and headed straight for us. "I'm Mrs. McMurry," she said with an endearing smile. "You must be Russell and Nancy. After talking to you on the phone, it's nice to meet you in person. I think I'm ready for you. Let's head back to my cubby. It's more private back there." Her desk had been cleared except for a manila folder with a neatly typed label marked Mr. and Mrs. Russell Zimmer.

As soon as we sat down, I noticed that she had several pictures of little children tacked to her wall. I couldn't help wondering who they were. *Were these children she had placed or did they need a home? Perhaps they were her own.*

"I'm sure you'll be pleased to know that everything checked out." My spirits soared. But just as we got down to the nitty-gritty, a co-worker from the next cubicle barged in to ask her a question. In a diplomatic way Mrs. McMurry explained that she was busy and asked if the situation could wait. I wanted her undivided attention and appreciated her tact in handling her co-worker.

"Now then," she said, "it strikes me that at twenty-three, the two of you are unusually grounded and mature."

I had always assumed everyone of our generation had similar dreams and aspirations, the same sense of urgency that we did to get on with their lives.

"Tell me, do you have any preference, boy or girl?"

Oh my God, I would love either one.

Russell jumped in. "We'd be happy with either."

Choosing the sex was never a consideration. *After all,* I reasoned, *if I were pregnant, I'd have no choice. Why should adoption be any different? With my puritanical beliefs, I felt that would somehow be cheating.*

"It strikes me that the two of you aren't afraid of responsibility. I understand you recently bought a home."

"Yes," Russell responded with unabashed pride. "We've got plenty of room for a baby."

I rattled on like an overzealous salesperson pitching a hesitant customer. "Our house has a great backyard with two fully grown almond trees. Lots more space than our old apartment. We even have a washer and dryer."

"That's wonderful," Mrs. McMurry said, subtly cutting me off. "Let me ask you, are you prepared to raise someone else's baby?"

"Uh-huh," I responded, in the careless slang I learned growing up in San Francisco. I corrected my sloppy presentation and answered with a more formal "Yes, absolutely." Then I gave a short dissertation, feeling as if I was on solid ground. "As you know, I teach school. I've taken lots of child development classes, learned lots about heredity and environment." And for good measure, I threw in my closing argument. "A child needs a good environment, and, fortunately, we can provide that."

Mrs. McMurry let it go. I could sense her sizing us up. Without being pedantic, she asked a string of questions about our educational background and our careers. In a non-committal manner, she remarked, "We don't have a baby for you at the present time, but I'll notify you just as soon as one becomes available that fits your profile."

Well, is that a yes? Did we pass her test? What does she think of us? It's sounding positive.

Then she rose, signaling the meeting was over. Russell and I were surprised that the interview ended so abruptly, but hesitated to ask further questions. Trying not to appear obsequious, we thanked Mrs. McMurry for her time and left.

What is our profile? I wondered. Suppose the adoption agency tried to match a baby to our physical appearance. Russell and I were physical opposites. His eyes were brown, mine blue. My hair was pencil straight and his wavy. He stood over six feet and I cleared the mark at five foot, three. I adored active sports and he never bounced a ball in his life. He was a perfectionist and workaholic and I was the laid-back, creative type.

The die was cast. The wheels of adoption began to roll. I needed to break the news to our families and closest friends. However, I did not tell anyone at school. Nothing happened for three more months. Fearful that they had forgotten us, I avoided the subject, trying to keep it low-key. But beneath the surface, I existed in a constant state of anticipation waiting for the fateful phone call.

Russell and I shared one car. So normally I hitched a ride with another teacher. But occasionally I would drop him off at the restaurant early in the morning, have breakfast there, and continue on to my school. One day during my lunch break, the impulse to shake things up at the adoption agency overwhelmed me. Never short on *chutzpah*, I called to inquire where we stood. The ultimate goal of my little ploy was to prod Mrs. McMurry, our social worker, into thinking of us as real people, not just an abstract application sitting idly in a *to do* basket.

CHAPTER 40

IT'S A GIRL

EVERYTHING WAS GOING pretty well for me at school except for wrecking a kiln—no small feat—and going way over budget on supplies for the faux stained glass windows for the Christmas pageant. My classroom, in reality an art studio with twenty-five to thirty kids five periods a day, resembled an anarchists' anthill. The overly enthusiastic students came at me from all directions demanding scissors, glue, paints, paper, and brushes. With less than two weeks to go until summer vacation, they needed to finish up their group projects: papier-mâché masks and free-standing robots. Large half-painted and drying sculptures were scattered on every available surface. A more experienced teacher would have known not to start multi-staged projects so close to the end of the school year. I had to admit, I was looking forward to cleaning the studio and then enjoying a carefree vacation. I had worked every summer and Christmas vacation during high school and held a part-time job while attending college. This would be my first extended, *do–nothing* break, and it was dangling out there like a carrot on a stick.

Supplies needed to be inventoried and reordered. The studio was thrashed. All the sticky counters and shelves needed at least two heavy-duty scrubbings, if not more. My plan was to enlist the students to clean-up and reorganize the room the last week of class.

One afternoon, wiped out as usual, I returned home desperately needing a nap. The telephone rang and I recognized the distinctive, professional voice of Mrs. McMurry, our social worker.

"How have you been?" she inquired.

"Fine. You know . . . busy with school," *That was an understatement if ever I heard one. I was drained and sorely in need of some vacation time.*

"Are you still teaching at the junior high school?"

"Yep. Still teaching art. Somehow I've managed to survive," I said, appalled at my flippant response.

"It sounds like quite an undertaking."

If only she knew the pandemonium that existed in my classroom. "It's fun. I can't believe I'm getting paid to do this job."

"Does Russell still own the restaurant?"

"Yes. Nothing's changed." Her questions were a little abrupt but I was in no position to do anything but answer them straight out.

"How's everything going in your life?"

"Everything's great," I reassured her, trying to convey a sense of well-being.

Finally she got to the heart of the matter. "Are you still interested in adopting a baby?" as if the possibility existed that we might have changed our minds.

What, are you crazy? That's all I ever think about. "Absolutely. Absolutely," I practically shouted. *My only goal was to be a mom.*

"Then I have good news. I may have a baby for you. She's three months old. I was wondering if you and your husband would like to see *her*?"

Her, it's a girl! What a ludicrous question. "Yes. Of course." I tried to project a serenity I didn't feel. I was dying of curiosity and wanted to ask no less than a million questions.

"Well, actually a caseworker in Sacramento is handling the baby," Mrs. McMurry volunteered. "I don't have all the details. The mother seems compatible to you in height and age. She's a hairdresser. She requested the baby go to a Jewish family."

"She's Jewish?" I asked incredulously.

"I believe so."

Our families, typical of their generation, carried on about marrying someone Jewish and obviously Russell and I abided by that custom. Though we were not observant, we were proud of our heritage. For that reason alone, we were prepared to raise our child Jewish. *Strange are the twists and turns of life.*

Her revelation turned out to be something we had not anticipated. According to strict Jewish law, a child born to a Jewish mother is considered Jewish. Not that we cared. When we filled out the paperwork we never made any specific demands—boy or girl, Jewish or non-Jewish. The two of us would have been thrilled with either sex, and as far as religion was concerned, it was a non-issue. All babies are precious. Our desire for a child of our own ran so deep, we would have been ecstatic no matter what background.

In passing, Mrs. McMurry slipped in another tidbit of information. "The baby's maternal grandfather was a doctor."

"A doctor. Really." Now that excited me. Immediately I jumped to the conclusion the baby, our baby, would be smart. With that last tidbit of information, I felt as if we had hit the jackpot. I jotted down the little nuggets of information. Almost as an afterthought, she threw in a vague reference to the baby being part-Hungarian. She remained virtually silent about the birth-father, only relaying the fact that he was six feet, two inches tall.

"There is one other thing . . ." Mrs. McMurry continued in a serious and softer tone. "I have to tell you there is a possibility that something might be wrong with the baby's heart. It may be nothing more than a heart murmur, but then again, there is the possibility that it could be more serious. Before you adopt her, you'll probably want to take her to your own doctor to be examined."

I felt a pang of anxiety, but when I drilled her for more information she assured me that she had passed on everything she knew. With all the positive news, I brushed aside the possibility of the baby being seriously ill. As usual, I had selective hearing.

"I'll talk to Russell and call you right back." As fast as my fingers could dial, I called him at the restaurant to relay the good news. Naturally I told him about the possibility of a heart problem.

Ever the optimist, Russell tried to reassure me, "If worse comes to worst, we can correct the problem with surgery."

Without having seen her, we spoke as if she were ours.

Fifteen minutes later I called Mrs. McMurry back. "Can we go up to Sacramento tomorrow to see the baby?"

"Not a problem. I've got another commitment. But I can make arrangements for another social worker, Miss Burns, to meet you. She works out of our Sacramento office."

Russell and I reacted in our usual rash, simplistic way. We ignored the warning and abandoned caution, allowing any doubts or restraint to dissolve like fat on a red hot barbeque.

Sometimes, when I reflect on the whole procedure, I'm shocked at our naïveté. In addition to the possibility of a heart problem, we never gave any serious thought to the birth-parents. We didn't know enough to ask the right questions. We wanted a baby so much that it never occurred to us to ask about the birth-parents mental or physical health, prenatal care, criminal records, intelligence, or educational levels. Looking back, it would have made sense to insist on a background check—especially if there was any alcohol or drug related issues.

Russell and I came of age listening to idealistic folk singers like Peter, Paul and Mary and Judy Collins. Neither of us could tolerate the smell of beer or hard liquor, much less cigarettes or drugs. Two goody-two-shoes, we were always compliant and respectful. Wrapped up in our own lives, we assumed everyone else grew up the same way. By today's standards, the limited knowledge Mrs. McMurry gave us was woefully inadequate. A school principal or credit manager receives far more information.

The facts we had were probably taken off some inter-office memo: three month old baby girl, possible heart problem, birth-mother a hairdresser, twenty-one years old, short, part-Hungarian, mother Jewish, grandfather a doctor, father over six feet tall.

We were comfortable with the fact that the baby would probably not take after either one of us. Russell's approach to life was orderly, sequential, and in constant motion. I preferred a more laid-back, serendipitous life-style. An early riser, he woke up singing. I, on the other hand, needed absolute silence—a newspaper and a cup of coffee to pry my eyelids open. Every day he made a *to-do* list and got it done; I floated through the day on a lackadaisical cloud. He worked sixteen hours a day in the restaurant; I returned from teaching and took a nap. Although diametrically opposite in style, we shared an underlying value system that emphasized work and family. Whatever the baby looked like, whatever her skills, she was bound to fit in somewhere along the continuum of our differing styles and personalities. With our indomitable spirit and youthful optimism, we convinced ourselves that we could easily mold a baby to our ideals.

CHAPTER 41

OUR BABY

RUSSELL AND I cranked down the front windows in our new compact car, a powder blue Ford Falcon, hoping to snag a cool breeze as we drove up to Sacramento to view our baby for the first time. Our spirits soared along with the 95 degree temperature as we traveled north on Highway 99, passing a steady stream of cars and trucks. Farms and orchards dominated the landscape. Confident in our future, we carried on an animated, non-stop conversation about *the* baby, *our* baby.

Tragically that day held both joy and sadness. Russell's father had congestive heart failure and landed in the hospital six days earlier and the family worried about his deteriorating condition. His life was slowly ebbing away. The impending adoption would be the happiest time in our lives, and provide a striking counterpoint for a grieving family worn down by illness and the shadow of death. With Russell's heavy foot on the gas pedal, and his determination to drive straight through to Sacramento, the trip took slightly more than two hours. He has an uncanny sense of direction and found Mercy Hospital without a hitch

Wrens darted in and out of the sycamore trees that grew near the small annex to the hospital. As we approached, Russell gripped my hand so tight that my wedding ring dug into me. We entered a generic space—an office barely the size of the walk-in refrigeration unit at the restaurant—and with about the same amount of charm. No decorations, not even a calendar hung on the gray cinder block walls. Our designated social worker, a slim, attractive woman in her early thirties, sat behind the solitary desk. Red curlicues overpowered her tiny face. It was easy to imagine the freckles that were once there. Miss Burns smiled. "You must be Nancy and Russell."

After the briefest of introductions, she gestured for us to take the only two seats remaining. The three of us carried on a bland conversation about the weather and our ride up to Sacramento. Miss Burns exuded a calm efficiency as she segued into the step-by-step adoption procedure.

Russell and I tried to appear placid and unrushed, but we sent telepathic messages to each other: *Enough already. Let's get on with it.* While she systematically explained the legal mumbo-jumbo, the only thing that dominated our thoughts was connecting with our daughter. It was like asking a starving person to go brush their teeth before giving him or her a slice of bread. After twenty minutes of tedium, we sensed it was about to happen. Parenthood was eminent.

It seemed like slow-motion as Miss Burns guided us out through the back door of the annex. A short breezeway connected it to the hospital and a maze of hallways. We entered an institutional room, made bright and cheerful by rays of sunlight pouring through elongated windows off to one side.

A surreal, dreamlike anticipation enveloped me, like a child about to open a pile of birthday gifts.

Suddenly she was there.

Our sweet baby, now three months old, was lying on her back in a wicker bassinet looking as bright as the planet Venus in a summer sky. Mesmerized, Russell and I just stared. As I gazed at her amazingly big eyes and perfect facial features, I gushed, "God, she's so beautiful!"

"Look. She's watching us," Russell exclaimed. Gigantic blue eyes followed our voices with curiosity. *Did she intuitively sense the significance of this first encounter?* As I gazed at her rich coffee and cream complexion, I assumed her birth-mother's family was Sephardic, that is, stemming from a Jewish ancestry from the Mediterranean or Middle East, rather than Ashkenazi, or eastern European. Olive skin instead of white.

With a professional eye, Miss Burns observed our reactions. Fascinated with the baby, we had forgotten all about her. She had been standing back discreetly, as inconspicuously as a light switch on the wall.

"Isn't she a cute one?" she finally offered. "Want to hold her?" Sensing my inexperience she gave explicit directions. "Cup her head like this," she said, picking the baby up gently.

"You're precious. Yes, you are," I murmured, immediately bonding with our beloved daughter. "Such a sweet, sweet baby."

Russell could hardly stand it. After a minute or two, we traded places. He cradled her, as if he were an experienced dad who had done this many times. "Look at you. Look at your big eyes."

After we put her back in the bassinet, I asked possessively, "Who's caring for her?"

"She's in a foster home. The folks are wonderful. She's receiving excellent care."

Foster care. It's not like being home. I made no comment but remembered that during my teacher training I had read studies about the growth and development of babies. To grow up well-adjusted, babies needed an abundance of love, tactile experiences, and interaction with adults. Right away I started to worry. *Was she getting the attention she needed?*

Miss Burns added, "There was some concern that she might have a heart problem. But since that first observation, the pediatrician thought everything checked out. For your own peace of mind, I suggest you have your own doctor examine her."

There wasn't anything to think over. It wasn't a business decision; it was a matter of the heart. Of course I was eager to take our daughter home that minute, but we had to address a few practical matters first. For starters, I needed to update my principal. He knew nothing about the pending adoption. Also, I was superstitious. Even though we had talked about adopting, until everything fell into place, I thought it best not to buy anything for the baby.

"Could we come and get her the day after tomorrow? I asked the social worker. Solemnly, almost prayer-like, I promised our baby that we would rescue her. *You'll be coming home soon*, I whispered silently.

CHAPTER 42

J.C. PENNEY'S

AS WE DROVE back to Modesto, our car whizzed past pink and white oleander bushes and purple agapanthus dividing Highway 99. Everything happened so quickly. There was so much to say and do, that our minds were overloaded.

"She's so alert," Russell gushed. "Did you notice, she never even cried? She really must be a good baby."

"She feels so soft," I said, "like a ripe plum. Russ, what are we going to do about a name?"

"I think we should name her after your dad." In the Jewish religion, tradition called for naming a baby after a deceased relative, but not using their name, only their initial.

I knew that would mean the world to my mother, who was still mourning the loss of my father. I thought about life's eternal cycles. It had only been a short time since my dad's death. His name was Daniel, so Russell and I bounced around girls' names beginning with the letter D. For a variety of reasons, we crossed them off. "I don't like names with tricky spelling," I explained. Then the teacher in me added, " . . . or that could be mistaken for a boy's names. And I don't like weird names that teachers have trouble pronouncing. Let's keep it simple. Just turn Daniel into Danielle?"

He repeated the name several times. "Danielle, Danielle. It has a nice ring to it. Like a beautiful French woman. Why not?"

Danielle fit the bill in every respect. I smiled inwardly, knowing how much it would mean to my mother. "Sold" I said with conviction. "Now . . . what about a middle name?"

We were both mindful that Russell's dad was not going to live much longer. "I don't like to talk like this," I said, "but if something happens to your dad, we can pick out a middle name for him."

The reality of his father's impending death brought tears to Russell's eyes.

Pretending not to notice, I continued. "If anyone asks us, let's just stall. Tell them we haven't decided on a middle name yet."

We mulled over the pros and cons of such an innocent deceit; then once again sat silently, our minds drained by the juxtaposition of happy and sad events. Another few minutes flew by before Russell snapped a small notepad from the visor and handed it to me. Then he pulled a Paper Mate pen from his shirt pocket. "Here. Start making a list of everything we need. Write down a crib, blankets, clothes . . . everything."

As I wrote, I began to panic. "How are we going to get it all in one day? She needs everything."

A meticulous planner, Russell said, "Don't worry. As soon as we get back to Modesto we'll go shopping. I think Penney's has all that stuff."

On weekdays, during the breakfast and lunch shifts, Etta, Russell's mother, worked the cash register behind the wooden U-shaped counter. As soon as Russell and I entered the restaurant, we spotted her. She was deep in concentration, putting the lunch checks in numerical order. Her pearlized reading glasses were perched halfway down the bridge of her nose.

Russell's initial greeting was one of concern. "How's Pop?"

"*Nisht* good," his mother grimaced, pushing her glasses up against her face with one finger. "Again, he's complaining about the swelling in his stomach and legs."

Up until the time of his illness, Russell's father had been the kingpin. Always a flashy guy, he was an incorrigible womanizer who lived a double-life. Unfortunately, he was also an inveterate gambler who blew his fortune in Las Vegas and the race track. He lived life to the fullest and always on his terms. He was a man's man and a rascal. His type was immortalized in Damon Runyon's musical, *Guys and Dolls*. Nevertheless, he was an old softy at heart.

After a few more details about his health, Etta's face brightened. "So . . . *nu*? Tell me, how did it go?"

Caught up in the moment, I tried to describe our day, but Russell continually interrupted, clarifying or adding his own version. We could hardly wait to go on our buying spree, so we gobbled down a quick sandwich and hustled over to J. C. Penney's, conveniently located kitty-corner to the restaurant. The antiquated department store, with out-of-date florescent lighting and old fashioned displays, was the only place in town to shop for a complete layette. We brought the bewildered saleslady in the baby department up to speed. And she knew just what to do. We scurried from one section to the next, trying to stay focused.

On the same day my aunt and uncle who lived in San Francisco showed up at the restaurant unexpectedly. Auntie Mollye, who played a major role in my life, was slightly over five feet, with hair dyed a fire engine red. And ever since I could remember, she had long, manicured fingernails to match. If a category five hurricane blew her away, not a helmet of shellacked hair would be out of place. Not once did I see her in anything but coordinated outfits with matching shoes and purses and just the right jewelry. With a quick tongue and a wicked wit, she never hesitated to give her opinion. But I loved her in spite of it. Always vain, her license plate simply read Mollye. Never mind that she was born Malka, to

Jewish immigrants from Lithuania. For years my dear aunt tried to teach me manners and how to dress.

My Uncle Mitch, a prince of a guy, sold wholesale costume jewelry. His territory happened to be the San Joaquin Valley, which included Modesto. He made his rounds three or four times a year and usually called us before coming to town. But for some unfathomable reason, this time my Auntie Mollye tagged along, hoping to drop-in and surprise us.

When Etta spotted my aunt and uncle walking towards her in the restaurant, she did a double-take. "For chrissakes, what are you doing here?"

After they shared their concern over Russell's dad, Etta realized that they had no inkling of the impending adoption. "Sit. Have something to eat. I have good news. Russell and Nancy are adopting a baby girl. Bringing her home the day after tomorrow."

"That dirty rat. She never said a word to me."

"Well, they just saw the baby today. Everything's happening fast. I don't think she had a chance. They just returned from Sacramento, had a quick bite to eat, and dashed over to Penney's to buy some things for the baby."

"I knew they were planning to adopt. But I had no idea they were about to bring a baby home. That's terrific. Mitch, let's run over there and surprise them."

Auntie Mollye asked the first salesperson she saw in the department store two questions. "Where is the baby department and where is the elevator?" For some reason, she was petrified of escalators.

I don't know what made me look across the room, but when I saw them heading towards us, I thought I was hallucinating. The sales clerk, a prim woman in a white collared black dress, didn't know what to make of the unexpected commotion. After we stopped with the congratulatory hugs and kisses, we clued them in. Piles of cellophane wrapped cotton sleepers, bibs, crib sheets and receiving blankets were strewn across every available space on the countertop.

My aunt and uncle had no children. They assumed the role of unofficial godparents, the guardian angels, to my brother and me.

They spoiled us with gifts that my parents couldn't afford, took us to the theater, and on weekend vacations that had been the highlight of my life growing up. Caught up in the magic of the day, they insisted on paying for the dark brown, walnut veneer crib and matching dresser that we had just picked out.

CHAPTER 43

THE PRINCIPAL

T HE NEXT DAY I returned to the junior high where I was teaching art, but my mind and heart were no longer in it. With motherhood looming, I was on top of the world. The exhilaration of seeing our baby for the first time and the outpouring of support from our family had suddenly taken precedence over my cush job. I made an appointment to see Mr. Williams, the principal, during my lunch hour.

His office, separated by a glass and wooden partition from the larger room, afforded us a modicum of privacy from the secretary, attendance clerks, and milling staff and students.

"Nancy, what can I do for you?" Mr. Williams asked, as I entered and helped myself to a chair in front of his desk.

The few times I had gone to his office were to ask for more art supplies. I'm sure he was anticipating the usual request. He had no inkling what had just transpired in my life. But I was planning to lay it all out for him and naturally assumed he would be happy for me. "Russell and I are adopting a baby girl. Tomorrow we're picking her up in Sacramento."

"That's real nice," he said, drawing out the *real* in that slow southern way, as he played with the turkey folds of skin around his neck. "I didn't know you were planning to adopt."

"Yeah . . . we're really excited. The timing couldn't be better. You can get a sub to finish out the year."

Mr. Williams' attitude changed. He did not appear at all happy with my proclamation. He wrapped one arm over the other and somehow managed to pull on his nose and sniffle. "Look, I'm happy for you'll, but you're gonna need to finish out this here school year. Like you said, school's almost over. Can't you just get someone else to take care of the baby 'til then?"

"I don't think so. I don't know any babysitters. But even if I did, I wouldn't leave her," I stammered, taken aback that he would even suggest it. Since the adoption was not yet a reality, I was having trouble referring to our daughter by name. I tried to explain. "You've got no idea how important she is to me."

He let my remark slide. "But I need you here." His congenial mood had turned sour. "You know you can't just up and quit anytime you want."

If that was a challenge, I took the bait. "Well, I plan to stay home," I said emphatically, then backed off. Taking another tack, I tried reasoning with the man. "You know when someone has a baby, they don't have to rush back to work the next day. Isn't this the same, only we're adopting?"

After another rebuke, I grew more obstinate. "Tomorrow we're picking her up. I can't finish the year. You'll need a sub. All they have to do is clean the room. And the kids can pretty much do that."

Unhappy with my mulish behavior, he bit his lower lip. In a carefully modulated but authoritarian tone he upped the ante. "Young lady, you signed a contract. Let me tell you something, either you'll finish out the year as agreed in your contract . . . or I'll see to it that you never teach again."

If trying to blackball me wasn't enough, I still harbored resentment from our first encounter. It happened a year-and-a-half earlier.

It happened at our very first meeting. He had burst into my life like a prickly cactus. The usual din of shuffling students turned quiet when Mr. Williams entered the bustling 6th grade classroom where I was doing my student-teaching. He whispered something to the master teacher and then headed in my direction. In his short sleeve shirt and rumpled slacks he looked like a small town sheriff in a television movie. Short and stocky with a buzz cut, he wore a nondescript tie that was too short and rested on his paunch.

He pulled me out of the classroom and led me to the school office so we might talk privately. I was surmising it had something to do with my student-teaching or college graduation. In the conference room adjacent to the principal's office we stood facing each other.

"I'm John Williams," he said, "and I'm principal at one of the junior high schools." With that, he sat on the edge of the conference table and left me standing. "I've been going over the records in the career center at the college. And it appears you have an extensive art background."

Aha, I thought, *it's about a job teaching art.* So naturally I began to promote myself. "Well, I love art and have taken art classes every chance I get."

"I see that," he said, noting the obvious. "It turns out our art teacher is leaving and I'm gonna have an opening next semester. Thought you might be interested."

Could it be I was going to get my dream job right out of college? My insides started to celebrate the possibility. I wondered if I should play it cool. "I'm very interested," I replied, suddenly jazzed on adrenaline.

Mr. Williams described what the job entailed and it was all that I ever wanted. Then he pulled a few papers from a beat-up leather briefcase, frowned, and switched gears. "I see here you're Jewish."

"Uh-huh," I replied, feeling somewhat unsettled by his comment.

I didn't think being Jewish was a disgrace, and probably marked it on some form. But I did not remember anyone at the college specifically asking about my religion. However, it suited my purpose to let the comment go.

"Well, I suppose you'll be wantin' to take off for them Jewish holidays."

Was that a statement or question? Of course I gave him the answer I thought he wanted to hear. "No, I never take off for religious holidays."

"Good," Mr. Williams sniffed, apparently pleased with himself for squeezing out a minor victory. He knew he had the upper hand and pressed on. "I suppose you think of yourself as the *Chosen People?*"

"*WHAT?*" I said, not sure that I heard him right. My eyes and forehead scrunched up in disbelieve. *Is that what he really believes?*

"You know, Jews as God's Chosen People?" he repeated.

The gist of his tone registered in my gut. Until this freakish encounter, I was shielded from religious pettiness by a cosmopolitan city, sophisticated friends and liberal universities. I had never before been confronted by outright prejudice.

"No," I said, showing some misgivings. "We don't believe we are the chosen people." But, in fact, I wasn't sure what millions of other Jews believed. I tried to recall what I learned in the one year I attended Sunday school. I could only remember two precepts: to perform *mitzvahs*, good deeds and *tikkun olam*, to help repair the world. And as far as I was concerned, they were completely inoffensive. *Who doesn't want to do good and help make the world a better place?* I was shocked that a school administrator, someone who tended to young children, someone that rose above the ranks of a teacher, could be so narrow-minded and brazen.

Satisfied with my weak-kneed answers, the principal finally let it rest.

Now, a year and a half later, when I walked into his office to let him know about the baby and requested the few remaining days off, I found myself once again butting heads. I still harbored shame for selling out, for being such a pushover when he dangled the art position in my face. This time was different. I was stronger and felt more sure-footed. Neither his threats nor his intimidation could stop me from being home with my daughter.

Mr. Williams said he would see to it that I never got another job teaching if I did not complete my contract. My mind whirled with anger. *There he goes again trying to intimidate me.* Not only did I disrespect the man, but knew I would never allow him to bully me again. Threatening to blackball me only succeeded in pushing my buttons.

Just before I returned to my classroom, I shot back, "If that's the way it is, it is! I don't care! For now, you better get a sub. Today's my last day."

By the time I got home my blood was boiling. I kicked off my shoes and immediately called Russell at work to vent my frustration. Always a good sounding board, he listened while I relayed Mr. William's threat. "Can he really keep me from teaching again?"

Russell had a way of making it all sound so simple. "I don't think so, but I'll check it out. One way or another, you'll get to stay home with Danielle. Everything will be all right."

That evening my aunt and uncle picked up some deli food and brought it to our house. After dinner, Marsha, Russell's sister, and her husband, Barry, came over to lend a hand. As much as she wanted to be with us, Etta, my mother-in-law, couldn't make it. After her shift at the restaurant, she invariably ran to the hospital to sit with Russell's dad. As far as I was concerned, Marsha and Barry, parents of three kids, held the master child-raising franchise. They were our only conduit to the mystique and care of a baby.

Marsha and my aunt oohed and aahed over the layette as we sat around the kitchen table removing the clear cellophane wrappings and tags.

"You know, you need to wash all this." Marsha, the maven of motherhood, instructed. "They've got to be sanitized."

What did I know? It never crossed my mind to wash new clothes. However, as a M-I-T, mother-in-training, I obediently picked up a pile and headed for the washing machine out in the garage. It did not take long to master the art of folding diapers into little triangles.

"You don't have to worry about it right away," my sister-in-law said, "but you will need a high chair."

Was there no end to our needs? "I think I've got enough Green Stamps saved," I replied, mentally calculating how many books it would take to redeem one.

"If you need more, I've got plenty," she offered.

The men—a traveling salesman, a restaurateur, and a scrap metal dealer—were not particularly handy with tools. But with good intentions, a little grousing, and an earnestness to get the job done, they managed to assemble the crib. Once completed, it sat in the middle of the room as we all debated which wall to put it on. Finally there was nothing left to do but clamp on a padded mobile. Out of sheer exhaustion the six of us stood zombie-like in the tiny bedroom listening to Brahms's Lullaby and watching the small pastel circus animals on the mobile twirling 'round and 'round.

Okay, we are ready, I thought.

CHAPTER 44

DANIELLE'S HOMECOMING

AWAKENING THE NEXT morning, the disappointments, heartaches, and red-tape were all but forgotten as we prepared for imminent parenthood. From this day forth we would have grown-up responsibilities. We would no longer be two newlyweds playing house, running out for a movie and pizza at the drop of a hat.

Russell, who had been managing the restaurant, left for work at seven o'clock in the morning to update his mother on a few situations to be handled that day. During the night my sister-in-law thought of a few addition needs. She called early and insisted I met her at Long's Drug Store on McHenry. Under her tutelage, I bought canned formula, baby powder, a tube of ointment for diaper rash, and a how-to book, *Dr. Spock's Baby and Child Care.* I had no idea what I was doing.

Highly emotional, Russell and I fought to balance our nervousness and the anticipation of becoming parents as we drove to Sacramento to pick up Danielle, *our* daughter.

"Hey, I'm a father," Russell crowed on our way home.

"Yeah, for the rest of your life," I added, as I nuzzled our precious, three month old daughter in my arms. In truth, we couldn't take our eyes off her for a minute.

"Russ, watch where you're going. You know we've got precious cargo riding in the front seat." Good-natured, Danielle must have sensed our timidity. Mercifully she didn't let out a whimper during the entire two hour drive. I'm not sure how we would have handled it if she had started to cry. Probably all-consuming panic.

The social worker had thoughtfully provided us with a canvas diaper bag—loaded down with a teething ring, one ready-to-use bottle of formula, an additional can of formula to get us started when we arrived home, and several terry cloth contoured diapers—quite avant-garde at the time. Fortunately we didn't have to use any of it.

Russell's father Harry remained in Modesto Memorial Hospital. We were anxious to show Danielle off and decided to stop there before taking her home. Gallantly Russell helped us out of the car. "Here, let me hold her?" he urged, as I passed our daughter to him.

We trampled gingerly through the tan bark and star jasmine growing in the wide flowerbed adjacent to the low-rise hospital wing. Harry had a corner room with a large picture window. When we reached it, our newly formed family squeezed as close to the plate-glass window as we could. Russell's father, wearing one of those silly hospital gowns, rose from his bed and shuffled to the window. Russell lifted Danielle up so his dad could see her face. Tears flowed down his ashen cheeks. He gave us the thumbs up sign and smiled.

After a few minutes Danielle began to fidget, letting me know she needed attention. On this impromptu visit, I suddenly realized what it meant to be a mother. It was there on the hospital grounds that I realized Danielle was not a play toy. With that tiny little whimper I got my first taste of responsibility. Her needs had to come before our own. Luckily, her calm demeanor permitted neophytes like us to break into parenting with a minimum of stress.

"Maybe she's hungry," I said with uncertainty.

We waved good-bye and the three of us headed home.

As planned, my aunt and uncle had arrived at our house while we were away. When they heard the car pull into the driveway, they rushed out the door to catch their first glimpse of Danielle. Early the next morning a splashy bouquet of fresh flowers was delivered to the house, courtesy of Russell's dad. With his waning strength, he personally contacted the florist. An avalanche of neighbors and close friends began their pilgrimage. By the end of the week, several teachers from my school had brought a gift from the faculty. From the very beginning, Danielle's homecoming was met with an outpouring of warmth and love.

President Kennedy used a rocking chair for his bad back. He spotlighted and personally revived the nation's interest in this old-fashioned piece of furniture. As soon as we brought Danielle home, I began to scout second-hand shops searching for an antique rocker. Eventually I spotted a graceful, turn-of-the century, birds-eye maple rocking chair in a dusty, used furniture store on Yosemite Boulevard. After restoring it, Russell and I often rocked rhythmically while giving Danielle a bottle. It was not uncommon for us to bicker about feeding her. We both wanted to do it. It was the epitome of peace and serenity to be tucked away in that simple little nursery cradling our daughter in our arms.

Several weeks passed and our ineptitude at handling Danielle had given way to a quiet efficiency. We packed our car with enough baby paraphernalia to last a month and the three of us drove to San Francisco to visit my mom. After my father passed away, an influential friend helped her land a sales job at Joseph Magnin's, an upscale women's specialty shop. Her work schedule and the fact that she did not drive, limited her time and mobility. But I knew she could hardly stand it, she was *plotzing* to see her first grandchild.

"She's gorgeous," my mom kept repeating over and over. "I can't stand it from her. Look at those big eyes." She labeled Danielle the little *mezuzah*, because we all sat around hugging and kissing her. Truly, it was akin to worshiping her.

Book Four

CONVERGENCE

CHAPTER 45

REUNIONS

OVER A SPAN of thirty years, U.S. presidents have come and gone. America has experienced untold tragedies and wars. And through it all, Russell and I have managed to stay married and raise three children. So jazzed about being parents, we wasted no time. We adopted Aaron just seventeen months after we brought Danielle home. Kelly, not adopted, arrived to our delight four years later.

Adoptions have changed drastically over the years.

Organizations have sprung up like wildflowers, providing opportunities for adopted children and birth-parents to reconnect. As this happened, I sat on the sidelines like a smug voyeur, observing the much publicized, sometimes dramatic reunions. I secretly prayed that I'd never have to deal with that situation. Though I would have been supportive, I was eternally grateful that neither one of our adopted children showed any desire to seek out their biological parents. There was a comfort-zone keeping things just the way they were.

No upheavals, no traumas.

At twenty-three, Danielle married Chris, her long time college sweetheart. An outstanding student, he had worked his way through school loading Coke trucks at 5 o'clock in the morning, working for engineers, and helping a professor in his lab. By sheer coincidence, or perhaps fate, Chris *and* his sister, Barbara, had also been adopted. So I had a bird's eye view when Barbara searched and connected with her birth-mother.

For her first face-to-face encounter, Barbara had originally consented to be on the *Sally Jesse Raphael Show,* a popular television reality show. Her adopted family accepted the fact that she was going to meet her birth-mother, but objected to making a public spectacle of it. Ultimately Barbara and her birth-mother met privately. They shared a short-lived intimacy until her birth-mother began hitting her up for money. In the final analysis, Barbara's childhood fantasy about a grand reunion had developed some unpredictably rough edges.

Not long after Barbara's reunion, Kelly, our youngest daughter, an opinionated Big City Girl, called from her studio apartment on the Upper West Side in Manhattan. She had just earned a Master's Degree in social work and was fixated on family dynamics. "Mom, you'll never believe what happened."

"No, probably not," I said, thinking anything was possible.

"Remember Rebecca? The one I used to go to camp with."

"I vaguely remember," I admitted, not sure where this was leading.

"Well, she was adopted as a baby."

My ears perked up. "I didn't know that."

"Anyway, she hooked up with an organization that helps adopted kids find their birth-mothers and fathers."

Fascinated with the story, I waited for her to tell me more.

"Her birth-mother gave her the brush-off. Apparently she's got other kids and just wanted to forget about her."

"Well, Kel, how would you feel getting a call like that? It could turn your life inside out. What was she supposed to say?" I pictured a frazzled housewife having to listen to a hellacious conversation with a flock of rambunctious teenagers and a haranguing husband sitting around the kitchen table while the rice was burning on the stove.

"Mom, my friend told me the organization that she went through actually gave her a script—what to say and what not to say. She told me that when she placed the call, the other person only has to respond with a *yes* or *no*."

"Kelly, face it. Who wants to get that kind of a phone call thirty years after the fact? Those records are sealed for a reason. Everyone involved signed a good faith contract. Suppose someone threw themselves into your life out of the blue? How would you feel?"

Undeterred, Kelly prattled on. "But wait. There's more. When she called her birth-father, he was totally happy. They talked for over an hour. And the next morning he sent her a dozen, long-stemmed red roses and a beautiful note. She called to thank him and they made a date to meet in person. Can you believe that? She's so happy."

The story touched my heart, moving me to tears. My voice cracked with emotion. I visualized the long-stemmed red roses and what her birth-father's acceptance meant after the cold reception from her birth-mother.

"I can't figure you out," my social worker daughter said, trying to psychoanalyze me. "You're all over the map. First you take one side . . . then the other."

"I know, honey. Sometimes I can sit on the fence and see both sides."

At that time I didn't know that these stories were a prelude to my own situation. Sometimes it's better not to see too far down the road.

CHAPTER 46

BRANDON, DANIELLE'S HALF-BROTHER

1998. **THIRTY PLUS YEARS** *had slipped by since Russell and I had adopted two children—Danielle and Aaron—and I gave birth to Kelly. Suddenly a young man named Brandon Barnett burst into our lives, claiming to be Danielle's half-brother. Through unswerving diligence and a few unbelievable strokes of luck, he found her. For me, he was the spoiler, the one who changed our lives forever. And when he did, it felt as if someone had thrown a can of red paint on a perfectly completed Rembrandt painting.*

At the time, Brandon was a young father in his thirties. It all began in Sacramento when his curiosity got the best of him. He had stopped his car in front of a bungalow in an old, rundown neighborhood. For ten minutes he sat in his car lost in a haze of youthful memories.

As a boy he had often pedaled his beat-up bike to this very spot and stood staring at his estranged grandparents' house. Back then he craved acceptance but lacked the courage to walk up and ring their doorbell. Neither his father, whom he never knew, nor his father's parents—his rightful grandparents—showed the slightest interest in him. He only knew what his mother had told him. Now older and wiser in the ways of the world, Brandon surmised it had to do with him being illegitimate.

Go for it, he said to himself.

He fiddled with the collar of his short sleeve white shirt before climbing the three stairs leading to the wooden porch, a few dead flowers in pots, and the front door. Not knowing what to expect, he hesitated before ringing the doorbell. Someone—he had forgotten who—had told him that his grandfather had died. But when the front door slid open, his eyes widened and he gasped inwardly. Only a torn screen door separated him from a gaunt and fragile man who resembled the ghost of Christmas past. His grandfather's uncombed chalk white hair matched the pallor of his face. A long, dangling tube trailed from his grandfather's nostrils to an oxygen tank anchored midway in the living room.

My God, the old geezer's not dead after all.

When Brandon explained who he was, the first few minutes were excruciatingly awkward. His grandmother, who overheard the conversation from the kitchen, suddenly rushed to her husband's side. Since they saw so few visitors, she invited him in. Brandon followed as his grandfather shuffled back to the living room in his bathrobe and slippers. Vials of pills and a magnifying glass rested on an aluminum TV table next to his club chair and torn hassock. Though it was perfectly light outside, the blinds were drawn and the uncirculated air smelled stale.

At first they sat like strangers, stiff and reserved, afraid to say what was on their minds. Grabbing the initiative, Brandon's grandmother, an abrasive woman who never held back, scolded him for not staying in touch.

As if it's my fault, Brandon brooded silently. *Communication goes two ways. Did you ever send me as much as a birthday card? Where were you when I was growing up?* He forced himself to listen as his grandparents complained about their multiple ailments. It did not take long before his grandmother started to talk about Gil, Brandon's father.

"You know, since I never knew my father, I've always wondered what he was like."

"Well . . . he was as smart as a whip," his grandmother bragged, immortalizing her son's best attribute. "But, Lordie, he got himself all jammed up. Gil was just a young kid when he took off for Spain. Maybe twenty-three, twenty-four, near as I can remember. Shoot, it was so long ago that I've forgotten exactly. Rarely ever comes back to see us. Teaches English, you know, in the Canary Islands."

Whenever Brandon's grandfather tried to add more than a sentence or two, he started to cough and spit up phlegm, leaving his embittered wife to dominate the conversation. With the advancement of years, and the feeling of entitlement to say whatever she wanted, her tongue loosened.

Eventually she let slip that in addition to fathering Brandon and his twin sister, her son had fathered two other girls.

"What do you suppose happened to them?" Brandon asked in a studied casualness.

"Can't say for sure. I remember Gil married a sweet Catholic girl, pretty little thing. She had a baby girl. Miranda, I think they named her. But, hell's bells, not long after she was born, that marriage busted up."

Trying to keep track of his peculiar family history, Brandon grew excited. "That baby, Miranda, or whatever her name is, that would make her my half-sister, right?"

"Well, I reckon so." His grandmother jogged her sluggish memory for more details. "Seems Gil's ex-wife remarried a few years after he left. If I remember correctly, she married one of the Sanchez boys. Roberto, I think. Yep, Roberto Sanchez. Geez, the last I heard they moved on up to Reno. Took the little girl with them."

Brandon let the name sink in. Miranda Sanchez. He pumped his estranged grandmother for more information. "What about the other one, you know, the other girl?"

"I can't say for sure. I think she was put up for adoption."

"By any chance, do you remember the mother's name?"

His grandmother strummed her forehead, trying to recall the details. "For the life of me, I can't remember."

"She was a Jew," his grandfather added in a derisive tone. "Supposedly her father was a doctor. Sherman, Shuman, something like that," he said and started to cough again.

"Do you remember where she lived?"

"Not far from here, but that was a heck of a long time ago," his grandmother lamented.

In dribs and drabs it all came out. In his head Brandon summarized: *my father was a real shithead. Got some Catholic woman pregnant and had to marry her. After the child was born he flew the coop. Got my mom pregnant and left her alone to fend for me and my twin sister. Then fathered another baby, another girl. And he never bothered to stay in touch with any of us.* He wondered, *Whatever became of those two half-sisters?*

Brandon worked the day shift at Horse Trader Sam's, a used car lot in Sacramento. It was mid-August and the hot air bounced off the asphalt and the chrome trim on the cars. Because of the heat, business was seasonally slow. So Brandon spent most of his time inside the small trailer-office sucking up the cold air coming from the air-conditioning unit placed in the lower part of the side window. The office was sparse. It held nothing more than a small metal desk, an armchair on rollers, two beat-up chairs for customers, a water cooler, phonebook and telephone.

Several days had passed since Brandon visited his grandparents. To keep busy, he pursued a systematic search for his two *half*-sisters. He thought he struck pay dirt when he located one *half*-sister in Reno. When they finally connected, he explained who he was and that they had the *same* father.

"No surprise there," his *half*-sister remarked in a jaded voice.

When he asked about his father, he hit a brick wall. "Sorry to disappoint you," she said, "but truth be told, from what I hear, he didn't stick around long. My mom told me they had to get married. And I was only eleven months old when he blew us off. Never saw the bastard. Hell, I don't know any more about him than you do."

As it turned out, she was the only legitimate child his father ever had.

Disappointed that his *half*-sister could be of so little help, Brandon was determined to find his other *half*-sister. He tried to recall the names his grandfather mentioned. Brandon was systematically calling every Sherman, Shuman, and Shulman in the Sacramento telephone book but was not having any success. As luck would have it, one Thursday his shift happened to overlap with another salesman, an immigrant from Germany.

When Brandon told him what he was doing, the German fellow made an off-handed suggestion. "Try spelling the name with a "*C*" or a double "N."

Brandon looked puzzled.

Grabbing a scratch pad off the desk, the man said, "Here, gimme your pencil." He printed the words: Schuman, Schumann, Schulman, and Schulmann. With additional avenues to pursue, Brandon persevered. It took diligence, but he worked his way down columns of names in the Sacramento telephone book, spelling the last name every which way. To those anonymous people, his calls were undoubtedly bizarre.

Brandon repeated the same spiel when he rang Pauline Schulman. "This call may seem a little weird, but I'm looking for a *half*-sister. Forgive my impertinence, but would you happen to know anything about a baby girl given up for adoption around thirty-three years ago?"

Pauline's heart palpitated wildly and goose bumps played havoc on her arms. She faltered. A procession of past heartaches splashed across her mind like roiling waves hitting the rocky coastline. Debating whether to open up, she finally figured she had nothing to lose. "Well . . . maybe . . ." she whispered, not sure what to say. "I gave a baby up for adoption around that time."

So used to being rejected over the phone, Brandon was shocked by her admission. Choosing his words carefully, he pressed on. "By any chance do you know a man named Gil?"

There was a palpable pause. "Uh-huh," Pauline finally admitted.

"Well, he was *my* father. And I'm looking for a *half*-sister."

Pauline immediately put two and two together. Of course she remembered the other children. She would never forget the excruciating grief they caused her years earlier.

"I just want to reassure you," Brandon said, "I don't have any ulterior motive. I don't want anything. I'm just trying to piece my family together."

In making these calls, he had been hoping to connect with somebody, anyone, who could lead him to his *half*-sister. *Life is strange,* he thought. *Five minutes ago neither of us would have dreamt of this intimate conversation. What were the chances that over thirty years later, the woman on the other line would actually be the birth-mother?* Not his, of course, because he was raised by his mother, but his *half*-sister's *birth*-mother. *What were the odds that she would still use her maiden name? What were the odds that she hadn't moved out of Sacramento?*

Brandon felt proud of his detective work. A perceptive, smooth-talking salesman, he wanted to put this stranger's mind at ease. He introduced himself and began sharing snippets from his own life.

"I'm married and have a little boy, Tommy. We call him T.J. He's a three year old terror," he said and chuckled, thinking of his son. "By the way, are you married? Have other kids?"

"No," Pauline replied ruefully, "I've never been married and she is, well . . . *was*, my only child."

Whoa, he thought. *Those were not the answers I was expecting.*

"Oh, it's such a long story," Pauline admitted sheepishly, skipping over the ugly years of substance abuse. "I was a basket case when I gave her up. Anyway, what's important is that I've turned my life around. I've been searching for my daughter for God knows how many years. I'm getting close." She rattled on about an agency that was trying to help. "I got the name of a lady who worked for the state. She had access to computer files on adoptions."

"What happened?" he asked, searching for more information.

"Promise me you won't tell anybody, okay? This is not for publication. I paid her a couple of hundred bucks, you know, under-the-table, to do some research. And she discovered my daughter was adopted by a young couple. The Zimmer's. They named her Danielle. Danielle Zimmer."

Brandon didn't know what to say. What he heard was good, like a half-eaten cookie, but he craved more.

"I've been trying to track Danielle down for a long time," Pauline continued. "Everywhere I go, I search the County Records. I found out she got married in Reno to a guy named Christopher Fuller. But everything stops there."

Bingo. Danielle Fuller. "You know, Pauline," Brandon said, "we're looking for the same person. If you want, maybe I could help you. Not to brag, but actually I'm a pretty good sleuth. I just found my other *half*-sister. Coincidentally, she lives in Reno."

Pauline suddenly switched gears. "Look . . ." and she searched her memory for his name.

"Brandon," he offered, catching her memory lapse.

"Look, Brandon, I could use your help. But only on one condition. You've got to promise me one thing; you won't contact her first. PLEASE. It's really important that I make that first contact. Remember that organization I was just telling you about? Well, they gave me a script. And I need to follow it exactly. If you say the wrong thing, you can really blow it for me."

CHAPTER 47

THE CONNECTION

BRANDON SURMISED that Saturday would be a good day to reach people. *They're usually not working,* he reasoned. In his quest to find his half-sister, he planned to call every Fuller listed in the Reno directory. He had discreetly torn out a section of *F* pages from the library's Reno phone directory and carried the papers to work in a large manila envelope. When he skimmed over the names, Christopher Fuller was not listed. But he figured one of the Fuller's could possibly be a member of Christopher's family. He dialed number after number and was stymied or rebuffed. Methodically he dialed another Fuller, bracing himself for another rejection.

"Hello," said the husky voice on the other end.

"Say, by any chance, do you know a Christopher Fuller?" Brandon asked, his leg tapping away like a metronome.

"Sure do. He's my son," said the warm, friendly voice on the other end of the line.

"Listen, I'm an old buddy from school," Brandon lied, trying to keep the pitter-patter generic.

"Did you go to UNR?"

"Sure did," Brandon said, circumventing the truth. "But my family moved away. What's Chris up to these days?"

"He just got an MBA from Stanford," Mr. Fuller bragged.

"No kidding. He was always the smart one. Where's he living now?"

"The Bay Area," Mr. Fuller replied, convinced he was being helpful in reestablishing an old friendship.

"And Danielle? What's up with her?" Brandon probed, hoping it sounded like idle chatter. Meanwhile his heart thumped like a big game hunter with the prey in the crosshairs of his scope.

"Oh, she's keeping busy. They've got a baby now and she's working. Coordinating special events."

"Gosh, it would sure be nice to catch-up. I'd like to give Chris a ring. You wouldn't happen to have his number handy?"

Mr. Fuller gave Brandon the telephone number, never suspecting he had just been scammed.

Brandon knew he needed to reach Christopher and Danielle before Christopher's dad did.

"Hello. Is this Danielle?"

"Yes . . . who's this?" She had no time to waste on an unsolicited sales pitch. It was a Saturday, mid-afternoon, and she was keeping an eye on her young son while cleaning the two-bedroom apartment she and Chris rented in Santa Clara.

The stranger on the other end of the line talked fast. "Please don't hang up! I know this is coming out of the blue, but I'm your *half*-brother. I just want to talk to you."

"I don't have a *half*-brother," Danielle rebutted, with undisguised belligerence. "Who are you and how'd you get my number?"

Not proud of the lies he told to track her down, Brandon knew he had to play it straight. *If I screw up, she'll slam the receiver down.* "Danielle, please listen for a sec. I know you're adopted, okay?"

The fact that he knew she was adopted grabbed her attention and sent a shiver down her spine. It was never hidden, but it was never an epic topic of conversation either.

"Listen carefully, Danielle, because it's complicated. But I swear I'm your *half*-brother."

Shaken, Danielle lowered herself into a chair at the kitchen table while clutching the telephone. She grappled with his pronouncement, uncertain she wanted to hear more. "I don't understand. Look, I don't even know your name."

"My name's Brandon," he enunciated clearly. "Let me explain. We have the *same* father, but *different* mothers. That makes you my *half*-sister."

Okay, she thought, biting her lip. *This is way more than I can handle.*

Brandon continued. "I swear to you, I'm not making this up. We have the *same* father, but *different* mothers. I've got a twin sister. Besides you and her, we have another *half*-sister. Also around our age. It's a long story but I tracked her down. I just spoke to her. She's married, has a couple of kids, and lives in Reno. She's an accountant at Mountain Marketing One."

"THAT'S SO WEIRD! This is freaking me out! Did you know that I used to live in Reno? When I graduated from UNR, my first job was at Mountain Marketing One."

"That is totally freaky," Brandon admitted. "I swear to God I didn't know you lived in Reno, much less where you worked. I only knew you applied for a marriage license there."

Brandon's disclosures drew her in. Danielle asked him again how they were related. And he repeated the fact that they shared the *same birth*-father, but had *different birth*-mothers.

It was slowly sinking in. Her curiosity whetted, Danielle listened as her *half*-brother filled her in. They discovered they had many things in common, especially their toddler sons. When Brandon got a sense that she had calmed down and he had gained her trust, he slipped in another shocker. "Danielle, I have something more to tell you, okay? I don't know how you'll feel about this, but when I was trying to track you down, I met your *birth*-mother."

Oh, my God!

"Hello, are you still there? Good. I know it's shocking, but she'd really like to meet you. But here's the thing," Brandon said, quickly backpedaling, "if you aren't ready for that, hey, I understand. I don't even have to tell her I spoke to you."

"I don't know. I really need time to think it over." A bunch of *what ifs* started to whirl through her mind. *Of course she had often wondered who her birth-mother was. But maybe it would be something better left alone?* At a crossroads, she refrained from talking, not wanting to ask the question she had suppressed all her life. Despite her best intentions, the key question spilled out anyway. "What's she like?"

"At first we spoke on the phone. Then we met for coffee. She seemed nice enough. You know, good people . . ."

"What do you know about her?"

"Well, for starters, her name's Pauline. She's never been married. Interestingly, she's got no other kids."

Danielle felt this might be her only shot and wanted to squeeze him for more information. "I've got to ask you this, what does she look like? I've often wondered."

"Short. Around five feet. Very attractive. Great bod."

"What do you mean? Can you be more specific?"

"Well, there's something about her eyes . . . they're pretty. But, truthfully, I didn't notice the actual color. She kinda reminded me of Dolly Parton. Long blond hair and, to put it bluntly, well . . ." and he hesitated, ". . . she's pretty busty."

Maybe it was the tension, but Danielle began to laugh. At last, something about her body resembled someone else's. "Do you know anything about my birth-father?" Then she corrected herself. "*Our* birth-father."

"Not much. He never married my mom. He was out of the picture from the get-go. From what I know, he's a real piece of work. His name's Gil. I got a picture of him as a young man."

"If you never met him, how'd you get it?"

Brandon explained his visit to his fraternal grandparents. "They're old. They live in Sacramento, actually not far from where

I grew up. It's a long story, but one day I sort of barged in on them. On a whim, I just rang their doorbell. They knew who I was but didn't really know me. Anyhow, they invited me in and we talked for a while."

Danielle stated the obvious. "Well, that must have taken a lot of nerve,"

"You know, it was something I had to do. I never knew my father. I was curious. His parents were nice enough. They even gave me an old picture."

"What does he look like?"

"If you want, I'll send it to you."

"I don't want your only picture."

"I don't mind sharing it. From what I've gathered, our father is a huge disappointment to everyone. I guess he loved the ladies. But apparently life got too complicated so he flew the coop. Landed in Spain. According to his parents, Gil has a really high I.Q. They told me he always loved to read. Had a thing about Ernest Hemmingway. He wanted to imitate his rough and tumble kind of life."

"Frankly he sounds like a real screw-up. Listen, Brandon, this is a lot of information to grasp in one day," she said, not precluding another conversation sometime in the future. "My son's getting cranky. I've really got to go." *I just learned the names of my birth-mother and birth-father, a brief family history, and found out I have a half-brother and two half-sisters.*

Brandon congratulated himself. In his search for family, he had achieved his goal. "Danielle, I hope we can talk again. This has meant a lot to me. Perhaps we can meet one day."

After he hung up the phone, he called his wife to tell her what he found out. Then he called Pauline, Danielle's birth-mother.

Even though Pauline was furious that he broke his promise to let her call first, she screamed through jumbled laughter and tears. "I don't believe it. You spoke to my daughter!"

As promised, several days later Brandon sent Danielle a friendly hand-written note and two photographs, one of himself with his wife and son and another of their father.

CHAPTER 48

SHOCKWAVES

THAT FATEFUL EVENING, Danielle relayed the news to me about her family ties—the *half*-brother and *birth*-mother. I hung up the telephone, too distraught to talk. Not sure where it would all lead, shockwaves of anguish exploded in my head. I sat motionless at my desk trying to sort it all out. For the moment I was incapable of explaining Danielle's disclosure to my husband Russell who continued to sleep peacefully on the couch with the television blaring. That night sleep came in short intervals—punctuated by wakeful bouts of *what ifs.*

During breakfast the following morning, I broke the news. Russell, a truly connected father, asked a few preliminary questions. Then he sat at the kitchen table brooding, staring out the window with a mournful look on his face.

Russell could not bring himself to talk about this revelation. I, on the other hand, became obsessive. That's all I wanted to talk about. Many afternoons when I got home from teaching—and he was still at work—I would phone Danielle just to discuss the situation. Kelly, our youngest, was also enthralled by the new family dynamics. She and I repeatedly rehashed every nuance. When I spoke to our son Aaron and Christopher, Danielle's husband, about the situation, I thought they would have shown a little more curiosity, even been happy for Danielle. But they were of one mind. They viewed the sequence of events with hostility and suspicion. No matter their personal views, I appreciated their kindness and sensitivity as they rallied around me.

To make the situation a reality, I felt the need to connect with Brandon, Danielle's half-brother. I needed to hear his voice and get a sense of who he was. Since he lived in northern California and we lived in the southern part of California, a face-to-face meeting was out of the question.

"Just call him, Mom," Danielle urged, after I badgered her with questions. "I told Brandon you wanted to speak to him and he's okay with it."

When I dialed his number and explained who I was, he read my mind. "I only wanted to meet my *half*-sister. It's nothing more than curiosity."

"Well, in a way, I'm as curious as you are, Brandon. But to be honest, I'm also angry. Part of me is sorry you ever contacted Danielle. It's not you personally, so don't get me wrong. But this has devastated our family."

"I'm sorry," he said sincerely. "I meant no harm."

"I know. This is about Danielle's *real* mother," I said and corrected myself. *Oops. I'm her real mother.* "She's *my* daughter." The point I was trying to make had nothing to do with Brandon, so I changed the subject. "Why don't you tell me about yourself?"

He spent twenty-five minutes telling me about his life, his family, and the father that abandoned him. Other than snooping, I don't know what made me ask about his fraternal grandparents.

"Well, like I said, growing up my sister and I lived with my other grandmother, my mom's mom. Actually my grandma helped raise me. But I don't know much about the other side, my father's parents. I believe they got married in Panama, came to the United States and he joined the Air Force."

Panama. That struck an unfamiliar chord. "Whoa. Hold on. They're from Panama? Are they Hispanic?"

"Yeah. I thought you knew that."

"No. Absolutely not. Not once during the whole adoption process did anyone mention that." *All this time I assumed Danielle's olive complexion and huge eyes were Sephardic characteristics. My God, I thought, what's it like for Danielle to discover she's part Hispanic? What if we had been bigoted parents carrying on about the immigrants . . .?*

By the time we hung up I felt like I had a handle on Brandon. He was a stand-up guy. Straight-forward, responsible and sensitive.

"Who were you talking to for so long?" Russell wanted to know.

"Brandon. Danielle's *half*-brother," I replied, anxious to fill him in on everything I'd gleaned.

"Oh . . ." Russell responded without enthusiasm, leaving no room for discussion. Still resisting this unwelcome intrusion, he refused to let down his defensive wall of silence.

CHAPTER 49

THE FATEFUL PHONE CALLS

I N A CONTEMPLATIVE MOOD, Pauline sat quietly in a
kitchen chair pulled alongside her Aunt Rose's sick bed. As the
sole caretaker, she grieved as her beloved aunt slowly wasted
away from cervical cancer.

Pauline's mind flooded with family history. Her mother
often spoke of their all-consuming sadness when they thought no
Hungarian members of their families survived Hitler's death camps.
And ultimately how joyous her mother and father had been when
they learned that her sister Rose and her cousin Esther survived
the Holocaust. Pauline knew that immediately following the war,
her parents brought the two frightened young women to America.
Growing up, she remembered how natural it felt with everyone living together in the big house in Shaker Heights.

Pauline balanced the telephone on her lap and fidgeted with
the silver locket her father had given her on the day he left for
prison. It had been many years since she had told her aunt about the
baby she gave up for adoption.

Having witnessed her long suffering guilt, Aunt Rose understood the importance of this moment. They had spent many hours
rehearsing it. Propped up with three pillows, Aunt Rose urged her
niece to go ahead and make the call. "You won't be sorry."

Pauline fantasized about this fateful phone call for years, but
it was going to be much harder than she expected. Part of her
wanted to back down and part of her wanted to plunge forward.
Terrified of being rebuffed, Pauline's courage flagged. *There's zero
room to screw up,* she reminded herself. The meetings that she had
frequently attended were supposed to help birth-parents and their
children reconnect. She could still hear the leaders' admonitions
being drilled into her head: *Go slow. The connection will be shocking.
Do not deviate from the prepared script. Above all, you don't want to spook
the person on the other end.*

It was Saturday, mid-morning. Danielle and her husband Chris
were planning to go to a Stanford football game later in the day. A
workout disciple, Chris had gone to the gym, leaving Danielle to
watch their son and pay the bills. All week she had been trying to
shake off the shocking conversation she had with her half-brother.
But, in spite of her best effort, random thoughts of Brandon and
her birth-mother keep creeping into her head.

"Hello. Is this Danielle?"

"Speaking. Who's this?"

"Danielle . . . This is your *birth*-mother." The word dangled
mid-air. There was a palpable quiet, an imperceptible stillness
almost impossible to bridge.

Danielle felt her heart sink. She knew she couldn't handle it. Not
knowing where this conversation would lead or who would get hurt,
a broad range of emotions yanked her in every direction—curiosity,
anger, but mostly resentment. For some reason talking to her half-
brother was far less threatening. "Look, I'm sorry," Danielle said, a
myriad of plausible excuses tumbling through her head. "I'd really like
to speak to you, but this just isn't a good time. I'm an event coordinator
and I'm right in the middle of a series of summer concerts. The first one
was last night and, frankly, I'm exhausted. It's too hectic right now."

Another awkward silence separated them. Neither dared to speak. Finally Pauline said, "I understand." With great sensitivity, she tried to shield Danielle from her profound disappointment. "Perhaps it will be less stressful at another time." Then, keeping to the script, she added, "I know how hard this must be for you. Would you mind if I called back sometime in the future?"

"Umm, well, okay," Danielle said, trying not to hurt Pauline's feelings. At the moment, her two-year-old son and her job were enough to deal with. Besides, a part of her worried about her parents and how they would react.

Almost a month to the day Pauline called again. Propped up with a little curiosity, the strained conversation lasted a bit longer although Pauline did most of the talking. "Danielle," she said in her sugar-sweet voice, "If nothing else, I'd like to give you a rundown on our family's health history. Someday that might come in handy."

Of course that piqued Danielle's interest. She had always wondered about that. "My dad's gone," Pauline explained. "He had Alzheimer's and Parkinson's. My mom passed away last year from cervical cancer. And now Auntie has it."

Danielle wasn't thrilled hearing these facts, but it was important information that she needed to know.

The conversation was short, but Pauline squeezed in as much information about her family as she could. "I have a sister, Ellie. We both live in Sacramento. Before my mom died, she and Aunt Rose lived side-by-side in a duplex. When my mom got sick, I moved in with her. Auntie still lives in the other duplex. Actually that's where I called you from that first time."

When Pauline inquired about her family, Danielle clammed up. "I'm sorry but I'm not comfortable talking about them."

"I understand," Pauline said, showing great restraint. "Anyway, I just wanted to give you some basic health information. May I call you again?"

The way it was put, Danielle didn't have the courage to flat-out say no. "I guess so," she offered weakly, more to be polite than out of conviction.

After a brief interlude, they reconnected. At this point Danielle realized the situation wasn't going to go away magically. It was up to her. Either she had to be firm and tell Pauline not to call or deal with it.

"I have some sad news to share," Pauline lamented. "Auntie passed away three weeks ago. I'm so disappointed. She never had the chance to meet you, but she knew I found you."

Not knowing what to say, Danielle ignored the latter comment. "Oh, I'm sorry. Your aunt must have been very special."

The awkwardness between Danielle and Pauline began to peel away after three or four additional phone calls. Overly informative, Pauline spoke bluntly about her father and how he wound up in prison, her problems with alcohol, AA, and her sobriety.

On one of those calls, Pauline couldn't resist asking the question that plagued her for years. "Danielle, dear, there's something I must ask. There was some question about your heart. Physically, I mean. Are you okay? No problems?"

"No problems. To tell you the truth, this is the first I heard anything about a heart problem. No one ever told me about that. I've always been pretty athletic. Played sports in school. Now I jog and work-out."

"Oh, thank God! I'm so relieved. Tears pooled in Pauline's eyes. "I felt so guilty. I've always wanted to find you, to explain why I had to give you up."

Danielle choked up.

"How would you feel about meeting me some day?" Pauline asked, trying hard to keep the tremor out of her voice.

Danielle's resistance wavered. *How can I say no?*

At Pauline's suggestion, they made tentative plans to meet in San Francisco for lunch and to take in a ballet, something that Pauline adored. But those plans fell through because of conflicting schedules. The postponement turned out to be a blessing, giving them several more opportunities to talk on the telephone and loosen up. Pauline demonstrated exceptional skill in playing her hand. She invariably left Danielle with options, handling her like a rare, delicate piece of porcelain.

When I heard how gently Pauline treated my daughter, my harsh view of her began to waver. I appreciated her sensitivity and non-confrontational manner.

CHAPTER 50

FIRST MEETING

I F HAPPINESS COULD BE measured by the rungs of a ladder, Pauline stood on the top, waving one hand triumphantly. To everyone she came in contact, she broadcast her plans to reunite with the baby she gave up for adoption. Reconnecting with her daughter dominated her waking thoughts. She wanted that first meeting to be flawless. Unfamiliar with the turf beyond Sacramento, she asked her friends and relatives to recommend a restaurant somewhere between Santa Clara and Sacramento, and finally settled for a restaurant on the Berkeley waterfront.

Pauline begged her sister to go with her. Ellie, who had stood by her sister over the years, agreed to drive her down in her new Chrysler, thinking Pauline's old clunker might not go the distance. For weeks before the *Big Day*, as they euphemistically tagged it, they rehearsed what to say, how to act, and what they were going to wear.

"I didn't worry this much before my own wedding," Ellie joked.

An hour ahead of schedule they arrived in Berkeley, hair teased to perfection and dressed conservatively enough to meet Queen Elizabeth for high tea. Filled with apprehension, Pauline announced to her sister, "I have to go to the bathroom. Find a gas station somewhere."

"We're almost there. Can't you wait and go when we get to the restaurant?"

"No. Suppose Danielle's waiting for us. I don't want the first words I ever say to my daughter to be 'I have to go to the bathroom.' That would be too humiliating."

So the two sisters drove through unfamiliar parts of town searching for a public restroom.

They did, however, beat the lunch crowd as they entered the upscale restaurant at the Berkeley Marina. Pauline juggled a bouquet of long-stemmed red roses, a Macy's shopping bag filled with several family albums, and her purse. No one was waiting. Pauline's eyes darted from the reception area to the dining room. There were only a few tables occupied—several men in white shirts and ties at one and another filled with three chatty gray-haired ladies.

"Check with the hostess, in case Danielle got here first," Ellie advised her sister.

The middle-aged hostess stood behind the stand sorting menus. "Excuse me," Pauline interrupted, "by any chance, did someone by the name of Danielle come in?"

"Danielle. No. I don't think so."

Pauline was unable to contain herself. "Well, today's a very special day. That's why I'm carrying these roses. Years ago I gave my daughter up for adoption and I'm going to meet her here for the very first time. I want everything to be perfect," she said, enunciating her *t's* as if she were taking elocution lessons.

"Well, that sounds very special. I'll make sure you have the best table," the well-groomed hostess winked. "I promise, we'll take good care of you." She reached over and patted Pauline's arm as if to say, "Don't worry, it's going to be just fine."

As the sun broke through a layer of clouds, tiny flickers of gold danced on the undulating waves in the bay. Pauline and her sister sat on a round settee in the large foyer surveying everyone who arrived. A flock of people arrived at the same time. A young woman with short, black hair drifted off to one side of the restaurant. She stood perusing the menu in a glass case attached to the wall.

"I think she's waiting for somebody," Ellie speculated, nudging her sister. "Maybe that's her."

"I'm scared."

"Go on. Just go over."

Pauline grabbed the roses and tapped the stranger on the back. As the woman turned she saw that she was Asian. "Excuse me," Pauline said, trying to recover from her embarrassment. "I thought you were someone else." She backed away and rejoined her sister. Then another fashionable woman in her mid-thirties came in, glanced at her watch, and stood waiting.

Again Ellie elbowed Pauline. "Go see if that's her."

Pauline picked up the roses and confronted the young lady. "Excuse me, but by any chance are you Danielle?"

"No," the spunky woman joked, "but if those flowers are for Danielle, I *could* be her!"

Sheepishly Pauline returned. "Ellie, would you cut it out. She's *my* daughter and I'll know her when I see her." From their vantage point, they continued to scrutinize the people as they sauntered in from the parking lot.

A short time later Pauline practically screamed, "That's her. I know it. I know that's her!"

A smartly dressed young woman, wearing a black and white hound's-tooth skirt and short black linen jacket, dashed towards the large oak door of the restaurant. As she entered, Pauline was there to greet her. "Danielle . . . is that you?"

"Yep, it's me," Danielle smiled, displaying perfectly straight teeth and an infectious smile. "You must be Pauline."

"Yes." Pauline tried to contain her emotions, but couldn't resist giving her daughter a hug that lasted an uncomfortably long time.

"Sorry I'm a few minutes late but there was all this roadwork when I got off the freeway. I got all screwed up."

"Yeah, I know. It's really confusing. Oh, I almost forgot. Here. These are for you." With that Pauline handed her daughter the bouquet of long-stemmed red roses. Pauline wanted nothing more than acceptance. She immersed herself in the moment, not sure if this would be the first and only time they would be together. "You're so beautiful. Precious," she fawned. After regaining her composure, she apologized. "Oh, I'm sorry. Let me introduce my sister."

After the introductions, Danielle startled them with her candid announcement. "Excuse me. I need to run to the bathroom. It's been a long ride."

As soon as she was out of hearing range, Pauline boasted, "Isn't she something?"

To relieve the tension, Ellie poked fun at her sister about their foray into Berkeley. "Yeah. We're the only *meshuganas*. We couldn't go to the bathroom here. No. We had to *schlep* around like two idiots looking for a gas station."

While the hostess checked on their table by the window, the three women masked their emotions. They spoke in generalities about the road construction and detour. Danielle exclaimed, "This is quite a view. I've never seen San Francisco from this angle. Look, you can see all the bridges. I never knew this place existed."

"This is my first time here, too," Pauline admitted.

The hostess led them to their table and handed them an extensive menu. Behind Danielle's back she gave Pauline another reassuring wink, letting her know everything was under control.

A few minutes later a solicitous waiter in a starched white jacket approached. "Would you ladies care for a cocktail? Or some wine, perhaps?"

Ellie ordered an apple martini, hoping it would take the edge off.

"How 'bout you, Danielle?" Pauline asked.

"Well, if everyone's having one . . ."

"Don't go by me," Pauline joked, inferring her membership in AA. "I've been sober for nineteen years, three months, and twenty-one days. If you want, go ahead. I'm okay with iced tea."

Pauline sat in awe. Nothing less than a miracle brought her to this day. At last, she was reunited with her daughter, that part of herself that she had missed for all these years. Her heart felt full again. There was so much to say, she hardly knew where to begin. "Danielle, I've always thought of you on your birthday. I would send my love . . . hoping somehow you'd feel it."

Danielle squirmed, unsure how to respond.

Undeterred by the silence, Pauline continued. "I'm curious. How old were you when you learned you were adopted?"

"I don't know. I guess I've always known. My parents told me I was chosen. Aaron, that's my brother, he's also adopted. When he was little he thought he hatched from an egg like a chicken," she said, hoping for a laugh to break the tension.

I could hardly wait to find out how it went. Riddled with curiosity, I called Danielle that evening. "Mom, I think you'll like her. She's really sweet." Always composed, Danielle has a Teflon disposition. She accepted the inevitable and, not given to hyperbole, she took that first meeting in stride.

I, on the other hand, wanted to hear affirmations. I needed to hear every compliment, every loving gesture, and every positive thing Pauline said. I'm proud that Danielle is my daughter and I needed assurance that her *birth*-mother felt exactly the same way.

With the passing of time, I felt less threatened and grew more accepting. But my heartsick husband—the most possessive father in the world—continued to close his ears and his mind, preferring not to know any details about Pauline.

CHAPTER 51

GIFTS

I N MID-NOVEMBER, Danielle was expecting her second child. A mere ten days before Joseph was born, she and Chris moved into a small tract home on a tree-lined cul-de-sac in Santa Clara. Winter in the desert of southern California is the busiest season for a spa and resort manager. So my husband Russell opted to stay behind and work when I flew up to the Bay Area to help Danielle. Immediately following Joseph's birth, it took both of us to keep up with the laundry, put food on the table, and tend to the children as a steady stream of friends dropped in to see their new home and baby.

One blustery Monday afternoon while the boys were napping, Danielle and I were on our hands and knees in the living room scooping up Kevin's Matchbox cars and blocks. Casually, as if she was asking me to turn on the microwave, Danielle posed the sixty-four thousand dollar question. "Mom, how would you feel if Pauline came down to see the baby?"

I struggled for the right answer. How was I supposed to feel meeting her birth-mother? To be sure, I was more than a little apprehensive. A mantle of unresolved angst hung over me. If I said no, the guilt would weigh on me for the rest of my life. I was afraid that a negative response would put an undue burden on my daughter's emotional well-being and forever leave a chasm between us. There was another aspect too. I was downright curious. As I evaluated the pros and cons, the inevitable response had to be, why not?

After breakfast the next morning, with my conflicted approval, Danielle picked up the telephone and invited Pauline for lunch that Friday. The only iffy element was the weather—unusual high winds and torrential rains. That day local television stations were constantly showing downed trees and flooded roads and advising people to stay home.

On Thursday the telephone rang. "I'll get it," I shouted from the kitchen where I had been folding two baskets of laundry.

"Danielle . . . ?"

"No, this is her mother," I responded naturally, assuming it was one of Danielle's friends.

"This is Pauline," she said, her soft voice sounding warm and friendly.

In my mind, I had always imagined I'd have plenty of time to think about it and compose myself before we had any personal exchange. *This is her mother,* I had stated so bluntly. As soon as I realized who I was speaking with, I felt contrite, as if I had rubbed her nose in it. I didn't mean to be unkind or cause her any needless pain. *It was all so confusing.* Then I tried to compensate for what I regarded as an embarrassing faux pas.

"Pauline, it's so nice to finally talk to you. Of course, Danielle and I are expecting you for lunch tomorrow. Yes. . . . I hope your car will make it. Uh-huh. The baby is beautiful. Kevin keeps running over to kiss the baby's feet."

The storm continued unabated. Friday turned out to be another nasty day with black skies and slashing rain. I looked at my watch. Just enough time to throw on a jacket and run outside to cut some lemons and greenery for a centerpiece. I was unloading the bucket onto a newspaper on the kitchen counter when I heard the doorbell buzz. *Oh my God, they're here twenty minutes early.*

Not sure of the protocol, I shouted to Danielle who was in the boys' room putting away a load of folded laundry. "Should I get the door?"

"No, Mom, I'll get it."

This was going to be an earth-shattering occasion and I needed to brace myself. *Take a deep breath. Inhale. Exhale. Release the tension.* I rarely cry from sadness or frustration, but fall apart at sentimental movies or observing poignant airport reunions. *Be natural. No tears,* I commanded myself. I wasn't sure how Pauline would feel—jealous or sad—if I boasted how precious Danielle was. Indecisive, I wasn't sure what to say.

Wet and bedraggled, two women in their late fifties stood at the front door. The shorter one wore a daffodil colored slicker and matching hat. The other wore a powder blue ski jacket and funky knit cap pulled down over her hair and ears. Each of them carried a shopping bag loaded with gift-wrapped packages. "Come in," Danielle offered, as if they were neighbors from down the street. "It's freezing out there."

Not sure who was who, I stood behind Danielle holding Kevin's hand. My feet were anchored to the floor and my antennas were up, ready to soak in every nuance of this incredible day.

Danielle seized the moment. "Pauline, this is my mom."

The shortest of the two, barely five feet tall, immediately came over and hugged me. "Nancy, it's so good to finally meet you. I've heard so much about you. And this is my friend, Judy."

The joy and happiness in Pauline's eyes and her openness immediately disarmed me, washing away my tension. "Here, let me take your coats," I offered, squishing their dripping raingear into the overstuffed hall closet.

Still cuddling baby Joey, Danielle guided us into the living room. Pauline and I sat side-by-side on the futon like two sparrows perched on a branch while her friend Judy balanced herself in the bentwood rocker. Kevin, the bewildered three-year-old, snuggled up on my lap, puzzled by all the commotion.

"Oh, look at that precious little one?" Pauline cooed. "He's sleeping so peacefully."

Danielle repositioned the baby so Pauline could see his face. "Would you like to hold him?"

"Oh, can I?"

Danielle handed her the baby, then excused herself to plug in the coffeemaker and pop the Spanish rice and turkey enchiladas into the oven.

"You have done an amazing job raising Danielle," Pauline began. "I thank God you were the one that adopted her."

Humbled by her kind words, I repeated what I told everyone. "Raising her was a breeze." I hesitated about revealing too much, and then thought *what the heck. I might as well let it all hang out.* "The adoption agency said your father was a doctor, so I figured Danielle came from good stock. You know, smart people."

There I sat—in my shapeless pants with the elastic waistband—sizing Pauline up. In her size 4 designer jeans with rhinestones on the back pocket and long, blond hair, she resembled a workout queen on infomercials. Trying to make each other comfortable, our obsequious remarks ping-ponged back and forth. In the meantime Judy sat in the rocker taking it all in.

"Judy, tell me, how'd you two meet?" I asked, trying to be inclusive.

"Well, actually, Pauline was my mentor in AA."

Danielle returned from the kitchen and plopped down in the big club chair. By this time Kevin had slipped off my lap and circled the gifts that rested on the hardwood floor.

"Kevin, honey, there are a few presents for you," Pauline said, setting two boxes carefully wrapped in blue and white Hanukkah paper in front of him. One contained a jack-in-the-box and the other a red fire engine with blinking lights and a loud siren.

With a round tin container in her hand, Pauline turned to me. "I baked these for you. They're Hungarian. My mom's recipe."

Pauline's desire to please touched my heart. "I never met a cookie I didn't like," I quipped, trying to disguise my pent-up emotions. I felt bad. I had nothing to give her in return. I had been so consumed just thinking about this momentous occasion, that a gift-exchange never crossed my mind.

Danielle and I sampled the delicate cookies and raved. Then Pauline grabbed another box and placed it in front of me.

"What's this? Another present?"

"Nancy, I wanted to give you something special. You know, to thank you for raising Danielle."

Danielle was the greatest gift and she had already given me that. It should have been the other way around. As I undid the bubble wrap, I discovered a music box with a porcelain angel holding an infant in the air. Trying to hold back the tears, I choked up.

"You're my angel," she said, her eyes sparkling with excitement. "Go ahead. Wind it up."

The angel and baby twirled around and around as strands of Brahms' *Lullaby* floated aloft. I took a few deep breaths as I recalled the little mobile we had attached to the crib the night before we adopted Danielle. It played the same lullaby.

Pauline retrieved another package and handed it to Danielle. Danielle tried to be gracious, but it was all too much. Sheathed in a blue jewelry cloth was an ornate silver candlestick. "Oh, Pauline, I can't keep this. It's way too valuable."

"Danielle, please. I want you to have it." Pauline said, her expression turning serious. "There's a story behind it. I never met my grandmother. But my mom told me my grandmother gave this *Shabbos* candlestick to her a few days before she left for America to marry my dad. My grandmother, who lived in Hungary, kept the matching one. She told my mom . . . 'til we meet again.' Not long after that my grandparents were killed by the Nazis. This is the one thing from the past that my mother had to hold on to. She always said one day I should pass it down to my family."

Whether by fate or divine intervention, Pauline's familial loop had been completed. It was all *beshert*. Destiny. Way out of my league.

I couldn't help thinking about Pauline and her inherent sweetness. Whatever happened in her tawdry past, it was apparent that her life had stabilized. She now had more discipline than I could ever have. She exercised daily, watched her calories, nursed her family, volunteered at an animal shelter and mentored her friends at AA. She fought for and deserved this happiness.

As she cuddled the baby, I studied her maternal extinct. Suddenly, as though my eyes were playing tricks, I noticed a tiny, pierced diamond, a mere sparkle like that of a firefly in the summertime, above her left nostril. She caught me staring. A bit self-conscious, she dabbed her nose with a tissue. "I don't have a cold," she explained. "I just got my nose pierced. Ellie warned me not to do it, you know, because of Danielle, but I did it anyway. I've always loved the way Indian women look. So feminine."

"It looks great," Danielle and I said in unison. Personally I marveled at her flare for the unconventional. Deep down I knew I was an uptight suburbanite, a conformist at heart.

Pauline turned to me. "Did you know my father was also named Joseph? Just like baby Joseph. Isn't that an amazing coincidence?"

"No kidding," I said begrudgingly, half-wishing it wasn't true. Yet there were so many twists and turns of fate playing out that I felt as if I had lost control.

CHAPTER 52

THE GENE POOL

MY CLOSEST FRIENDS followed the on-going saga of Danielle's biological mother. Every last one of them wanted to know how I was handling it. Some projected themselves into the situation, claiming they would never speak to the woman. To my way of thinking, Pauline was not a pariah, and obviously I didn't listen to them. After the initial shock, I had ample time to recover. Slowly, in incremental steps, I came to realize neither my life nor Danielle's would fall apart because of Pauline. I found Pauline endearing. She was trying so hard to fit it.

Periodically Danielle spoke to Pauline, her biological mother, on the telephone. One day, after getting better acquainted, Pauline urged Danielle to travel up to Sacramento, her turf. "Why don't you drive up here with the kids and meet my whole family . . . and Franco. They're dying to meet you."

Danielle wracked her brain trying to remember all the family names, but finally had to say, "I'm embarrassed. Who's Franco?"

"Well . . ." Pauline paused, "he's not exactly family. He moved in with me not long ago. We've had an on-again, off-again relationship. I guess I didn't tell you about him. He's a wonderful man. We met years ago at AA and we've been pulling each other out of funks ever since. Well, anyway, I can't stop raving about you and the boys. So, naturally he wants to meet you. You can bring your mom too."

At first Danielle hesitated, not because she was unwilling to meet Pauline's family, but with a baby that needed constant attention and a rambunctious three year old, the two hour drive did not sound all that appealing. Danielle mentioned Pauline's offer to me. I still can't figure out why I was so gung-ho on the idea, but I was. Perhaps it was the *yenta* within, the busybody that craved more insight. "Let's do it," I urged. "I'll help you with the little guys."

Danielle and Pauline hatched a plan for a get-together. Pauline knew she had captured my heart, but was no rube. She understood the men in our family were still not enamored with her. To her credit, she side-stepped their resentment, never letting on how hurt or disappointed she felt. I tried to reassure her that they would eventually come around.

At the end of June, in a stifling heat wave, Danielle and I, along with the two boys, drove north to Sacramento. As we rode along Interstate 80 listening to Raffi singing *Wheels on the Bus Go Round, Round, Round* and other children's songs, I tuned out. I couldn't help comparing my life to Pauline's. I had a husband, three well-adjusted children, and four grandchildren. How rich and rewarding it has all been.

As navigator I barked out instructions according to MapQuest. Exiting off Florin Road, Danielle drove through a ranch-style neighborhood lined with trees. After a few frustrating attempts to find Pauline's duplex, Danielle turned into a cul-de-sac to make a U-turn. As we headed back towards the main drive we noticed an older woman on foot, heading in the same direction as the car. We both sensed her wary eyes.

"Stop," I said, "ask her for directions."

Danielle rolled down her window. "Excuse me. We can't seem to find this address."

The cautious woman, in her late seventies, looked carefully at the address. In a thick accent she asked, "Who are you looking for?"

When Danielle told her, her face brightened. "Ah, you must be Danielle. When I saw you driving around, I thought it might be you. But I wasn't sure. I'm Esther, Pauline's aunt. I'm heading over to her house right now."

"Esther, I've heard so much about you. Want a ride?"

"No, no. Pauline's house is just at the end of the block." Esther peeked into the back seat and clapped her hands. "Such *shtarkers*. Such handsome boys. They're dahlink." she exclaimed, sounding exactly like Zsa Zsa Gabor.

Danielle, who has a heavy foot on the pedal, found the duplex and roared into the driveway. I held my breath, thinking she was going to crash into the garage door. But, fortunately, she left an inch or two. *I feared hitting the garage door would not make a very good impression.*

Esther, who had chosen to walk the half-block, reached the car as we started to unload. "You didn't bring your mom?" she queried, sounding disappointed.

"This *is* my mom," Danielle explained.

"This is your mom? You look so young." Turning to me, she said, "I thought you were one of Danielle's girlfriends."

Who could not love a woman like that? Could anyone be more charming? I knew immediately that I would love Pauline's family.

Joseph, who had barely mastered the art of walking, toddled alongside us. Kevin grew timid, not sure who the lady was or exactly where he was supposed to go. Danielle, taking charge, rapped lightly on Pauline's front door. On the brink of meeting Danielle's biological gene pool, I tried to center myself. In an ironic way, it was the culmination of Pauline's dreams and my initial nightmare. *The blessing and the curse.*

Yet, in my heart, I knew somehow it was all meant to be. It reminded me of one of my favorite folksongs: *All My Life's a Circle.*

No straight lines make up my life,
And all my roads have bends,
There's no clear-cut beginnings,
And so far no dead-ends.

Thirty-three years earlier in Sacramento events happened that rippled out and profoundly transformed my life. After numerous attempts to abort, Pauline, an unwed mother, decided to give her baby up for adoption. To ease her conscience she had asked one of the nuns at Mercy Hospital to place her baby with a Jewish family. And in Modesto, at about the same time, Russell and I filled out a form at the impersonal social service department. In the little square marked religion, we wrote in Jewish, never dreaming that would make a difference.

Russell and I will never be sure who set us up with Danielle, but we will always be grateful that it happened. We had the joy of raising a beautiful child whose sweetness radiates from within. Now, as a grown woman, a wife and mother, she was returning— more or less—to the source.

Our arrival caused massive chaos. We managed to plop Kevin down on the carpet in the living room and lay out several bags of action figures and rubber dinosaurs for his amusement.

Danielle apologized. "Joseph's a little stink bomb right now. Can I can change him somewhere?"

While Pauline led Danielle and the little one to her bedroom, Esther and I sat on the sofa in the cozy living room. Over the hum of the air conditioner, we struck up a casual, but polite conversation. Esther's face lit up as she spoke. "Pauline can't stop raving about Danielle. You've no idea how happy this has made her." She reached over to touch my arm.

It was then that I spotted the chilling numbers tattooed to the inner side of her left arm, indelible reminders of Auschwitz and Bergen-Belsen. Following the letter A, there were six numbers. I froze, not knowing what to say. I wanted to reach over and hug her, to tell her how I felt, but couldn't, for fear I would inadvertently stir up nightmarish memories.

I felt a profound sorrow for the six million Jews slaughtered for no other reason than being Jewish. I had always wondered what great artists and scientists, inventors and potential leaders died in the Nazi camps. I remembered reading somewhere that a statistic is a fact without any tears. *The Diary of Anne Frank* erased those abstract numbers and created a human being, a young girl to whom readers could relate. But sitting alongside Esther, a survivor, destined to wear that navy blue tattoo to the grave, was even more compelling.

Pauline's friends drifted in and out of the house. Danielle and I were treated with utmost respect, like visiting celebrities. We were flattered by the attention, but sensed we were on display, like Rodin sculptures on loan to a foreign museum. Pauline's sister Ellie, a plump, easy-going woman, left her real estate office early just to be with us. Her husband, Wyatt, who had over the years urged Pauline to drop her search and get on with her life, stopped by with his sidekick, a fluffy shih-tzu named Woochi. With his lapping tongue, the rambunctious, playful dog proved to be a perfect distraction for the boys.

When we sat down for lunch, Danielle held Joseph on her lap and tried to eat.

"I'm sorry I don't have a high chair," Pauline apologized.

A wiggly kid, Joseph grabbed at everything, salad, lasagna, the utensils and the lace tablecloth, anything within his grasp. In the meantime, Kevin kept putting black olives on his fingers, causing everyone to chuckle. Eventually Danielle deposited Joseph on the carpet. Fascinated with the dog and eight cats, he chased after them until they scampered under the furniture.

"Six of the kitties are mine," Pauline explained. "I'm babysitting two more. Their owner didn't want them anymore and brought them to Happy Tails. I volunteer there once a week. So I took them home."

Pauline followed my gaze to the center of her breakfront where there was an enlarged photograph of Danielle at twenty months. I remembered snapping that picture. *How in the heck did she get it?*

Pauline went into the same spiel that by this time I had heard over and over again. "You know Danielle was eighteen when I started tracking her down. By then I had finally overcome booze and drugs. This lady in San Francisco—the one I paid under the table—well, she worked for the state and had access to a computer. She told me Danielle was adopted by a Jewish couple that lived in Modesto. Remember, that's how I got your last name."

Even though I had heard all this before, it was particularly poignant sitting at the table with my daughter and her birth-mother. The entire conversation centered on Danielle. She sat at the dining room table stoically, as if we were talking about Mary Poppins. I wondered whether she was just being polite, curious about all these details, or wished she could disappear and not have to listen to it all over again.

"Well, anyway," Pauline continued, "my mom and I drove down to Modesto, you know, trying to track down information. We looked in the telephone book but couldn't find your number listed."

"By then we were long gone," I commented. "We had returned to the Bay Area. I think Danielle was only three or four when we left."

"Oh, that explains a lot," Pauline said, as she glanced up at the photograph. "We went to the synagogue. We spotted your father's name listed on the memorial board, but no one knew where you were. But we were determined. So we drove to the Welfare Department and a social worker looked up your file."

Always cynical about bureaucracies, I was surprised they could find the records after so many years.

"The social worker told me she wasn't allowed to give me any specific information," Pauline continued, "but for some reason, I guess she felt sorry for me. She handed me this picture."

"Pauline was pathetic," Ellie snickered. "She showed it to everyone she met."

"I carried it with me for years. When it started to fray, I had it enlarged and framed. That's what you're looking at."

I remembered taking that picture to finish up a roll of film. "We used to spend a fortune on photographs when the kids were little. Russell and I thought everything they did was a Kodak moment." When I brought that roll in to be developed, the camera shop made duplicates. Usually I sent the extras to my mom, but that particular pose, with an ugly troll doll, was not one of my favorites. But I didn't have the heart to throw it out. So on a whim, I sent the copy to our social worker thinking she might like to see how much Danielle had grown."

Bored with all this women talk, Ellie's husband Wyatt placed his cloth napkin next to his plate and stood. "Sorry to run ladies, but I need to head home. Start dinner. Hey, everybody, remember dinner's at six-thirty. You've got four hours to digest your lunch before we eat again." Referring to Danielle and me, he said, "Brace yourself. There's a lot more family to meet."

With so much at stake, there had been an insurmountable tension during lunch and everyone was exhausted. Esther claimed she needed to go home and take a nap. Danielle's allergies started to flare up from the dog and multiple cats. "You'll have to excuse us," she announced. "The boys are getting fidgety. They need to rest and I'm going to lie down with them."

Ellie did not go home to help Wyatt. She kicked off her shoes, stretched out on the couch in the living room and dozed.

I did not know if it was orchestrated or not, but suddenly Pauline and I were left alone. After we straightened up the kitchen, Pauline grabbed a shopping bag that had been sitting near the breakfront. "Let's go outside so we don't wake anyone," she whispered. We sat on the patio at a round redwood picnic table, protected from the blazing sun by a green and white striped umbrella.

Pauline carefully removed a well-worn leather scrapbook from her shopping bag. Although the photos were faded and some newspaper clipping were brittle, she attempted to show me her family page-by-page. Perhaps she sensed that I could only absorb so much, because after a while she shifted gears.

This time her eyes glowed with amusement. "Did I tell you I got a new car? Well, it's not exactly new. Wait 'til you see it; it's in the garage. But we can't go through the kitchen. You'll see why in a minute. I've got to open the garage door from the outside."

Dominating every inch of the garage was an eye-popping fire-engine red '57 Caddy convertible with elongated fins, polished chrome, and cherry red leather upholstery. It was easy to imagine Pauline tooling around Sacramento like a Hollywood starlet with the top down. In my mind's eye, I pictured her wearing a white halter-top and matching oversized sunglasses, with her long, blond hair blowing in the wind.

"This is one snazzy car," I said, appreciating its classic lines. "A collector's item."

"When I went to trade-in my old clunker," Pauline giggled, "the sales guy took me out on the lot to show me some other car. Then I spotted this beauty, right out of the 50's. I knew I had to have it."

For me it was like *déjà vu*. Russell's dad—before he went belly-up—drove the same car and model, only his was pink and mauve. On formal occasions, like our high school proms, Russell borrowed his father's Cadillac, one of the most elegant cars of that era.

That evening at her sister Ellie's home, Danielle and I were treated to a Norman Rockwell style dinner. More relatives were gathered in the family room when we arrived with the boys. After introductions, wine and a few hors d'oeuvres, we crowded around the extended dining room table for an informal family-style dinner. It was a virtual United Nations. Wyatt, our gracious host, was a Southern Baptist from Oklahoma. Ellie, our hostess, was once an overindulged, pampered Jewish girl from Cleveland. Their daughter was married to a personable Asian man with a gregarious personality. Pauline's significant other, Franco, a proud Hispanic veteran of Viet Nam, sat to my right. Down at the other end was Missy, an unmarried, pregnant niece who owned a drive-through coffee hut. An assortment of live-in boyfriends and girlfriends with multiple religious and ethnic backgrounds filled the extended table with lively conversation.

No one had a problem with diversity.

But it struck me as a far cry from the insular, repressive, and judgmental mores that dictated our lives just thirty or forty years earlier. Everyone there was effusive—warm, funny, and direct. But most of all, accepting.

The next morning as Danielle, the boys, and I drove back to the Bay Area, I felt as though I had just added a new branch to our family tree.

CHAPTER 53

THE INVITATION

SUMMER, FIVE YEARS LATER. Russell and I rented a condo in Sunriver, a small resort community near Bend, Oregon. Our entire family—children, spouses, and grandchildren—linked up for a couple of boisterous weeks in July. One afternoon while the rest of the clan set off on their bikes, Danielle and I looked forward to sharing a few hours of solitude. Drained from the constant clamor of the kids, we plunked ourselves down on the couch in the living room for a simple mother-daughter visit.

Calmly, with minimal fanfare, Danielle made an announcement. "Mom, I talked to Pauline. She and Franco are getting married. And you and dad will be invited to the wedding."

Oh great, I thought, *how am I going to get Russell to go. He's so stubborn.* He still refused to incorporate Pauline into his life.

"Mom, Pauline asked me to be her matron-of-honor."

Six years had passed since Pauline and I met. Over time a genuine friendship flourished. She opened up her heart and entrusted me with her family's extraordinary history and the most intimate details of her life, including her mercurial relationship with Franco. They had a tumultuous, on-again, off-again relationship. One day she called every hospital in Sacramento searching for him. On another day she had planned to kick him out. Franco and Pauline's paths first crossed at AA meetings. They had forged a meaningful friendship and in the process found love. By helping each other, they had struggled and ultimately triumphed over their dependencies. For her sake I hoped the marriage would work, especially after learning he had previously been divorced three times.

At sixty-one, Pauline had traveled a long, bumpy road. She had fought hard to overcome the obstacles thrown her way. The more I thought about it, Danielle's role in the wedding felt right. When Danielle was present, I could literally feel the joy radiating from Pauline. She did not have other children and never would. Her devotion to the daughter we shared, gladdened my heart.

But, still, my husband Russell could not bear to utter her name. When forced to discuss her, he referred to Pauline antiseptically, simply as Danielle's birth-mother. He studiously avoided asking about her. He refused to connect a personality, a voice, or a history to her. He built an impenetrable wall, not easily pierced. In the beginning, when Pauline called the house and he happened to answer the phone, he was cold. He would simply say "For you" and pass the phone over without so much as a "How are you?"

"How does Russell feel about me?" Pauline would sometimes ask, like a little girl seeking approval, even though she knew the answer.

That question always put me in a tight spot. Though I couldn't lie about it, I didn't want to hurt her feelings either. "He'll come around sooner or later," I promised, hoping for the best.

Nevertheless, Pauline persevered. Whenever we spoke, she never failed to ask about his health. Whenever she sent holiday cards, they were hand-picked and addressed to both of us. Always sweet and thoughtful, she sent heartfelt notes when we lost my aunt and a year later, Russell's mother.

I roared when a whimsical, three-paneled invitation to Pauline and Franco's wedding arrived in the mail. In her teasing, tongue-in-cheek way, Pauline frequently referred to herself and Franco as Beauty and the Beast. Even the message on their answering machine said: "You have reached the home of Beauty and the Beast . . ." The invitation reflected their personalities. One third of the invitation showed Beauty and the Beast kissing. The center gave the time and place, along with a wily reminder that Pauline represented Beauty and Franco the Beast . . . lest we forget. And the third panel showed beauty kissing not the Beast but a Prince.

Franco did the calligraphy and it was letter perfect. Using silver ink, he printed our names on the interior envelope, complete with a personalized, hand-drawn Star of David, and flanked on either side by the word *shalom*. I couldn't help but wonder if his Christian friends had landed a cross on their invitations.

Franco possesses a broad, portly frame and a swarthy complexion. Although he has the steely core of a Viet Nam veteran who has experienced heavy combat and emotional scars to prove it, he is basically a caring and sensitive man. He understands and whole-heartedly supports Pauline's devotion to Danielle.

When I met Franco in Sacramento, he gave me the sweetest, personally written letter I will ever receive. In thoughtful and loving words, Franco explained what Pauline's reunion with Danielle meant to her. And in the envelope, he included several impressive photos of himself in combat gear in Viet Nam.

Predictably, attending Pauline's wedding became a contentious family issue. This would be the first face-to-face meeting between Russell and Pauline. "Are you going or not," I finally asked Russell with growing impatience, ". . . because I have to respond?"

Russell complained he wasn't going to know anyone and made a few lame excuses why he couldn't attend the wedding. When I announced that I planned to go whether or not he did, he finally relented. For reasons only he could answer, his obstinacy finally began to dissolve. Maybe he needed the six-year grace period to give his raw emotions time to heal or maybe he just came to accept the inevitable. Over the years, he couldn't help overhearing flattering snippets about Pauline. I was shocked the first time he referred to her by name. Perhaps it began to register in his mind that she posed no threat to our family. Perhaps he realized he would always be Danielle's dad.

CHAPTER 54

ONE FAMILY

F OR THE LATE Sunday afternoon wedding, Russell and I flew into Reno, Nevada and rented an SUV. As we sped along the loop road, Russell's cell phone rang. All I could hear were Russell's multiple exclamations: "Danielle, I can't believe it! You've got to be kidding!"

From the smile on his face and the enthusiasm in his voice, I figured it was good news. All I knew was that before the wedding, Danielle and Pauline planned to get their hair done and then run through a quick rehearsal.

"What's going on?" I was dying to know what caused such a positive change in his demeanor.

When he hung up, Russell was laughing. He explained that after Danielle and Pauline got their hair done, they linked up with the groom and his best man. And for the first time they all met Reverend Ricky, the person Pauline had hired to perform the wedding ceremony at the Chart House Restaurant. He owned the wedding chapel at Harvey's Hotel and Casino and performed ceremonies there and around the Tahoe basin. Up until that meeting, Pauline had never seen him in person. The details had been arranged over the telephone. With all their back and forth calls, she repeatedly crowed about her matron-of-honor, the daughter she gave up for adoption and then found.

When the wedding party linked up for the rehearsal at the Chart House, Danielle met Reverend Ricky. She immediately recognized the name and face, but not the title. Many years had passed since their last connection.

"Before I got married," she explained to him, "I was Danielle Zimmer. You worked in my dad's restaurant. When my friends and I would stop by, you used to give us ice cream." Twenty years earlier Russell had opened a restaurant in Burlingame and hired Ricky Maloof as the manager and maitre-d. Ricky has striking good looks, a dark complexion with coal black eyes, and the ability to charm a recalcitrant recluse. Unfortunately the restaurant folded and all of us, including Ricky, wound up in the Lake Tahoe-Reno area, where Ricky started his own restaurant.

After Russell and I moved to southern California, we lost touch. We had absolutely no idea that he had started a full-service wedding chapel. It was absolutely incongruous that Ricky—a consummate outdoorsman who had taken my son fishing and tried to teach me to scuba dive—became known as *Reverend Ricky*, the majordomo of Lake Tahoe weddings. Apparently no divinity degree was needed to perform marriage ceremonies in Nevada, simply a license.

He and Danielle embraced warmly and chatted for a few minutes about this extraordinary coincidence. Danielle brought Ricky up-to-date on her relationship to Pauline—even though he had already heard it many times—but never got the connection since Danielle's last name had changed after she married.

In anticipation of meeting an old friend, Russell's attitude perked up. We pulled into the parking lot early. Within minutes Danielle drove up in her metallic grey SUV with the bride-to-be on the passenger side. Underneath her diaphanous veil, Pauline's blond hair cascade beyond her shoulders. Pearls pinned randomly in her hair created an ethereal glow, like an aura in a Botticelli painting.

Danielle stopped the car and ran around and opened the door for Pauline. She made sure the flowing bridal dress did not catch on the door or the train drag on the ground. The sixty-one-year-old bride, as svelte as a twenty-year old, had a childlike innocence. Her white, Victorian gown—fashioned of silk, lace, and pearls—perfectly enhanced her tiny waist.

I stood in awe as Pauline theatrically mouthed the words, "Ah . . . you must be Russell. It's nice to finally meet you. Thank you for being here." She played the role of the gracious bride, at once magnanimous, dramatic, and sexy.

"It's nice to meet you too," Russell replied gallantly, as if this was an everyday occurrence. "You look beautiful." Just like that, in an anti-climatic way, without blaring trumpets, without fanfare, Russell's Cold War dissolved into peaceful coexistence. It flowed so naturally that no one had the time or inclination to dwell on it. Pauline had far more pressing things on her mind.

In her next breath, she held her hands up, fingers splayed, and said with a degree of urgency, "I don't want Franco to see me. Is he around?"

Eager to keep the nervous bride calm, I replied, "Haven't seen him."

"Mom," Danielle directed, "take Pauline inside the restaurant and stay with her. I'll be right back. I need to park the car." With that, she handed me Pauline's delicate evening bag. "Don't lose it," she warned. "Her credit card is inside."

My God, I better not lose it if she's planning to pay for the whole she-bang with that one piece of plastic. I helped Pauline sail into an unused portion of the restaurant, hidden away from the other guests.

In the small banquet room used as a hideaway, I lavished praise on the jittery bride. Exhilarated, Pauline jabbered on about the wedding. "I was with my mother when I bought this gown seventeen years ago. I was going to marry someone else, but I broke it off because I really loved Franco. But I always adored this dress. Did you notice the back? It has seventy cloth-covered buttons. I just had it refitted for the wedding."

I wondered what she had refitted since there wasn't an ounce of flab on her. It dawned on me that age has nothing to do with the desire for a traditional wedding. For six months Pauline and Franco had systematically searched for the perfect wedding site. It was obvious that a myriad of details went into this moment.

"This is my first marriage if you don't count the time I was married for twenty-eight days when I was just a kid," Pauline giggled, knowing she had understated the facts just a bit.

"That didn't count," I agreed, not knowing the circumstances. From my vantage point near a long, narrow window, I had a birds-eye view of the guests beginning to file in one level below us.

"Today is the *yarhzeit* for my Auntie Rose," Pauline remarked. "Her day of remembrance. I didn't know that when I picked the date. Isn't that amazing?"

I nodded, knowing that she had been extremely close to her aunt and that she passed away shortly before Danielle had a chance to meet her.

Pauline continued to chatter. "Guess what? There are twelve steps to walk down. I counted them at the rehearsal this morning." I must have looked baffled because she added, "You know . . . like AA's twelve-steps."

We spoke about the coincidence that our friend, Ricky Maloof, would be performing the service. "When I started to make the arrangements for the wedding," Pauline explained, "I was supposed to speak to someone else. But Ricky answered the phone. And I just loved the sound of his voice. Right then and there I made up my mind. I wanted *him* to perform the ceremony, no one else."

Danielle finally breezed in to take over the care of the bride, her birth-mother. As a professional special events coordinator—known affectionately by our family as Boss Lady—Danielle has always paid meticulous attention to the minutest details. *Every bride would be well served to have a lady-in-waiting like her.*

Danielle handed me a new assignment. "Mom, go downstairs and check on the ring bearer." After wishing Pauline luck, we clasped hands for a moment, not daring to embrace for fear of smudging her make-up.

As soon as I reached the terrace lawn behind the restaurant, an usher approached. "The bride's or groom's side?" he asked. Looking at the seated guests, the answer was obvious. One of eleven children, Franco's large Hispanic family overflowed on his side of the aisle. Only a few relatives sat on Pauline's, along with friends from AA and Happy Tales, the animal shelter where she volunteered.

Fragrant pine trees fanned out and framed this idyllic panoramic view. The crystal clear water of Lake Tahoe reflected the cloudless blue sky. At four in the afternoon, the sun was out, but it wasn't too warm. A white trellis decorated with an overabundance of pale pink roses and baby's breath anchored the spot where the bride and groom would stand.

I had no sooner been seated, when a young woman with an old-fashion wicker basket of flowers handed me a delicate corsage and Russell a boutonniere. A touching gesture. Classic Pauline. Her subtle way of making us feel like family. We would be hard pressed not to love her.

A disc jockey stood off to one side playing an instrumental rendition of *You Are the Wind Beneath My Wings.* When everyone was seats, the best man and Danielle appeared. Danielle's pink and white bouquet and her pastel print dress complemented the best man's black tux. With perfect posture and winsome smiles, they resembled the figurines atop a tiered wedding cake.

Russell and I fixated on Danielle, like the rooting section when the home team takes the field. Silently we shouted, "Go Danielle!" She and the best man waited for their cue and then slowly walked up the center aisle.

Just when I thought it couldn't get any better, there was a break in the music. Anticipation crowded the air as *Mendelssohn's Wedding March* began. All eyes focused on Pauline as she stepped onto the landing one flight above. She paused dramatically, and then descended the twelve steps like a poised show girl from the Ziegfeld Follies.

Franco, who had been standing in the center facing Reverend Ricky, turned and scooted over to greet her. At the foot of the staircase their eyes locked, and he offered her his arm.

At last, her knight-in-shining-armor had arrived.

Two adorable flower girls dressed in pink frocks followed behind, holding Pauline's long, flowing train as she and Franco slowly marched up the aisle together.

Reverend Ricky, himself of Lebanese descent, did an impressive job blending their Catholic and Jewish backgrounds. Lending a spiritual quality to the ceremony, he recited a meaningful Navajo wedding prayer. And instead of sipping wine—a no-no for recovering alcoholics—Pauline and Franco held separate candles and lit one together to symbolize their new life. Then he explained a Jewish tradition where the groom stomps on and shatters a glass.

When everyone heard the glass popping, shouts of *mazel tov*, the Jewish equivalent of congratulations broke the silence. After the ceremony, the bridal party posed for photographs. First Pauline rounded up Danielle, Christopher, and their boys—then came over to Russell and me. "I want you both to join us in a family portrait."

At dinner Danielle and the best man lauded the bride and groom. Franco spoke next. He captured our hearts with humor, poking fun at his *psycho*-bride.

Then Pauline stood and thanked everyone for being there. Once again she repeated how blessed she felt to have her daughter as matron-of-honor. In a soft, serious voice she made a modest request. "I would appreciate it if everyone would stand, hold hands, and join me in reciting the *Lord's Prayer.*" Chairs scratched the floor as we rose.

I stood between Russell and Pauline's Aunt Esther. As I clutched their hands, I had an epiphany. Life is a circle. It had all come together for Pauline: the daughter we shared, her friends and loved ones from every walk of life, from every religion, and every nationality. The perfect wedding. She was living out her dream. And we were all part of it. Somehow it was all *beshert*, it was all meant to be.

Book Group Discussion

1. When Mama was left alone to raise Joseph, what were some of the inherent difficulties she had to overcome?

2. In his break-up with Maureen, was Joseph unduly influenced my Mama?

3. The Holocaust affected the Schulman family in what ways?

4. Did Joseph change for better or worse after Mama's death?

5. Do you think Joseph was guilty or not guilty of perjury? How did this event alter the Schulman's life?

6. Who sets moral standards? How do the standards of the 60's differ from today's standards?

7. Do you think Pauline was weak or courageous giving up her child?

8. Do you believe in open or closed adoptions? Why?

9. Is there any difference between a child tracking down a birth-parent or a birth-parent tracking down a child?

10. Do you believe in coincidence or fate? And what part did either play in Pauline finding her daughter?

11. There were multiple blessings and curses. Can you name a few?

12. Is there any person in this story that you can identify with more than another?

ACKNOWLEDGEMENTS

It has been said that it takes a village to raise a child. I found that it takes far more than that to complete a book.

I am grateful to the Palm Springs Writers Guild for motivating me. And thankful to the many friends who pushed me forward with their words of encouragement: Jane Cutler, Fay Katlin, Carolyn Valez, Rutika Gaber, Lorraine Highkin, and Gloria Blum. Much appreciation to Jackie and Jay Benson, Harriet Goldberg, Jerri Schubert, Nancy Cantor, Cecily Silbert, Shari Winicki, Beverly Schatz, Barbara Hurst-Schatz, Seana Jollo, Cynthia Shapiro, and all the rest who plodded through my multiple drafts.

I am deeply appreciative to Kathy Schindel and Leslie Conley for helping to create order out of chaos and to Sissy Kaplan, whose idea I used for the cover. I am beholden to Irene Tritel, who read my manuscript more times than I can remember and continually prodded me to dig deeper.

For forbearance and patience reading my short stories, I thank Steve Gurvitz, Judith Cohen, Bonnie Linn, Susan Horenstein, Ellie Frankel, Margie Nunan, Linda Sue Rosefsky, Barbara Wyse, Linda Stewart, Anneke Delen, and Nadine Legarza. And a special thank you to Ceil Hermann and Barbara Rose Brooker for your detailed advice.

I am humbled by the openness of my daughter's birth-mother who has shared her life story and that of her family. She has succeeded in overcoming many challenges with sincerity, sweetness, and grace. And I am proud that she is now part of our family.

I am especially grateful to my son for his infinite patience sorting out my computer messes and to my two daughters who rooted me on. Most of all, I appreciate and love my husband, who constantly endured my frustrations, made sure I had plenty of paper and back-up cartridges for the printer, stood in line at Fed Ex and the post office to mail out copies, and spent more than his share of lonely nights in front of the TV. This project is yours as well as mine.

Made in the USA
San Bernardino, CA
17 July 2013